*Liberalism and American Identity*

*Lib*

★ ★ ★ ★ ★ ★ ★ ★

*eralism*

AND AMERICAN IDENTITY

★  ★  ★  ★   PATRICK M. GARRY

THE KENT STATE UNIVERSITY PRESS

*Kent, Ohio, and London, England*

© 1992 by The Kent State University Press, Kent, Ohio 44242

*All rights reserved*

Library of Congress Catalog Card Number 91–30840

ISBN 0-87338-451-2

Manufactured in the United States of America


**Library of Congress Cataloging-in-Publication Data**

Garry, Patrick M.

Liberalism and American identity  /  Patrick M. Garry.

p.    cm.

Includes bibliographical references and index.

ISBN 0-87338-451-2 (alk. paper) ⊗

1.  Liberalism—United States—History.    2.  Liberalism—United

States.    I.  Title.

JA84.U5G29   1992

320.5'1'0973—dc20        91-30840


British Library Cataloging-in-Publishing data are available.

*To my brothers and sisters and the liberal education they gave me:*

*Mary Jane*
*Kate*
*Daniel*
*Thomas*
*Maureen*
*Joseph*
*Anne*

# Contents

# Introduction:
# The Task Ahead—Rediscovering
# the Liberal Tradition

The majority of American voters alive today voted at one time in their lives for Franklin Roosevelt, Harry Truman, or John Kennedy. Indeed, for most of the twentieth century, liberal leaders and activists like Roosevelt and Truman dominated American public life. Liberals rescued America from the Great Depression and shaped the building of the postwar world. All the major political accomplishments of the century were inspired by the liberal impulse. In effect, liberal values had come to define the American spirit.

Despite this proud history, however, liberalism was not a popular creed during the 1980s. The three presidential campaigns of the eighties witnessed increasingly sharper attacks on liberalism. During the 1988 campaign, liberal candidates fearful of political defeat even denied any association with liberalism. Conservatives, on the other hand, disregarded America's liberal heritage and claimed to have taken permanent control over the political agenda and to have captured the American political identity. As they did in the 1920s and 1950s, conservatives proclaimed the political death of liberalism.

The decade of the nineties, however, is already bringing some wrenching problems and dilemmas to conservatives. After having railed against government regulation of business, conservatives must now confront the largest financial scandal in U.S. history. The savings and loan bailout will cost the American public, in one single payment, more than the food stamp program did during its entire existence. After having vehemently preached their dedication to democratic values and movements during their support of the Nicaraguan Contras, conservatives have watched the Bush administration stand idly by as the Chinese government brutally massacred the country's democratic movement in Tiananmen Square. America, though the international beacon of democracy for the first two hundred years of its existence, no longer seems to be the leader of the world's democracy movement. The real heroes of democracy are outside the United States, in places like the newly democratized Eastern Europe.

At home, the challenges to a democratic government and society continue after a decade of neglect. With jobs moving overseas, with income inequalities dangerously widening, and with educational costs skyrocketing, America is drifting away from its image as a land of opportunity. Environmental pollution threatens the livability of the land that we pass on to future generations of Americans. Race tensions, drug-related crimes, and blighted urban housing are creating social tensions reminiscent of the turbulent sixties. The economic marketplace heralded by conservatives as perfectly efficient and self-regulating has been less the arena of equal opportunity for all Americans than it has the tool of manipulation by individuals like Ivan Boesky and Michael Milken. And crises in the banking and insurance industries loom as a reprise of the savings and loan fiasco and threaten further worsening of the largest budget deficit in history. As House Speaker Thomas S. Foley recently observed: "We are in need of a crusade to move this country forward. And if I have a criticism of the president, it is that he is not exercising the call that needs to be made to this country to deal with the problems of our cities, to face the difficulties of American education, to develop a health care system that serves all Americans."[1]

The question is whether these crises to the conservative leadership and agenda will translate into a rejuvenation of liberalism. History proves that such a rejuvenation will not happen by default. Nor should liberals desire such a result. The first task for liberals in gaining control over the political agenda is to return to their political foundation and to renew the liberal philosophy—a philosophy whose label often served as a badge of defeat for politicians in the 1980s. Indeed, shortly after the 1988 election, an essay in *Time* magazine predicted that the Democrats were helpless "until they can shake the taint of '60s liberalism."[2]

The challenge to liberals lies not simply in finding new ideas, as Gary Hart so often preached. The challenge is not merely to devise political strategies to win elections. Instead, the challenge is to energize the ideological roots of liberalism from which ideas and political success stem. Fundamentally, this means that liberals must define their ideological identity—for ideology provides the name tag by which the public comes to know and understand liberal policies and programs.

Contrary to what many political media consultants might claim, ideology is becoming more important in contemporary politics. As political issues become more complex and interrelated and as solutions to social problems become less obvious, the electorate must look to and rely on a candidate's ideology. Campaigns based simply on issues can be deceptive and inadequate, since all of the issues could never be adequately analyzed. An ideology, however, provides a continual outlook and frame of reference which will in turn guide the resolution of political issues. And in a world changing with increasing rapidity, an ideology connects the past with the future by interpreting the past and using it to guide the future.

Ideology also brings to politics a moral and social vision. It forms a link between the identity and aspirations of a people and the workings of their government. It unifies individuals under a common purpose and under some common identity. Indeed, as the decade of the nineties began, the liberal ideology was unifying societies around the world in making great changes toward democracy and individual freedom.

It is often said that Americans are a pragmatic people, unresponsive to ideological politics. This is partially true. Their pragmatic nature leads Americans to distrust ideological extremes. Yet within the bounds set by these extremes, American politics has contained a highly ideological core. America is the only nation founded on an ideological creed—a creed set forth in the Declaration of Independence.

Americans have historically demonstrated their commitment to ideological causes. The antislavery campaign, the crusade for decent working conditions and for an end to child labor, the movement to end property qualifications for the right to vote, the battle against prejudice and discrimination, and the drive for international peace have all been set in ideological terms. The success of each resulted from an intense moral fervor and passion, and from an idealistic vision of the American purpose.

Indeed, the power of conservatism in the 1980s derived from a strong and clear ideology, notwithstanding the fact that the conservative program often failed to fulfill that ideology. A dedication to democracy, to moral strength, to the integrity of the family and the community formed the pillars of the conservative vision. Comparisons of that vision with the perceived liberal ideology revealed the weaknesses and emptiness of the latter and reflected the popularity of the conservative ideology among the American public. During the 1988 election, the public saw liberals as flag-haters, criminal-panderers, and defense-weaklings. It is hardly surprising, therefore, that liberals could not even unite their own followers, much less the American public, under this negative ideology.

Unfortunately, during the last two decades liberals have increasingly retreated from the ideological arena. After having dominated American politics and political discourse for most of the twentieth century, liberalism seemed exhausted. Consequently, it lost its ideological edge. Liberals talked less of liberal values and ideas and more of pragmatic political programs. Into this ideological vacuum conservatives stepped. As a result, the ideological definitions of liberalism in the 1980s came not from liberals but from conservatives.

During the nineties, and in preparation for the 1992 election, liberals must articulate the true liberal philosophy. They must redefine it after a decade of slander by the conservatives. Yet they need not create some new ideological identity, they simply must rediscover it from the liberal tradition of America's past. By rediscovering their ideology, liberals can recover their vision and purpose. It is this vision and purpose to which the public looks in electing its leaders. Indeed, political campaigns and elections are in large part social exercises in defining the American purpose and identity. And ideology, rather than an amalgamation of political programs, provides such purpose and identity.

Ideology matters in America. It matters perhaps because America is still such a relatively young nation with a relatively fluid society. It matters perhaps because for so much of its history America was the only democratic society in a world so hostile to democracy. Perhaps for all these reasons Americans continually want a definition of themselves as a society and of their purpose as a nation. Consequently, every election is about ideology, purpose, and identity.

Americans hold a strange mixture of both conservative and liberal sentiments. Yet their liberal side has withered as liberals have backed away from ideology. Indeed, the story of politics in the 1980s may not be so much about the ascendancy of conservative ideas as it was about the absence of liberal ones.

If the future is to be different, however, liberals must again seize the realm of ideology. Liberalism must regain the ideological identity that proved so powerful for so much of the twentieth century. Liberals, however, should not wait for yet another disastrous election before undertaking such an endeavor. In 1992, at the very least, liberals must meet their primary task of firing the nation's ideological vision, of articulating their political ideals, and of optimistically defining their differences with the conservative agenda.

Ideology does not derive from a complicated philosophical process. Ideology in American politics essentially involves defining a sense of what it means to be "American." Conservatives did so in the 1980s. Liberals did so in 1960. And FDR did so in 1932. Unfortunately, liberals recently have been too afraid of the very term "American." Yet, with this fear, how can liberals hope to govern a society and nation known as America?

Just as Franklin Roosevelt did more than a half century ago, liberals must first answer the basic question of what is "American." The answer to this question will frame all others: are social justice programs "American"; are civil rights and equal opportunity "American" concerns; is a progressive tax structure "un-American"? The answer to this question will also define liberalism in terms beyond and greater than mere political promises and economic programs.

The notion of what is "American" does not have to be the same notion as that adopted by conservatives. Yet it is no answer for liberals to simply avoid defining America in terms of a social or ideological identity. However uncomfortable liberals might be with the presence of social and moral issues in modern American politics, they cannot simply refuse to recognize the importance of cultural politics.

The American voter seeks from his or her political leader a sense of America. If liberals do not provide this sense, conservatives will—just as they did throughout the past decade. What liberals must not forget is that the conservative vision set forth in the 1980s was not necessarily the "American" vision; but without a clear liberal vision, Americans have no ideological alternative.

America is a diverse, pluralistic society. As a country of immigrants, its population makeup undergoes continual change. Liberals have always recognized this aspect of America. But if liberals do not also recognize an "American" ideological identity or vision, they become powerless to lead an American nation and essentially concede that social unity is impossible.

Voters want more from politics than simply economic benefits. Yet contemporary liberals have primarily focused their liberalism on economic issues. A "money liberalism" has evolved; the equality of money has replaced traditional liberal values, such as the equality of opportunity, as the foundation of the liberal agenda. Consequently, the language of compensation has overridden the language of values and ideology in the liberal dialogue.

As a result of this nonideological "money liberalism," liberals have tended to view individuals strictly as economic actors and have consequently fashioned their political policies to primarily satisfy

economic interests. American voters, however, are more than economic actors. When they enter the voting booth and when they in-
teract as a community, they do so as citizens. And citizens occupy a
much broader category of individuals than do economic actors: they
have ethnic backgrounds and communal identities. This is why so
many people during the 1980s continued to vote for Ronald Reagan
even though national policies were not benefiting them economically. In many ways, Reagan appealed more to the public's dreams
than to its budgets. This appeal to dreams and ideals characterized
liberalism throughout much of the twentieth century; and as the century ends, liberals must once again formulate a vision and ideological
identity that will inspire the political will of a nation.

In forming an American vision, liberals must remember that democracy requires a public mandate and consensus. Consequently, liberals must formulate an American vision to which a majority will
adhere. This challenge was highlighted in the July 15–22, 1991, issue
of *The Nation,* in which many prominent liberals wrote about their
definitions of patriotism. To the majority of the writers, their feelings of patriotism revolved around the right of the minority in
America to dissent. Few defined patriotism in any affirmative or consensual values. Like the Democrats in the 1988 election, these liberal
writers reflected liberalism's current problem in defining a national
vision or identity. A nation of dissenters hardly makes a workable
democracy dependent on majority rule. Thus, in the decade ahead,
liberals must renew an ideology capable of inspiring and leading a
democratic nation. Liberalism must reverse the public perception
that it is indifferent, if not hostile, to the cultural and social sentiments of most Americans. It must reassert itself as an ideology of the
majority, rather than as the beliefs of a select minority.

During the twentieth century, Franklin Roosevelt, Hubert Humphrey, and John Kennedy led America with a liberal banner. That liberalism came to symbolize America. It symbolized the nation's
highest aspirations and ideological yearnings. That connection between liberalism and the American identity is a connection that liberals today must once again make.

The task ahead for liberals is to return to the liberal tradition to
resolve the fundamental campaign issue in 1988—the meaning of liberalism. Indeed, in the public mind, the liberal label probably still
connotes the negative and "un-American" image as defined by the
conservatives. Despite the political onslaught against liberalism in
the 1980s, it is surprising that liberals still have not asserted a bold
defense of their philosophy—a defense this book undertakes.

With the luxury of space and time, this book sets out to provide a more complete defense to the conservative attacks on liberalism than was given during the political campaigns of the eighties. Chapter 1 discusses the plight of liberalism in the 1980s and articulates the need for a rediscovery of the liberal tradition. Moreover, it notes the irony of the 1988 attack on liberalism by examining the underlying support of liberal programs among the majority of American voters, who seem to be suspicious not of liberal policies but of the liberal label.

Chapter 2 explores the nature of historical attacks on liberalism and attempts to discover those elements of conservatism which lead it to an often fanatical and reactionary assault on liberalism. Indeed, a strand of conservatism apparently truly fears liberalism and suspects it of dastardly intentions. Seen within this historical context, the 1988 campaign appears to be less a public indictment on liberalism and more a recurrent feature of conservative rhetoric.

A definition of liberalism appears in chapter 3—a definition the public has not been given in the eighties. This definition is then supported and clarified by a historical examination of liberal leaders and accomplishments. This liberal tradition, set out in chapters 4 and 5, demonstrates the important contributions and "Americanness" of liberalism in the United States.

This historical examination of the liberal tradition in chapter 4 focuses on the actions and beliefs of certain American political leaders who were, during their time, generally considered to be liberal. It does not, however, seek to definitively place these individuals on an ideological scale of liberalism. The question of whether, and to what degree, these individuals have earned the liberal identity is not addressed here. Instead, a historical analysis is used to derive and articulate certain recurring themes or components of the American liberal tradition. The discussion centers on political figures who have generally been termed liberal and highlights their liberal beliefs and actions, which in turn help define the American liberal tradition. Unquestionably, Franklin Roosevelt and Harry Truman advocated certain "conservative" ideas or took certain "conservative" actions; but such ideas and actions do not make up the liberal tradition. Thus, the historical inquiry into the liberal tradition attempts to avoid the problem of definitively classifying the liberalism of each individual.

The brief historical examination of liberalism, although not a complete analysis of the American liberal tradition, also does not recognize many of the leading liberals of the postwar period and liberals identified with certain causes and movements, such as the women's movement, the civil rights movement, and the social justice movement. The discussion is confined, with a few exceptions, to the beliefs and programs of American presidents, thus avoiding the need to equally recognize individuals representing all of the major interests of liberals. Unfortunately, a reliance on American presidents for an illustration of the liberal tradition ignores a great many men and women who through their work and beliefs have implemented the liberal creed. However, the focus on elected presidents does demonstrate the popular acceptance of the liberal principles espoused by these presidents.

During the past decade, liberals have been preoccupied with reacting to conservative attacks. A regular feature of conservative political rhetoric has been the distorted and exaggerated comparisons of liberalism with conservatism. Throughout the twentieth century, conservatives have consistently downgraded liberalism far more than liberals have exploited the weaknesses of conservatism. Yet comparisons can be valuable, and liberalism can also be defined by what it is not. Chapter 6 compares the beliefs and values of liberalism with those of conservatism.

In the 1980s, conservatives sharply criticized liberalism for its lack of concern for American values and community. Chapters 7 and 8 respond to this criticism and explore the values of liberalism and the liberal support of community. This discussion demonstrates the historic liberal nurturing and advocacy of American values and community, and it further reveals the nature of the liberal ideology in American politics. This ideology is further explored with a discussion in chapter 9 of the liberal approach to four contemporary issues—defense, crime, abortion, welfare. This discussion not only presents an ideological response to some of the specific conservative denunciations of liberalism during the 1980s, but it demonstrates how the liberal ideology translates into public policy on certain political issues.

Throughout the eighties, conservative attacks greatly twisted and distorted the tenets of liberalism. Yet these attacks received the support of a public grown weary of "interest-group liberalism," with its constant demand for rights of particular groups and for an ever-increasing, ever-expensive federal bureaucracy. To most Americans, interest-group liberals focusing primarily on the victims of America had nothing good to say about America, found nothing of value in American beliefs, and contributed nothing toward social and political unity. Chapter 10 explores the political problems caused by interest-group liberalism during the last twenty-five years. The historical roots and political consequences of this deviation from the mainstream liberal tradition are analyzed, along with the challenges ahead for liberals who must reclaim their political philosophy from the grip of interest-group liberalism.

One primary challenge is to harmonize the American liberal tradition with a present-day liberal ideology. Moreover, to define and articulate their ideology, liberals must welcome free and open debate within their ranks, just as they prescribe it for democratic society as a whole. In this context, the ideas of modern "neoliberals" must be openly examined in light of the American liberal tradition. Such an examination and comparison is discussed in chapter 11. The issue is whether the "neo" prefix implies "new" or "not quite." Have the neoliberals simply adopted some conservative images in order to painlessly escape the negative perceptions of liberalism, or have they attempted to move liberal policies forward and in a manner consistent with the liberal tradition? The neoliberal policies and politicians have curiously stirred a backlash of hostility from many self-proclaimed liberals. Instead of welcoming change and new ideas, liberals in the 1980s have tried to isolate neoliberals. Yet, throughout the debate over neoliberalism there has been little focus on the American liberal tradition and on the articulation of an ideology consistent with that tradition. Absent from the debates over liberal policies has been an attempt to formulate the liberal ideology.

For the last decade or two, liberalism has become increasingly estranged from the American public. The generation of Americans who grew up politically during the New Deal and New Frontier eras remember a liberalism that was energetic and positive and as "American as apple pie." For the generation of Americans who lived their youths during the 1960s, liberalism was "hip" and "in," and conservatism was "square" and establishment oriented. Today, that generation still remembers with fondness the liberalism of its past but cannot see the relevance of liberal principles to contemporary politics.

The generation of first-time voters in the 1980s has never known the liberalism that inspired much of the political history of the twentieth century. To them, the only popular liberals are those of some past generation who are no longer alive. They see liberalism as something their parents or older siblings once flirted with and which went terribly awry. Their political hero is Ronald Reagan, whose nemeses were "those liberal politicians." And so, after the last several decades, all of America, including liberals, must become reacquainted with the true foundations and beliefs of American liberalism—a political philosophy that has itself defined America.

## CHAPTER ONE

# The Decline of Liberalism in the Eighties

## The Attack on Liberalism in the 1980s
## and the Closing of the American Mind

On the surface, the decade of the 1980s was a time of rediscovering America. The flag flew higher. Expressions of patriotic pride became more commonplace. President Reagan promised that America's leaders would more forcefully defend American values. Allan Bloom wrote in *The Closing of the American Mind* that Americans reaffirm the values and ideals which have formed the national identity.

As the decade of the eighties came to a close, however, so did the American mind. The attack on the "L-word" (liberalism) during the 1988 presidential election closed the American mind to a vital part of its identity and to a rich source of its national ideals. Contrary to President Reagan's promise, the leaders of the attack on liberalism struck a blow at the heart of a tradition of American values reaching back to the Declaration of Independence. The attack was more than a campaign against a political opponent; it was an attack on the American identity.

The crescendo of attacks building throughout the 1980s culminated in the 1988 crusade against liberalism. These attacks were more than just a sign of a resurgent conservatism; they reflected a deliberate attempt to remove the liberal tradition from America's political identity. To the degree the attempt succeeded, it blurred the American memory to the inspiring ideals of its beginnings.

Liberal beliefs influenced the birth of America, and the liberal philosophy reflects the dreams and visions that such early Americans as Thomas Jefferson held for the new nation. From the time the pilgrims first arrived more than three centuries ago, America has been a nation identified with a mission and founded upon an idea. America was the land of the free. Unlike the nations of Europe, America was not just an area of land defined by geographic boundaries nor a location of a certain ethnic or racial group of people. The American dream defined America; and the liberal belief in freedom expressed that dream.

The survival of the American dream and mission depends on a respect for the liberal beliefs that have made up that dream and mission. The attack on liberalism in the 1980s demonstrated the need for rediscovering the true liberal tradition and the American identity based on that tradition. Despite all of the conservative claims in the 1980s that they stood for what was truly American, they rejected an important part of the American identity by distorting and ridiculing its liberal tradition. Critics of liberalism in 1988 weakened the historical connection between liberalism and the American identity and portrayed liberalism as the enemy and a threat to the American way of life. Yet throughout the twentieth century, liberalism had repelled America's enemies and strengthened the American way of life. Liberals had guided America through the crises that threatened defeat of the American mission: two world wars, the Great Depression, the Cold War, and the civil rights struggles. If, as the conservatives claimed in 1988, liberalism was for all practical purposes politically dead, what is America to do when it once again needs liberal beliefs and values to sustain it through times of crisis?

The 1988 election also demonstrated the close relationship between a political philosophy and the real world of American politics. Although political philosophies often seem unnecessary in today's politics of glitzy media presentations, all of the millions of dollars of media spots in 1988 could not offset the impact of the attack on the "L-word," which demonstrates the importance of ideology in American politics.

The political conflict between liberalism and conservatism has outlined the course of American history. Together, the two political ideologies frame the American political identity. Though they are competitors, liberalism and conservatism cannot exist independently. The identity of each depends upon that of the other. Therefore, the attack in the 1980s on the very existence and legitimacy of liberalism creates serious implications for the American political identity.

## The Attack on Liberalism:
## Mudslinging the "L-Word" in the 1988 Campaign

The 1988 presidential campaign quickly became a referendum on the "L-word." Its main focus centered on the ideological identity and popularity of liberalism. Besides recording the victory of George Bush, that election seemingly revealed the depths of public opinion—perhaps the lowest in this century—to which liberalism had fallen. Indeed, the election appeared as much a public judgment on liberalism as it was a preference poll on the two candidates. In that judgment, the public certainly seemed to give a thumbs-down to liberalism, though it really had no other choice.

Liberalism in 1988 had no advocates or defenders, just adversaries and attackers. Only a minority of the American public knew what the "L-word" really meant. Thus, on closer examination, the 1988 election may have reflected not a public indictment on liberalism, but the failure of liberals and Democrats to articulate and defend their ideology.

Despite the gloomy predictions of its critics, the American connection with liberalism is far from severed. Though the 1988 election ended with the defeat of Michael Dukakis, it did not extinguish the liberal tradition. To avoid such a fate, however, liberals must recover the spirit of liberalism that inspired the leadership and accomplishments of Franklin Roosevelt, Harry Truman, and John Kennedy. The first step in that recovery requires an appreciation of the negative images and definitions currently associated with liberalism. Those negative images and definitions came to light in the 1988 presidential campaign.

The 1988 election demonstrated the fundamental role of ideology in American politics. The public was not concerned with discussing specific issues when the ideology question remained unanswered. The campaign involved more than issues; beliefs and vision were at stake. Therefore, within days after the Democratic Convention, an issueless campaign suddenly became a ping-pong game of the "L-word": George Bush charging that Michael Dukakis was an "L" and Dukakis denying the charge.

The "L-word" subsequently became the scandal of the 1988 presidential campaign, and like all scandals the media played it in the headlines:

"L-WORD" BECOMES CURSE OF CAMPAIGN

BUSH PRESSES ISSUE OF RIVAL'S LIBERALISM[1]

Ironically, the "L-word" scandal arose in a campaign that began with two Democratic candidates dropping out amidst such personal scandals as adultery and plagiarism. Dukakis, like anyone accused of scandalous activity, spent most of the campaign denying and running away from the dreaded liberal label.

While the story of the 1988 election was the "L-word," the narrators were the conservatives. The Democrats let the conservatives do all the talking about liberalism, language that was not very complimentary. The Dukakis campaign correctly perceived that the liberal label can be dangerous. The danger, however, results not from an inherent deficiency in liberalism, but from the silence of liberals in the face of conservative attacks.

The only images and definitions of liberalism in 1988 came from the conservatives. They announced that liberals would cripple the national defense and let cop-killers, rapists, and drug-dealing thugs run free. George Bush proclaimed that "the 'L-word' and the 'L' has failed [and that] liberalism failed America because it lost faith in the people."[2] He proudly stated that he was "not a big 'L-word' candidate" and that he was "more in tune with the mainstream." Indeed, the 1988 campaign often appeared as a conservative effort to forever purge America of the memory and "mistake" of liberalism. The message was not just that liberal policies did not fit current problems. Conservatives went further and proclaimed that liberalism in the American system was fundamentally and morally flawed. Liberalism did not belong; it was "un-American."

While dictionaries define liberals as reform-minded activists committed to individual freedom, politics in the 1980s has provided different definitions. As one voter said, "When I think of liberal, I think of socialist—a kind of anti-American feeling." Polls showed that the public's sense of liberalism "tracked pretty close to George Bush's definition of liberalism." One political observer admitted that his sense of "what a liberal is today is pretty much what George Bush has defined a liberal as."[3]

Though praising the liberalism prevalent in the first two-thirds of this century, conservatives defined modern "liberals" as outsiders to that tradition. President Reagan, while defending Roosevelt and Truman, claimed that Dukakis was not in their mold but instead was pursuing the "Carter-Mondale liberal agenda," even though Jimmy Carter had been the most conservative Democratic president since Grover Cleveland. Therefore, besides negatively defining liberalism, conservatives in 1988 identified liberalism with the least popular of the Democratic presidential candidates of the last twenty years.

While the Republican path to victory in 1988 was a crusade against liberalism, the Democrats sought to ignore political ideology and particularly their own liberal traditions. Although John Kennedy won the presidency in 1960 proudly proclaiming his liberal beliefs, Democrats in 1988 avoided even the slightest mention of liberalism. Consequently, the full story on liberalism was never told; and most of the American public had no idea what the "L-word" really meant. Despite the constant disparagement of liberalism, the Democrats seemed uninterested in educating or persuading the public, simply arguing that ideological labels served no useful purpose.

The Democrats' avoidance of the liberal label only seemed to give credibility to the conservatives' attack on the "L-word." According to one writer, "When Mr. Bush bullied Dukakis about being a liberal, the latter seemed to imply that the charge was very unfair because he . . . really stood for nothing." During the campaign, George Bush "had painted a big 'L' on [Dukakis's] forehead, and absent some positive credo of Dukakis's own, it was likely to stick."[4] It did. But it was not the definition of liberalism that Dukakis's mentor, John Kennedy, would have accepted. And so, in the midst of a year in which our nation celebrated the anniversaries and accomplishments of national heroes like John and Robert Kennedy, Martin Luther King, Harry Truman, and Franklin Roosevelt—all well-known and respected liberals—Americans heard from the politicians that liberalism was a failure and disgrace.

Even though the Democrats were running away from the "L-word," a ground swell of support arose from a diverse segment of the American population still proud of the liberal label. Editorials advocated the value and power of liberalism."[5] Others recounted the historical tradition of American liberalism. Yet this defense came too late and without sufficient depth. The attack on liberalism was succeeding. In a *New York Times*—CBS poll conducted shortly before the election, 15 percent of the voters considered themselves liberals, the lowest figure in decades. This low point in the popularity of liberalism culminated the political drift of the eighties.

## The Plight of Liberalism in the Eighties

For liberals, the decade of the eighties was a long decade of disappointment. The assault on liberalism seemed to gradually intensify throughout the decade, with the final blow clearly coming in 1988, which came as no surprise. Though liberals had experienced similar but less severe attacks in 1980 and 1984, by 1988 they still had prepared no response or defense. This passivity resulted from Reagan's liberal-bashing campaigns, after which liberals became increasingly tentative and defensive. These campaigns seemed to convince Democrats in 1988 that any association with liberalism would be fatal. So instead of redefining and defending their beliefs, many Democrats avoided ideology and retreated to wage strictly an "issues" campaign. Consequently, despite the conservative failures and problems of the eighties, the liberal ideology was so unclear and negative in the public perception that liberalism was the philosophy on the defensive in 1988. Even though conservatives had occupied the White House for sixteen of the twenty years since 1968, Reagan and Bush succeeded in convincing the voters that all the national ills arose from liberals and liberal policies.

If Reagan was "the teflon president," liberalism in the 1980s was the adhesive political philosophy. Every liberal criticism of Reagan's policy slid off the teflon coating and instead adhered to the liberal label. When fighting the record budget deficits, the liberals were stuck with the charge of being big spenders. They were further stuck with the criticism of being weak and timid on national defense when they questioned the U.S. role in Nicaragua; and when they spoke out for the unemployed and the children living in poverty, they were stuck with an antibusiness label. Though they may have been correct on the issues, liberals had not articulated a clear vision of their own ideology. Without this vision, and handicapped by the distorted definition of liberalism offered by conservatives, the liberal positions on the issues went unnoticed at best and lacked credibility at worst. When they do recover the liberal vision, they will also see that the modern conservative ideas—from flag-burning amendments to further tax cuts—are increasingly losing power and credibility.[6]

Throughout the 1980s, liberals reacted to the conservative attacks by believing that Reagan's victories were primarily a sign of his personal appeal—the popularity of "the Great Communicator." Never in their debate with Reagan conservatives did liberals face the American public to assert and defend the principles of the liberal tradition that have been so powerful and influential in American history. Instead, liberals withdrew from the political arena and fought their battles within the courts and federal agencies. Therefore, by the time of the 1988 campaign, the American public had not been given any positive image of liberalism for at least a decade.

The combination of liberal retreat and conservative attack naturally produced a steady loss of popularity for liberalism. Throughout the 1980s, the number of persons calling themselves liberals continually declined. Moreover, the slide in popularity of liberalism has continued for the last two decades. From 1955 to 1978, the percentage of self-described liberals among the voting public fell from 53 to 23 percent.[7]

The plight of the Democratic party during the 1980s has also contributed to the identity crisis of liberalism. Of course, the Democratic party and the liberal label are not automatically synonymous. Policies of the Democratic party are not always liberal policies, nor does the party platform always express the liberal philosophy. Likewise, Republicans are not always adversaries to liberalism. Throughout the party's history, many prominent Republicans have been liberals; and the party itself has sometimes followed a liberal philosophy. Undoubtedly, however, Democrats today are far more likely to be liberals than are Republicans.

The dilemma of the Democratic party and its search for a national political message and strategy ties in with the quest to define and defend the liberal philosophy. Since 1980, the Democratic party has been nearly paralyzed by its continuing search for its own direction. This paralysis naturally followed in the wake of the steadily declining popularity of liberalism. During the last decade, Democrats have approached each presidential election seemingly convinced that they have at last redefined their ideology. And after each loss, they have set out once again to rediscover their vision. Following the Carter/Mondale loss in 1980, for instance, the party sought to redefine and reinvigorate its message and sponsored numerous study commissions. All these studies, however, have failed to produce a clear direction or identity. Caught in an identity crisis somewhat similar to the one they faced in the 1950s, both liberals and Democrats have appeared stymied by an unresolved introspection.

The solution to the public-opinion beatings liberalism has taken in the campaigns of the 1980s, as it did in the campaigns of the 1950s, is not to hide from the liberal label and hope it goes away. It will not. Conservatives will not let it, or at least they will not let their negative image of liberalism go away. Moreover, liberalism can be a strong ally, as it was to liberals like Roosevelt, Truman, and Kennedy. But it does not automatically exert its influence; it requires strong spokespersons. As liberalism is a more dynamic philosophy than conservatism, its advocates must work harder to keep articulating its principles. Therefore, the solution to the problems of liberalism in the 1980s, as it was in the 1950s, is to rediscover the basic values of the liberal tradition and to articulate and apply them to the present age.

## Confusion within the Liberal Ranks:
## A Comparison to the 1950s

American history tends to be categorized into decades. The 1980s have now joined the decades of the 1950s and the 1920s as periods marked by conservative attitudes and a relative lack of liberal influence. The question of the similarity of periods, however, remains unresolved, since for a closer connection the 1980s must lead to a period of liberal prominence just as did the 1920s and 1950s.

Many comparisons have been made lately between the decades of the eighties and the fifties, and liberals tend to actively promote such comparisons. They hope that the country will come out of the conservative eighties and enter a more liberal nineties, just as it did in the sixties after the conservative decade of the fifties. Therefore, the struggles of liberals in the 1950s as they built the foundations for a revival of liberalism in 1960 may have some applicability to the struggles of liberals in the 1980s and the challenges they face in the 1990s. Furthermore, the revival of liberalism in 1960 offers a great hope that liberalism can recover from the 1980s.

After twenty years of liberal reform and leadership, America in 1952 turned on a more conservative path under President Dwight D. Eisenhower. Recognizing the passage of the New Deal era, liberals underwent a process of refining and adapting that brand of liberalism to the new age. But never throughout the conservative fifties did they completely back away from or ignore the liberal label, as Dukakis did in 1988. Instead, they sought to improve and strengthen it. Of course, liberalism had not fallen in the 1950s to as low a point as it apparently fell in the 1980s. Back then, it was the conservatives who were still somewhat defensive about political labels and who tried to appear more liberal by supporting various New Deal programs. In that era, "liberal" was a much more coveted label.[8]

To once again achieve prominence for liberal values and programs, liberals today have even greater need to define their ideology than did liberals in the 1950s. Liberals must defend their philosophy, not be defensive about it. Avoiding liberalism and the liberal label will only delay the reemergence of liberalism.

The present challenge to liberals is to define their post-1960s future, just as liberals in the 1950s pondered and articulated in the 1950s their post-New Deal future. Indeed, the reflections of one liberal, Arthur Schlesinger, more than three decades ago holds uncanny relevance to the present and deserves to be quoted at length:

If we are going to build a satisfying life at home for ourselves and our children, the production of consumer goods will have to be made subordinate to some larger national purpose. . . . The hallmark of the '50s has been the belief that what is good for one's own private interest is good for all. Charles E. Wilson gave this idea its classic formulation when he suggested that what was good for General Motors was good for the Country. . . . But people can't fool themselves indefinitely into supposing that the national interest is only the extension of whatever serves their own power and pocketbook. . . . If the hallmark of the '50s has been the belief in the sanctity of private interests, the hallmark of the '60s, I suggest, may well be the revival of a sense of the supremacy of the public interest—along with the realization that private interests and the public interest often come into harsh conflict. . . . One of the singular developments of the last decade was the rise of the notion that government was somehow the enemy. This was not George Washington's attitude toward government, nor Alexander Hamilton's, nor Andrew Jackson's, nor Abraham Lincoln's. The great American statesmen have all seen government as one means by which a free people achieves its purposes. But in the '50s we tended to support that a man engaged in making money for himself was in nobler work than a man serving the community (and that the more money he made, the greater his wisdom and virtue). That attitude will diminish in the '60s. Young men will go into public service with devotion and hope as they did in the days of TR, Wilson, and FDR. Government will gain strength and vitality from these fresh people and new ideas.

The issues of the new period will not be those involved with refueling the economic machine, putting floors under wages and farm prices, and establishing systems of social security. The new issues will be rather those of education, health, equal opportunity, community planning—the issues which make the difference between defeat and opportunity, between frustration and fulfillment, in the everyday lives of average persons. These issues will determine the quality of civilization to which our nation aspires in an age of ever-increasing wealth and leisure. A guiding aim, I believe, will be the insistence that every American boy and girl have access to the career proportionate to his or her talents and characteristics, regardless of birth, fortune, creed, or color.[9]

As Schlesinger recognized then, the liberal philosophy and its historical tradition remain unchanged, but liberal policies must adapt to present needs and issues. In the battleground of politics, however, the essential framework of a political philosophy can be blurred. In the 1990s, as in the 1950s, the blurring of the liberal philosophy must be cleared away.

In avoiding ideological labels in 1988, liberals and Democrats only contributed to the confusion of liberalism and further blurred its meaning. They ignored the vital role that political ideology has played in American politics. They forgot the historical lesson that political ideals "are central to American national identity and have played a critical role in shaping American political evolution and development."[10] Ideology has always been a powerful ingredient in presidential elections. In fact, so powerful is the sway of ideology that the negative image of the liberal ideology in the 1980s caused a decline in the public support of liberalism even though the American public strongly supported the liberal programs and concerns of their government.

This underlying public support of liberal programs provides a striking irony to the 1988 election and the apparent success of the attack on the "L-word." Given this irony, a rehabilitation of the liberal ideology becomes all the more vital. It is the key to reviving liberalism in the coming decade.

### The Irony of the Attack on Liberalism: Public and Conservative Support of Liberal Programs and Leaders

Rediscovering and defending the principles of the liberal ideology, more than any other task, will revive liberalism among the American public. The climate is ripe. The basic support of liberal beliefs and programs exists. That support was evident even during the 1988 attack on liberalism, when, in the midst of assailing the ideology, the Republicans praised the liberal heroes of the twentieth century. Neither Bush nor Reagan had any problem accepting the liberalism of John Kennedy, Harry Truman, and Franklin Roosevelt. In a speech given at the University of Notre Dame, Bush said that these persons practiced a "liberalism that was committed abroad and concerned at home, a liberalism that spoke for some good things like civil rights." Reagan claimed that his own concern for children, health care, education, average families, and the environment put him squarely in the mold of Roosevelt and Kennedy. Thus, even conservatives in 1988 recognized a liberalism that had not failed America, a liberalism they could respect and honor. This conservative embrace of Roosevelt and Kennedy liberalism, however, yields several questions: What is good liberalism and what is bad liberalism? Should we return to the liberalism of FDR and Truman? Have conservatives now adopted that "traditional" liberalism of Roosevelt, Truman, and Kennedy?

Even more ironic was the prevalence of liberal themes in the Bush campaign and inaugural address. While painting liberals as weak and lacking the will to impose discipline, Bush spoke of a "kinder, gentler America." He promised government involvement to remedy social problems in such areas as the environment, child care, the homeless, and the affordability of higher education—all traditional liberal concerns. Bush also pledged to protect Social Security, that liberal program of the New Deal, and to expand the health insurance system. Although he lambasted the growth of government, Bush promised to use government to help solve social problems.

In his inaugural address, Bush continued his liberal-related themes. He pledged a compassionate government, attacked individual selfishness and materialism, and promised to improve civic and social morality.[11] Contrary to Reagan four years earlier, Bush blamed the nation's troubles not on the failure of government but on a lapse of civic virtue. And while Reagan equated liberals with government and talked of government as the enemy, Bush spoke of it as a positive force for a stronger America.

Another irony of the 1988 conservative attack on liberalism lay in the problems encountered during the Reagan era. Within just a two-year period preceding the 1988 election, the Reagan administration experienced one problem after another: the Iran–Contra scandal and its fallout surfaced; the shaky economy and its Reaganomics foundation finally blew a gasket; criminal investigations and indictments continued against administration members on a scale surpassing even the Nixon and Harding administrations; and a resounding defeat was handed to Reagan's ideologically conservative Supreme Court nominee, Robert Bork. Indeed, Reagan's "morning in America" had seen farmers starving, working families falling further behind, the AIDS scare escalating into a plague, and—with American jobs disappearing overseas—American store shelves increasingly displaying foreign goods.

In contrast to its antiliberal campaign themes, the Bush administration quickly adopted a more assertive and affirmative government posture toward some of the festering problems left over from the Reagan era. Indeed, the economic permissiveness of the Reagan era unsurprisingly coincided with scandals and abuses in the private business sector. A bankrupt thrift industry, scandals in the futures pits, and revelations of stock market manipulation and rampant insider trading all have combined to cause a loss of public confidence in the financial services area and have prompted a public clamor for more regulation. Even former Securities and Exchange Commission

(SEC) chairman David S. Ruder defended the new activism in financial regulation and argues that "the attitude that the market will regulate itself is inappropriate for the stock market."[12] Likewise, in the environmental area, the increased governmental activism of the Bush administration followed the public outcry over such events as the Exxon *Valdez* oil spill, the publicity over cancer-causing chemicals on fruit, the continuance of acid rain emissions, and the increasing severity of the depletion of the earth's ozone layer. Therefore, despite his attacks on liberal activism, Bush has felt it necessary to move away from a conservative hands-off approach to business and toward a more liberal agenda of affirmative government, another irony of the 1988 attack.

The attack on liberalism also contradicted the broad public support for many liberal programs and concerns. These programs have become especially important with the resurgence of serious social problems during the Reagan years and the resulting public demand for government action. For instance, while the conservatives press for unfettered freedom for American business, the public has begun calling for more government supervision of the securities industry, especially in the wake of the Boesky scandal and the October 1987 stock market crash. The public has also begun questioning the wisdom of conservative moves to deregulate certain industries. In the aftermath of the bankruptcy filing of Eastern Airlines, the *New York Times* reported the public's concern that deregulation had led to a decline in competition.[13]

The list of liberal programs strongly supported in 1988 goes on. A clear majority of Americans want to address the homeless problem and favor government programs to do so. By a two-to-one margin, the public agreed with Dukakis that employers should be required to provide their employees with health insurance. Despite the conservative attack on liberals for their advocacy of gun control legislation, 91 percent of the public supported a law requiring a seven-day waiting period before a handgun could be purchased. In a poll released shortly before the election, more than 63 percent said that environmental protection and arms reduction should be a "top priority" for the next administration.[14] According to a *Los Angeles Times* poll, 60 percent of those who considered the budget deficit the most important campaign issue voted for Dukakis, as did the 67 percent who considered the issue of ethics in government the crucial issue.

The public's support of liberal programs in 1988 was not an abnormality. The American public has continually demonstrated such support. Since the New Deal called upon government to act in the public interest, the public has consistently favored sustaining or even increasing current levels of government spending for social services. An overwhelming majority has continually supported increased spending in areas like health and education. Public opinion studies show that the American public has accepted the idea that the way to solve certain problems is through government action. Indeed, many believe that the government is the "only force potentially available to control or regulate the problems produced by . . . the self-interested, income-enhancing motivations of people," even if it is sometimes inefficient and wasteful.[15]

Polls show that liberalism does not suffer from a lack of public approval of its programs and policies, but rather from a distrust of the government. Ironically, this distrust has resulted from the abuses committed during times when conservatives have been in charge of the government. Public distrust of government began with the clandestine conduct of the war in Vietnam and continued during the inflation and Watergate crises of the 1970s and the covert foreign operations and Iran–Contra scandal of the 1980s. Much of the public's hostility toward government, which certainly has not been allayed during the 1980s, rests on the belief that "most government officials are crooked." Thus, public discontent with government has not necessarily involved a direct opposition to liberal policies, such as aid to the underprivileged, regulation of certain aspects of the economy, and protection of the environment. Furthermore, in voting for tax-cutting measures the public often expresses a desire "not for less government but for less wasteful and more effective government."[16]

Besides the broad public support of liberal programs, polls also indicate that the trend in public opinion over the past generation may be toward greater liberalism, even if the public still is uncomfortable with or uncertain about the liberal label. Public opinion experts Ladd and Lipsett have found that, contrary to the assumption that Americans have moved away from liberal values toward conservative attitudes, public opinion has not made a consistent move to the right and that most Americans have remained liberally oriented in the economic and social areas. Other pollsters have likewise found that, despite the conservative attacks on liberalism, the Reagan years have not been matched by a shift to the right in public opinion. Indeed, contrary to the perceptions of an overwhelming mandate, Ronald Reagan received only 51 percent of the popular vote in 1980. Furthermore, shortly before the 1988 election, 69 percent of the public said that it made no difference to them if a candidate were described as a liberal.[17] Though this response is difficult to explain, perhaps it reflected the respondents' memory of the great liberal tradition and programs in American history, even if they associated present-day liberalism with the negative images put forth by conservatives.

To explain the public support for liberal values and programs and of a liberal Congress, many political analysts have recognized that the American public is "operationally liberal"—they like the activities and accomplishments of liberalism more than they like the label of liberalism.[18] In his recent book *Cycles in American History,* Arthur Schlesinger documents the historically strong public support for affirmative government programs to address social and economic problems. Yet despite this tradition of public support of liberal programs, conservatives in the 1980s generated an ideological fear of liberalism among the public.

Conservatives have often cast themselves as opponents of the "liberal threat." They have frequently conjured up images of extremism associated with liberalism. Yet throughout American history it has been the extremists of both the right and left that have attacked liberalism—the foremost proponent of freedom—as their greatest enemy. Indeed, during the twentieth century, liberals have vigilantly fought against the extremist tendencies that have brought down many other liberal democracies across the world. Perhaps that is why liberals are so often attacked by ideological extremists.

Given the history of conservative attacks on and suspicions of liberalism, the 1988 campaign does not appear particularly unique or surprising. Furthermore, by considering the history of conservative fears and reactionary rhetoric, the present assault on liberalism may simply reflect a well-established conservative tactic and tendency, rather than a public indictment on the failure of twentieth-century liberalism. Perhaps, then, the public suspicion of liberalism in the 1980s results from decades of conservative attacks. Nonetheless, by recognizing the historical propensity of conservatives to denounce liberalism and the nature of those attacks, liberals must also see the need to assertively defend and define liberal values and policies, otherwise liberalism will continue its fall from grace as a result of conservative criticisms. For throughout American history, liberalism and its advocates have endured exaggerated and emotionally charged accusations from the Right.

## CHAPTER TWO

# A History of Attacks on Liberalism: Patterns of Hysteria and Reaction

## The 1988 Attack—Another Occurrence in a Long History

The 1988 conservative campaign was a culmination of eight years of attacks on liberalism, which began as far back as 1964. Liberals should have known what was coming. Yet the more criticism conservatives directed at liberalism, the less forcefully liberals defended their philosophy. When Dukakis finally let on that he was a liberal in the Roosevelt-Truman-Kennedy mold, he fell into the conservative trap by not defining liberalism nor clearly stating its foundations. He simply tried to grab the image of historic liberal heroes. Since Dukakis lacked the popularity of an FDR or JFK, he made it easy for the conservatives to answer simply that he was no JFK or FDR. Lloyd Bentsen had already taught that lesson to the Republicans.

Although the 1988 attack on liberalism focused on creating a negative legacy of certain liberal programs and leaders of the last decade, it also followed the historical pattern of earlier and similar attacks. The 1988 campaign was not the first presidential campaign to witness such an attack on liberalism. Liberals have often been used by conservatives as a target of blame for nearly every serious problem or crisis in America. The fear of liberals by aristocrats and conservatives began in the days of Thomas Jefferson and Andrew Jackson.

Jefferson was reviled in his time as being an atheist and adulterer. Conservatives also labeled Jeffersonians as "democrats," a derogatory term associated with the French Revolution. During the campaign of 1828, Jackson's opponents argued that he, by advocating an expansion of democracy, posed a grave danger to the future and survival of America.[1] His opponents, who mistrusted the will of the majority and sought to tightly control the executive branch by the wealthy elite, attacked Jackson for his belief that the president stood for all the people. Today Jackson is considered one of our great presidents.

Likewise, Theodore Roosevelt has gone down in history as a bold and courageous leader, not as a dangerous radical. However, in the campaign of 1912, Roosevelt's opponent, conservative Republican William Howard Taft, charged that Roosevelt's supporters were "destructive radicals." And while in office, Roosevelt had been branded by the conservative press as having given "more encouragement to state socialism . . . than all that frothy demagogues have accomplished in a quarter century of agitation."[2]

Roosevelt was a Republican and a liberal. His New Nationalism program involved progressive reform, direct democracy, conservation of natural resources, women's suffrage, and federal regulation of monopolies—programs all eventually enacted. Nonetheless, Taft argued that he, rather than Roosevelt, should receive the Republican nomination so as to prevent Roosevelt "from wrecking the Republican party" and "changing it to a radical party from a party of moderate liberalism."[3] The Republican party of eighty years ago, however, was much different than it is today. In the election of 1912 even the conservative Taft recognized the deep changes that had taken place in the American society and economy and realized that strict laissez-faire in the face of powerful monopolies no longer constituted an adequate model for society. In contrast to the Republican president in 1988, Taft acknowledged that the days of unbridled corporate acquisition and social irresponsibility were gone forever.

In 1920, the Republican party made a significant shift away from the democratic and progressive reforms of Theodore Roosevelt and Woodrow Wilson. Warren Harding's campaign slogan was "back to normalcy." He said that "America's present need is not heroics but healing; not nostrums but normalcy."[4] In many ways that statement characterizes the key differences between liberalism and conservatism. Of course, in 1920 the conservative philosophy assumed a world stable enough to maintain serenity and normalcy. They closed their eyes to conditions which in nine years would plunge the country into its greatest economic crisis.

The Republican party did not stray from its conservative path and in 1924 nominated Calvin Coolidge. "Silent Cal" did not believe in government action; he preferred to let business take care of America. Republican senator Robert M. LaFollette, campaigning against Coolidge on a Progressive platform, was denounced by conservatives as a dangerous radical.

The conservative fear and denouncement of liberals continued on a heightened level through the 1920s. Even though by 1928 the Republicans had held the presidency for eight years, they still campaigned against the "liberal threat" and characterized liberals as dangerous extremists. Running against Republican Herbert Hoover in 1928, Al Smith, a Catholic, drew heavy attacks from anti-Catholics and was characterized as representing the "forces of hell." Conservatives labeled his proposals for farm relief and public power as horrendously socialistic. As a liberal in the 1920s, Smith favored individual freedom, free speech, states rights, and an end to bureaucracy and Prohibition. Nonetheless, Hoover charged Smith with taking the road to socialism.[5]

Hoover won the election, and the stock market fell apart the next year. With Hoover unwilling to take government action, America sank into the most severe depression in its history. Franklin Roosevelt campaigned on a promise to take action against the Great Depression. True to form, Hoover called FDR's New Deal proposals radical, socialistic, and un-American. Conservatives even branded FDR as dangerously liberal in comparison with Al Smith, who was also vying for the nomination and who four years earlier had also been charged with socialism.[6]

Roosevelt won the election of 1932 but continued to endure accusations of communist influences. During the 1936 campaign, the Hearst newspapers accused FDR of being surrounded by a "communist entourage." The *Chicago Tribune* proclaimed that "Moscow Orders Reds in U.S. to Back Roosevelt" and stated that an FDR victory would put "Moscow in the White House." The Republican vice-presidential candidate attacked FDR for "leading us toward Moscow." FDR did not lead America toward Moscow; he led the country out of the Great Depression and preserved America's freedom and international democracy in World War II. Yet, as late as 1949, Hoover still called FDR's New Deal policies "a disguise for the totalitarian state" and claimed that America was "on the last mile to collectivism."[7]

These kinds of inflammatory accusations were continually hurled at both Roosevelt and Truman during their administrations. Conservatives described their policies as un-American and communistic. Nonetheless, both presidents enjoyed great popularity among the general public. In fact, the only "group in American life that had opposed Roosevelt and Truman with near unanimity [was] the business community."[8]

Rather than confront and debate the real tenets of American liberalism, conservatives have throughout this century connected liberalism with socialism. Since the 1920s, following the Bolshevik revolution in Russia, conservatives have linked American liberalism with European and Russian radicalism. Contrary to the conservative fears and inflammatory attacks, however, a strong socialist or radical movement has never existed in America. Furthermore, American liberalism in its basic philosophy and values is completely antisocialist. Nonetheless, because liberalism often stands for change, thus associated with "foreign" ideas, the socialist label imported from Europe has been tagged on American liberalism. According to Louis Hartz, the conservative fear of "foreign liberalism" has prompted an irrational "nativist" reaction to American liberalism. Indeed, conservatives historically have argued that their creed is the true American ethos and that liberalism is somehow "outside the American ethos" and "un-American."[9]

### The Conservative Reaction against Change, Democracy and "Foreign" Ideas and People

Throughout history, conservatives have not only painted liberals as dangerous, but have also attacked change as something destructive. Yet, no change for the better has ever taken place that has not been resisted by prominent and well-intentioned individuals.[10] American history contains many examples of conservative resistance to necessary and worthwhile change.

At the time of the American Revolution, John Adams estimated that at least one-third of the population opposed it. The proponents of universal voting rights for all white males "met with like resistance." In the early nineteenth century, conservatives greatly feared the western expansion and the disruptive effects of geographic and social mobility. Having no taste for changes in the social order, conservatives opposed national acquisition of new territories and supported property qualifications for voting and restrictions on immigration. They questioned the wisdom of majority rule, "claiming that the masses could not be trusted to exercise power unselfishly."[11] To conservatives, the true function of government was not to defend liberty but to protect property. They believed that the nation's future depended on the support of the wealthy and propertied elite. During America's first century, conservatives hinged their political philosophy on a defense of property and rule by the elite, whereas liberals stood for individual liberty and democratic rule.

In the debate over slavery in the mid-nineteenth century, conservative proslavery forces called the abolitionists "atheists, socialists and communists." The demand for free public schools "encountered obstacles almost as stubborn."[12] Conservatives objected to public education and argued that free education would cause laziness in poor children, result in government interference in the parent-child relationship, and, through the establishment of public schools, pave the way for the establishment of a state church.

In the twentieth century, during the administrations of Wilson, Roosevelt, Truman, Kennedy, and Johnson, conservatives opposed all of the necessary and valuable political changes. The twentieth-century conservative opposition to change has been particularly emotional and reactionary. Change has been branded "un-American." Yet this opposition to change has in itself conflicted with the American experience. Historians, for instance, have established that not until the World War I era did "Americanism" become identified with a commitment to the status quo.

Liberalism as a philosophy of change and progress has suffered reactionary attacks during times of social change and instability. Throughout history, just as America needed liberal policies to help it through periods of change and instability, conservatives have attacked liberals instead of the actual underlying social problems. Periods of such national turmoil and reactionary attacks on liberal democratic freedoms by conservatives occurred as early as 1798 when, in the wake of the French Revolution, the Federalists enacted the Alien and Sedition Acts. These acts punished persons who criticized the government and attempted to squelch the political activity of the Jeffersonians, whom the Federalists feared were out to destroy American society. In effect, the acts outlawed the kind of political activity that the colonists had used to break away from England. Under the subsequent administration of Thomas Jefferson, those acts were repealed and democratic freedoms restored.

A conservative reaction against change and democratic freedoms occurred again in the mid-nineteenth century when a great wave of immigrants came to America from Ireland and Germany. An anti-Catholic and nativist sentiment rose up against the immigrants, and conservatives sought to exclude these immigrants from American society and politics. The nativist fear motivating this conservative response—and even existing with the conservative fundamentalism of today—saw America as a fragile paradise susceptible to destruction from within. Conservatives, then and now, viewed America as threatened by sinister and conspiratorial adversaries and believed that the American way of life was in danger.[13] They used this fear to appeal to persons who were frightened and disoriented by the rapid change brought on by urbanization and industrialization. Yet, instead of addressing these changes, conservatives ignored and exploited the changes by promising comfort and community through causes that claimed to be distinctively patriotic, even though those causes—like the anti-Catholic crusade of the 1850s—violated fundamental American concepts of freedom.

The nineteenth-century crusade against immigrants also stemmed from the conservative fear of immigrant radicalism. For instance, the anti-Catholic prejudice associated subversive danger with the Irish Catholic ethnic group. To fight this supposed radicalism, the American Protective Association, founded in 1887, sought to curb Catholic political power, and the Immigrant Restriction League campaigned for literacy tests which would deny the vote to the new immigrants.

The social upheavals created by World War I and the Bolshevik revolution unleashed nativist passions in conservatives which resulted in the post-war "Red scare" and the Ku Klux Klan resurgence. During the "Red scare," United States Attorney General Mitchell Palmer arrested without cause thousands of people suspected of any disloyalty or Communist leanings. One person was jailed for writing in a letter "I am for the people, and the government is for the profiteers." Unpopular ideas, rather than illegal acts, fell under attack. In Palmer's wake came public panic and vigilantism. Eventually calm prevailed and America returned to regarding its democratic liberal freedoms with respect. According to Arthur Schlesinger, the historical pattern in times of national crisis has been hysteria followed by repression and eventually remorse; after the period of remorse, America once again embraces liberalism.[14] A similar pattern occurred in the McCarthyism of the 1950s.

Hysteria has always served as a catalyst for reacting against freedoms; it is a useful "weapon for the enemies of a free society" and in the long run "will be fatal to the vitality of our free institutions." Yet history has demonstrated that each liberal victory in upholding freedom makes it harder "to destroy freedom in the next age of fright and hysteria."[15] America's experience in its periods of repression and hysteria reflect the liberal lesson that Americanism is not a totalitarian faith imposing a single political dogma and requiring absolute adherence.

Conservative reactionary nativism, like the anti-Catholic crusade and the Palmer attacks, has been a response to periods of rapid change and the perceived threat to traditional values posed by such changes. Beginning in the twentieth century, this conservative reaction changed in its perception of the threat to traditional American values: un-American ideas, rather than un-American peoples, now posed the danger. While passage of immigration restriction laws represented the "old style of nativism," linking foreigners with radicalism, the "Red scare" and McCarthyism focused on the danger of "foreign ideas" and reflected the new style of nativism. This new style of conservative nativism began by decrying liberalism as soft on communism. It resulted in the New Right campaign of the 1970s and 1980s against a host of domestic subversives, such as secular humanists and other "evil proponents of modernity."[16] The new style of conservative nativism has prompted such antiliberal crusades as the rigid fundamentalism of the Moral Majority. To modern conservatives, the liberals' rejection of school prayer—rather than the epidemics of AIDS, drug use, and institutionalized poverty—poses the real threat to the fabric of American society.

Related to the conservative fear of liberalism and change is the conservative suspicion of robust public debate. The history of twentieth-century conservatism has demonstrated a continual reaction against free speech and press when those rights have come into conflict with other "social order" interests. Since open debate always challenges the status quo, the conservative hostility toward change translates into an opposition to debate. But the conservative fear of debate seems to go even deeper, to a fundamental mistrust of what harm individuals might do with information and ideas. Unlike liberals, conservatives appear to have a pessimistic view toward the outcome and dynamics of a free flow of information—perhaps because social control is difficult without some control on information. For instance, during Reagan's term secrecy and censorship greatly increased: the Freedom of Information Act was narrowed; lifetime censorship agreements were imposed on thousands of government employees; and previously illegal surveillance activities of the FBI and CIA were legalized.[17] These controls and censorships have been justified by preying on the public's fear of terrorism and crime. However, it is perfectly possible to fight crime and terrorism and still uphold and respect our traditions of free expression established more than two centuries ago.

The history of conservative attacks on liberalism raises questions about the 1988 campaign against the "L-word." Did it, as conservatives suggest, represent a fundamental popular opposition to liberalism? Or was the 1988 attack just another historical example of conservative attacks against liberals? In 1988, many problems confronted America after eight years of neglect. Even more than these problems, there was a national identity crisis: once the proud, independent economic leader of the world, America was now its largest debtor. According to historical pattern, conservatives in 1988 did not address the underlying problems and national crises, but directed their focus to an attack on liberalism. Will the 1988 conservative campaign be ultimately judged to have distorted the true meaning of liberalism, as have previous campaigns? How much of a part of the American political tradition has liberalism played? And how does this tradition compare with the conservative labeling of liberalism as "un-American"? Finally, if even the conservatives accept and respect the liberalism of FDR and JFK, as Reagan and Bush suggested, then what has happened to liberalism in the last twenty-five years? Should we return to the liberalism of JFK?

To address these questions, liberalism must first be defined in a rational context, free of the influence of emotional yet compelling images like the flag. The answer is not simply to return to a "rosier past," as many Democrats believed after the 1988 election when they urged a return to the tradition of JFK.[18] Indeed, if that tradition is not clearly defined, such a desire is just nostalgia.

## CHAPTER THREE

# The Liberal Political Philosophy

## The Need for Ideological Identity

Liberals have overcome all of the conservative attacks of the past. They have done so by reminding Americans of the value and promise of the liberal philosophy and by returning to the basic principles of the liberal tradition. However, liberalism has never prospered in the American esteem when liberals have failed to clarify their ideology and vision. For instance, not until liberalism recouped its vision in the 1960s did it recover from the doldrums of the 1950s. The 1988 election witnessed the failure of liberals to define their political philosophy. Moreover, history demonstrates that liberalism will continue to be the kick ball of conservatives until the liberal creed is clarified in the public's mind. Though liberalism has many forms and varieties and, hence, is difficult to define as a single ideology, the great need for such definition exists because of the frequent and successful use by conservatives of negative images of liberalism in the 1988 campaign and throughout the 1980s in general.

Ideology plays a powerful role in the national political arena. As the Democrats learned in the 1980s, an emphasis on specific issues is no substitute for a weak or unclear ideology. Indeed, as the modern world grows more complex and issues become more complicated and obscure, the public must increasingly rely on political ideology as a guide for political action. And with the media often focusing on irrelevant and even inaccurate personality images of candidates, the public is left with only its perception of the candidate's political ideology.

Political ideology also expresses the public's view of the national identity. In each presidential election, the voters not only choose a president but make a statement on the American identity and view of the world. Indeed, ever since the first American colony was established more than three centuries ago, Americans have been continually searching for a deeper understanding of the national identity and character. A significant part of that identity lies in the liberal tradition—a tradition with roots in the ideals underlying the Declaration of Independence and the Constitution.

The liberal ideology connects the liberal American past with the present and offers a vision of the future. But without a clear vision of that ideology, Americans cannot make that essential connection with traditional liberal principles. Furthermore, since liberalism as a philosophy encourages change and dynamism more than does conservatism, it is all the more important for liberalism to adapt and be clear during changing times.

## The Confused Ideological Identity of Liberalism

Sometime in the late sixties, and certainly by 1972, liberalism seemingly lost its ideological identity. The liberal philosophy became unglued and lacked a cohesive focus. As set forth in more detail in chapter 10, liberalism increasingly became a fragmented collection of interests and groups. The broadening influence of principles gave way to the narrowing effect of specific interests. The connection between present-day liberalism and the historical liberal tradition weakened. Liberalism became more a party platform than an ideology.

As liberalism wandered from the basic principles and ideological identity of the liberal tradition, it lost the central focus of its message. Without that focus, the liberal dialogue drifted increasingly to the Left. This drift blurred the differences between liberalism and the Left, and liberals failed to clarify their opposition to radical leftist notions, such as those underlying Soviet communism. Consequently, the liberal identity was articulated by spokespersons and groups who were so leftist that neither FDR nor JFK would have considered them to be within the American liberal tradition.

This increasing confusion over the last two decades as to the liberal identity was a result of the turmoil within the liberal ranks and the conservative attacks on liberalism. The identity crisis of liberalism also resulted in part from the great successes and overwhelming popularity of liberalism throughout the twentieth century.

The success of liberalism in the post-Depression and post–World War II eras in some ways bred the problems of the eighties. Because of their earlier successes, liberals lost sight of the need to articulate to the public the fundamental tenets of their philosophy. Instead of supporting policies that would follow in the liberal tradition, liberals slipped into pushing the programs of certain "liberal" constituent groups. Liberalism came to be defined in terms of specific issues or groups, instead of in terms of its ideological outlook and philosophical beliefs. Thus, the generation of baby boomers who came of age politically in the seventies and eighties have had little experience in defining or articulating liberal values and the liberal tradition in America.

In the 1970s and 1980s, liberalism also lost a part of its political dimension. Increasingly, it became merely a creed for groups and individuals who wished to defy social or cultural creeds and customs. And many "limousine liberals" adopted liberalism as a sort of cultural game to play or as a mark of independence from their conservative, wealthy acquaintances. All the while these individuals and groups were attracting great attention due to their social standing, liberalism appeared less and less the political creed that had inspired popular leaders like Roosevelt, Truman, and Kennedy.

To resurrect and energize the ideological foundations of their political philosophy in the 1990s, liberals must openly explore the history of liberal thought and reach a consensus on the broad, philosophical basis of liberalism. Only after reaching this basic definition of liberalism should liberals then debate the particular policy approaches for various specific social problems or issues. Yet many "liberal" politicians reject such a course and insist on narrowly defining liberalism by specifying it as the "proper" stand on particular issues. This approach tends to close down debate among liberals about which policy positions should flow from the philosophical beliefs of liberalism. Moreover, by rejecting debate and abandoning ideology the liberal ranks lose a vital force of innovation and growth.

## The Foundations and Principles of the Liberal Ideology

An examination of the American liberal tradition reveals the fundamental philosophical composition of the liberal ideology—a composition still relevant and applicable today. Liberalism, America's oldest political philosophy, contains two basic beliefs or concepts. The first is a belief in the freedom and dignity of the individual—a belief which inspired the Declaration of Independence. From this respect for basic individual freedoms also flows a belief in the power and potential of the individual. Possessing the power of reason and the capacity for virtue, individuals who are free to develop their talents and potential hold the only key for social progress. Liberalism has always placed its trust for the future in the individual, not in any privileged class or institution. It recognizes that during too much of human history have such classes and institutions repressed individuals and retarded social growth. The liberal faith in the individual also accepts the reality and value of change. Since it is inevitable, and since only individuals are capable of rationally channeling it into progress, change will bring progress as long as individuals are free. Thus, the liberal belief in the individual produces an optimistic belief in the future.

The second strand or basic belief of liberalism focuses on the political organization of society. This political strand of liberalism, however, still revolves around the individual. Liberalism holds that political government must be based on the consent and direction of the governed—a "social compact" among individuals in society. Therefore, the only legitimate government in such a social compact is one directed by the individual—a democracy. A liberal democracy envisions a government created by equal and freely consenting citizens who with other free and equal individuals direct the government through majority rule. Thus, the individual forms the bedrock of the liberal political order.

Liberalism, with its emphasis on the individual and on democratic government, distrusts concentrated power which could enslave or rule the individual. Since all political power resides ultimately in the individual, any form of government other than a democracy would threaten that power. Likewise, concentrations of economic power stronger than the democratic government could further weaken the power and freedom of the individual. Consequently, liberalism has sought to preserve, in the face of larger social and economic aggregations of power, the individual's capability to direct the social, political, and economic life of the nation. When Andrew Jackson fought the monopoly power of the National Bank in 1832 and when John Kennedy opposed the concerted actions of the steel companies in 1962, each demonstrated a liberal commitment to democratic rule and an opposition to unchecked economic power in the hands of a few.

The political goals of liberalism are primarily two-fold: first, to open and enlarge opportunities for individuals and, of course, to preserve individual freedoms; and second, to perfect the democratic functioning of the political system. This second goal is fulfilled both by increasing the numbers actually participating in the political process and by clearing away roadblocks to the fulfillment of the majority will. The benchmark of the liberal political process is whether it accomplishes the political will of the majority, not whether it fulfills some doctrine or economic interest not chosen by the majority. This latter purpose has often characterized American conservatism.

The two basic concepts of liberalism are interrelated and interdependent. Each needs the other. To preserve the democratic social compact, the majority cannot take away certain vital individual rights and freedoms necessary to preserve individual political equality. Through democratic action, the ideals of self-realization and self-respect are expressed in terms of what individuals want their society to produce for them.[1] Thus, democracy is freedom to pursue both individual and community goals.

Liberal political theory follows the Judeo-Christian belief in the free will of human beings. Each person possesses the freedom and the capacity to choose their actions, to choose between right and wrong; but they can only attain "right" if they are free to choose. Likewise, liberalism believes that political action can only be "right" if the governors (the individuals) are free to choose. On this fundamental belief, political liberals and conservatives often differ. Conservatives harbor a strong tendency to sacrifice individual freedom for the sake of social order and conformity, and they frequently criticize liberals for being too concerned with rights and freedoms rather than with obedience and duties. Conservatives base their criticism of the liberal "freedom" position on the claim that such freedoms must be tempered and restrained for the health of our democratic society. This argument, however, ignores the lessons of history and the political philosophy of the constitutional framers, as well as present-day experiences in other countries seeking to encourage democracy. For instance, in the Chinese democratic protests in the spring of 1989, the protestors called for greater individual freedoms of speech and press, realizing that these freedoms were essential for a more democratic society.

The two strands of American liberalism underlie the two founding documents of the American nation—the Declaration of Independence and the Constitution. The belief in individual freedom and dignity contained in the Declaration states that "all Men are created equal, that they are endowed by their Creator with certain unalienable Rights, that among these are Life, Liberty, and the Pursuit of Happiness." The American commitment to democratic rule is articulated in the Preamble to the Constitution, which expresses the aim of democratic government "to form a more perfect union, establish justice, insure domestic tranquility, provide for the common defence, promote the general welfare, and secure the blessings of liberty to ourselves and our posterity." Thus, the liberal principles of individual equality and liberty, as well as the positive role of democratic government, are recorded in America's birth certificate.

The liberal philosophy also envisions a similarity between the individual experience and the political experience. A belief in the rationality of the individual mirrors a liberal faith and optimism in the democratic political process. An awareness of the reality of change in individual life carries over to an acceptance of the necessity of change and of the value of experimentation in politics. An optimism for the future characterizes the liberal belief in both the individual and the political system. The liberal trust in the rational ability of the individual translates into a trust of a democratic government to achieve positive results and to better the life of society and its members. With a respect for the opinions of each individual, and with the faith that truth will result from the airing of diverse opinions, liberalism welcomes the active political debate and strives to open up the democratic process. These beliefs inspired Roosevelt to overcome Hoover's fear of government action to combat the Great Depression and motivated Kennedy to set America on a renewed course of economic and social progress.

The basic tenets of liberalism briefly outlined here broadly set the parameters for the liberal philosophy. It is a starting point; and the starting point is indeed a very broad one. While some may want a liberalism defined narrowly to include only certain interest groups, such a definition would serve to exclude rather than include followers, to favor a certain privileged few rather than the general interests of society, and to freeze a narrow definition of liberalism at a certain point in time and prevent it from adapting to the changing future. Similar to its prescription for democratic government, liberalism must itself be a broad, inclusive concept. As Schlesinger has stated, "liberalism, in the broad sense, is an expression of the total national experience."[2]

Nor can liberalism be narrowly defined in terms of specific issues. The American liberal tradition reaches back more than two hundred years; and while the present political issues have changed, the basic foundation of liberalism remains intact. The liberalism that prompted the New Deal has not changed, even though its policies and prescriptions for different issues may have changed. The two single most important issues facing our government today are reducing the Cold War tensions while promoting a democratic international order and restoring strength to our economy. Throughout history, however, different issues have taken top priority. While liberalism must address these issues, it should not be solely defined in terms of its specific prescriptions for specific problems. A collection of economic measures does not define a philosophy. Yet, though liberal policies need constant scrutiny and occasional revision, liberal principles such as individual freedom and opportunity and the integrity of democratic rule are timeless.

## Distinguishing Liberalism from Conservatism

Conservatives would probably deny that liberalism could be accurately characterized and distinguished by a belief in two basic principles: individual freedom and democratic society. Conservatives instead would claim that those principles are true conservative principles. Although they may vehemently argue this point, they cannot avoid the lessons of history and the American conservative tradition—a tradition which has consistently opposed liberal efforts to expand freedom and strengthen democratic rule.

The contrast between liberalism and conservatism can be succinctly drawn by comparing the primary focus of each philosophy. The definition of "liberalism" can be even further simplified and abbreviated to "a belief in the individual." The conservative creed, on the other hand, can be concisely characterized as a belief in social institutions.

The liberal focus and trust lies with the individual—protecting her freedoms, strengthening her political power, and enlarging her opportunities within society. The aim of the New Deal was not to create federal bureaucracies, but to help the individual combat a national economy that was out of control and impoverishing the individual. As liberals recognize, a belief in the individual requires a belief in freedom, democracy, and social justice.

Contrary to liberalism, the conservative focus concentrates on protecting existing institutions in society and in promoting social order, even when enforcing social order conflicts with individual and democratic freedoms. The primary social institution protected by conservatives is the economic and corporate system. In fact, the only area of individual freedom ardently defended by conservatives is what they call "economic liberty." Yet this "liberty" is not the freedom of individual opportunity and competition as much as it is the immunity from any democratic political decisions that may alter the existing distribution of economic wealth and power. The conserva-

tive advocacy of economic liberty results more from a desire to uphold the existing economic institutions and the social distribution of
wealth than from a belief in individual freedom. Thus, under the
guise of freedom, conservatives often defend monopolistic corporations from any democratic supervision.

The connection of liberalism with the individual and conservatism
with social order explains in part the historical tendency of conservatives to fear and attack liberals. Individual freedom and power pose
a threat to an unchanging social order, yet a certain degree of social
chaos and change accompanies freedom. Indeed, the conservative
rulers of European nations of the nineteenth and early twentieth centuries feared and avoided democracy because of its threat to the traditional social order. This fear of the competing ideology does not
characterize liberalism. Liberals are not suspicious of social order;
they welcome it. In contrast to conservatives, however, liberals seek
order within a democratic society recognizing individual freedoms.
They seek a community of free individuals, not one based on rigid
classifications of individuals.

Several obvious and well-established traits result from the conservative belief in social order and the liberal belief in the individual. Focusing on social order, conservatism emphasizes the past, the status
quo, and an unchanging economic system. Believing in the freedom
and power of the individual, liberals value change, are optimistic
about the future, and encourage an active democratic government.

Emerson distinguished liberalism from conservatism as the philosophy of hope and the future versus the philosophy of memory and
the past. Schlesinger describes liberalism as believing that history is a
process of change and that social change can improve the quality of
life. Conservatives, however, resist change and embrace it only as a
last resort, especially when change "threatens the existing distribution of power and wealth—because they believe that things are about
as good as they can reasonably be expected to be, and that any change
is more likely than not to be for the worse." Schlesinger further defines a conservative as one who has "grown fond of the order which
liberals have forced on him."[3]

The liberal belief in change and in optimism for the future also reflects a liberal commitment to build for the future. The American
liberal tradition has been characterized by its commitment to providing a better life for succeeding generations. To liberals, it is
not enough that the present generation is better off than the last; it is
also important that the next generation live in an even better world.
Conservatives have traditionally not held such a strong belief in the

future; their focus has been more on the past and the present. For instance, Reagan in 1984 asked only if Americans were better off in 1984 than they had been in 1980; he did not talk about whether Americans in the future would be better off because of his policies. Indeed, the Reagan administration deliberately cut taxes to make the voters in the 1980s "better off" than those of the 1970s. But to do that, the federal deficit had to be increased enormously. Conservatives used a massive federal deficit to purchase some short-term prosperity, but they levied the cost of that deficit on future generations. Contrary to any liberal program of the past, the conservative agenda of the 1980s required future generations to pay for the current generation's luxuries and irresponsible living. Indeed, for the first time in our nation's history, the next generation faces the prospect of a declining standard of living; and this decline is the legacy of the conservative program of the 1980s. Yet the budget deficit is only one example—although a striking example—of the failure of conservatives to plan for and value the future.

Throughout the twentieth century, conservative thought has centered on the principles of continuity, order, and stability. These principles contrasted sharply with the liberal emphasis on the principles of freedom and experimentation under Wilson and Roosevelt. The contrast reflects not only a different attitude toward change, but a different belief or optimism in humanity's ability to achieve progress from such change. To liberals, this ability results from the exercise by free individuals of their rational powers. Conservatives, however, distrust such free play in society and favor a more static, rule-oriented society, organized according to certain nondebatable "moral" principles. Although they favor moral reform over individual freedom, conservatives do not trust individuals, families, and private religion to conduct such voluntary reform; instead, they seek it through the compulsory arm of the state.

Classical conservative movements have been elitist, anti-democratic, and aristocratic in outlook. Conversely, the struggle by the "humble members of society" against domination by the economic elite has been the "consistent motive of American liberalism." Conservatism also tends to look on legitimate social protest as the mischief of agitators rather than as a sign of a problem to be addressed. This focus revolves around the conservative identification of a "particular status quo with the survival of civilization."[4] However, social conflict in America has been minimized precisely because the status quo has not been rigidly maintained with classes of people cementing into an inflexible caste system. In the American "way of life," the fluid economic system has made the class system relatively loose, but that feature has always been adversely affected during conservative periods, most recently the Reagan years.

The conservative public philosophy fears the loss of the "American way," and to combat that danger it seeks to impose discipline and responsibility.[5] As a way of resisting change, "discipline" has been used as an excuse for rigid inflexibility. The conservative advocacy of discipline and social order has reflected an uneasiness with the two basic strands of liberalism—democracy and individual freedom. With its fluidity and its responsiveness to the needs of the average person, democracy renders social control difficult. Likewise, individual freedom injects the power and spirit of change into society. Unhindered democracy and individual freedom pose a threat to certain core conservative interests that require a somewhat controlled, unchanging social and political environment. Curiously, conservatives have argued that such an environment is necessary for maintaining the "American way," even though the American Revolution was a revolt against such a "way."

## Defining Liberalism through the Example of History and the American Liberal Tradition

For centuries, philosophers and political observers have sought to define liberalism. Their attempts at definition have revolved around philosophical, and often abstract, arguments. The more the attempts, however, the less the acceptance of any one definition or theory. Yet as liberalism grows more abstract, obtuse, and undefined, the conservative attacks against it increase and the public support of it decreases.

In the 1950s, as in the 1980s, an uncertainty prevailed around the liberal ideology. Then, as now, conservative attacks ensued. In response to those attacks and in the wake of the conservative decade of the 1950s, Senator Eugene McCarthy set out to clarify the liberal ideology, to determine whether an authentic American liberalism existed, and to assess it as force in American politics. As he recognized then, "This task would be much easier if there were an established and clear definition of liberalism."[6] The same task and need for definition exists today.

Although any single definition of liberalism will be open to dispute and disagreement, an examination of the liberal tradition in America provides a meaningful and tangible view of American liberalism. Such an examination will also reveal the differences between the liberal and conservative traditions. Exploring American history and the liberal tradition will gradually yield an accurate picture of liberalism. The process will resemble piecing together a jigsaw puzzle: after enough pieces are fitted together, the general picture or theme of the puzzle is apparent. For liberalism can only be seen and evaluated through history. Furthermore, looking to the liberal tradition to discover the meaning of liberalism will also reestablish and strengthen the ties of present-day liberalism with its historical tradition. In the last several decades, the ideological crisis of liberalism has resulted in large part from an erosion of its historical component. During the same period, the strengthening of historical roots and values has brought about a resurgence in conservatism.

The success of conservatives in the 1980s resulted from more than just Reagan's personality and communication skills. Since the early sixties, conservatives have been striving to define their political philosophy in terms of enduring American principles. They have broadened the historical basis of conservatism. The conservative creed has become the creed of Lincoln. In deepening their historical identity, conservatives have, unlike liberals, acquired a more ideological message and identity. Conservatives today do not narrowly define themselves in terms of constituent groups (i.e., corporate and military interests) nor in terms of specific issue stands (i.e., opposition to stricter environmental or health protection). They identify conservatism as the ideological progeny to the principles and ideals of Abraham Lincoln.

To reach an ideological consensus on liberalism, liberals today must go back to the basic tenets of the liberal philosophy and integrate its long historical tradition with their present ideological identity. By expanding the historical memory of liberalism, its fundamental political philosophy becomes apparent. This broader, philosophical identity of liberalism arises in large part from a historical view of the American liberal tradition. This tradition also demonstrates the degree of popular acceptance of liberalism throughout America's history.

CHAPTER FOUR

# The Liberal Tradition in America

## Liberal Accomplishments and Victories in American History

Liberalism has played a vital role in American history. Most of the significant political events and achievements in our history owe their occurrence to the liberal impulse. To review this history of accomplishments is to begin to grasp the power and influence of American liberalism.

The founding document of United States political history is the Declaration of Independence, an eloquent proclamation of liberal principles. The Declaration asserted the liberal beliefs in individual sovereignty and natural rights—rights which individuals inherently possessed and which could not be taken away by government. These beliefs had convinced the colonists to break from England. Thus, the Declaration of Independence stands as a lasting statement of the liberal foundation of American politics.

Liberals once again had to fight for basic freedoms when the Federalists passed the Alien and Sedition Acts in 1798. The acts punished criticism of the government and threatened Thomas Jefferson and his Democrat-Republican party. They not only abridged the hard-won freedoms of the Revolution, but they choked the democratic process. Jefferson defeated Adams in the next election and repealed the acts. The Alien and Sedition Acts, however, were just the beginning of a long history of conservative attempts to limit free speech.

During the first decades of America's nationhood, liberals kept up the crusade to expand democratic freedoms. Andrew Jackson, the seventh president, worked to lower the suffrage requirements so that more people could participate in democratic politics. Conservatives throughout the eighteenth and nineteenth centuries, on the other

43

hand, opposed the extension of political rights and argued that property possession was a prerequisite for political participation.[1] Jackson's belief in the independence and equality of the individual was also reflected in his opposition to economic privilege and monopoly—a liberal cause that would resurface during the presidencies of Theodore Roosevelt and Woodrow Wilson.

The nineteenth-century westward expansion reflected another aspect of the liberal outlook in American history. As liberals envisioned, this westward expansion, which was opposed by conservatives, would provide economic opportunity and independence to the immigrants streaming into the country. Liberals believed that as American institutions of political democracy extended across the land, freedom and liberty would be broadened. While feared by conservatives for its disruptive effects on social order, America's westward expansion also symbolized the liberal faith in progress and optimism in the future. Liberals trusted the inhabitants of the new areas to govern themselves outside the influence of the older elite.

In the mid-nineteenth century, during the height of the westward expansion, a liberal reform movement also occurred. The reform efforts included establishment of a public education system, abolition of slavery, improvement of working conditions in factories that employed young girls, and the right of women to vote. The reforms also responded to the growing centralization of society. While conservatives favored a centralized society for economic and industrial purposes, liberals wanted a more decentralized society, which would give people more control over their local affairs.

This nineteenth-century reform movement previewed the great reform period of the late nineteenth and early twentieth centuries. This liberal-inspired reform movement responded to the harsh conditions caused by rapid industrialization and urban crowding. Commonly referred to as the Progressive reforms, the reforms included regulation of the railroads and other monopolies, development of agriculture, reform of the civil service system, health regulation of the meat-packing industry, extension of the vote to women, a crusade against political machines, and improvement of factory working conditions and hours for children. During the Progressive Era, the growth of industrial monopolies began somewhat to redefine the policies of liberalism, which had previously favored a limited role for the national government. Now it had become apparent that private industry, as well as government, could repress individual freedom and opportunity and could weaken the democratic governance of society.

Even during the conservative era of the twenties and the return to "normalcy," the Progressive reforms were generally accepted and sustained. To conservatives who still opposed the reforms, however, the preservation of social order became more important than the integrity of democratic processes and the constitutional principles of liberty. During the 1920s, conservatives launched a nationwide campaign against free speech and targeted for attack those espousing unpopular or nontraditional beliefs. Conservatives during this period also rejected the social compact notion of government in favor of a state based on tradition and social order. They succeeded in placing control of the nation's political system in the hands of the wealthy and the business interests.

Outside of the Civil War, perhaps the greatest threat to our national welfare and survival came during the Great Depression. In response to this national calamity, conservatives opposed any substantial governmental action, arguing that it would destroy capitalism and encourage individual dependency on the government. Meanwhile, hundreds of thousands of Americans lost their jobs, their homes, their savings, and even their lives. Liberals, on the other hand, advocated a more activist response by the government. With both private business and voluntary relief agencies crippled by the Depression, liberals realized that without government involvement millions of Americans would stay hopelessly trapped in poverty.

Under the New Deal, liberals enacted public works projects and put thousands to work. The long-neglected, poverty-stricken farmer was given a new opportunity, and programs like rural electrification were enacted to help develop and strengthen the agricultural economy. Programs were also developed to assist the children, the aged, and the handicapped—those left out of the economic marketplace. Consequently, New Deal liberalism led Americans to understand that the government's obligations extended beyond supporting business and financial institutions and that the average American could request and rely on the government to solve social problems.

Coinciding with the domestic crisis posed by the Great Depression, an international crisis loomed in Europe. Just as with World War I, democratic nations looked to America as an ally. Despite the conservative isolationist impulse, liberals realized that America and the rest of the world could no longer remain separate. Not only did liberalism sustain America through the war, but it strove to create a prosperous and peaceful postwar world governed by the rule of law rather than military might. Although conservatives had defeated Woodrow Wilson's attempt to gain America's entrance into the

League of Nations after World War I, post–World War II liberals prevailed in their attempt to form the United Nations. Liberals also saw that America's national defense hinged on the defense of democracies abroad. Through NATO and the Marshall Plan, American liberalism helped transform a war-torn Europe into a region of prosperous, stable democracies protected from Communist takeover.

Following the war, America faced other crises at home. The decade of the conservative fifties had focused on conformity and adherence to traditional rules. Political activity was discouraged, but business was exalted. The message was, as it was under Calvin Coolidge, that what was good for business was good for the country. Unfortunately, many Americans were not prospering, as was General Motors. Significant pockets of poverty existed in rural areas, urban slums were imprisoning their inhabitants, and blacks and other minorities were politically and socially segregated. Despite these increasing social tensions and problems, however, conservatives continually expressed the "desire to operate a pure [economic] marketplace situation without any social responsibility."[2]

The liberals of the sixties attempted to bring a sense of social responsibility to the economy. After its unrestrained freedom in the fifties, business had left gaping holes in the social fabric. The liberals of the sixties tried to reinvigorate the social contract. They sought to impose a sense of social responsibility along with the right to operate in the economic marketplace. As with the New Deal, government stepped in to rectify obvious problems and inequities within the economic system. The government programs of the sixties, though addressing new problems, often rested on principles of the past. The Job Corps program, for instance, combined the traditional democratic idea that education could provide an equal opportunity to participate in the marketplace with the New Deal notion that government could help in expanding the marketplace.[3]

Postwar liberalism not only employed government to achieve social justice goals but also saw the potential of democratic government to encourage social progress. Government assistance to the arts and to scientific research contributed to America's worldwide leadership in these areas. Indeed, the U.S. space program and the first successful moon landing in 1969 demonstrated the vast potential of the liberal vision.

Since the 1960s, many social problems and challenges have come to our attention. Yet while conservatives have denied or ignored these problems, liberals have been seeking solutions. Civil rights were guaranteed for blacks, and desegregation was outlawed. Voting restrictions were erased. Educational opportunities were expanded. Extreme poverty in cities and rural areas was addressed. And the environment finally received governmental protection. All of these reforms and accomplishments, as with similar ones over the last two centuries, were led by liberals and opposed by conservatives.

## Classical Liberalism and the Birth of America

When conservatives attack modern liberalism they are not criticizing the entire American liberal philosophy. Indeed, the modern conservative political philosophy is an outgrowth of the liberal philosophy referred to as classical liberalism and to which America's founders ascribed. This liberal philosophy guided American political development in the eighteenth century, through the break with England, and into the nineteenth century.

In the late nineteenth and early twentieth centuries, as partisan politics matured, two strands of political dialogue developed out of the American classical liberal philosophy and formed the basis of the modern conservative and liberal creeds. It was not until America had sufficient experience with its liberal democratic government, however, that it could then nurture two distinct and competing philosophies within that liberal orientation. Consequently, both modern liberalism and modern conservatism have roots in classical Jeffersonian liberalism.[4]

The roots of classical liberal thought reach back to the time of the Hebrew prophets and such Greek scholars as Aristotle and Socrates, all of whom promoted the idea that individuals could reach their full individual and social potential only if freed from the tyranny of arbitrary, external restraints. Historically, such restraints took the form of rigid social caste rules and an absolutist dictatorial political system. To the early liberal thinkers, individual freedom meant social progress.

In seventeenth- and eighteenth-century Europe, feudalism governed the social and political order. The social system, along with aristocratic political rulers, governed every aspect of an individual's life. Society was organized into classes, and the individual was subordinate to his or her class and the rules and opportunities available to and governing that class. It was a well-ordered caste society.

Eighteenth-century classical liberalism, however, opposed such social structures and lack of individual freedom. Liberalism flourished in the emerging European middle class, which wanted greater freedom and believed that the independent will of free individuals should direct society. The middle-class liberals rebelled against a "directed society." The concept of laissez-faire reflected this liberal desire for greater freedom, envisioning a society free of all constraints and presuming that all people had equal opportunity to compete. The eighteenth-century middle-class liberals thought that such a system would produce a classless society with social harmony among equal individuals.

Classical liberalism, in effect, strove to enhance the "life chances" of citizens and to break down barriers to an individual's full access to "citizenship rights."[5] Contrary to the rigid social system of the time, liberalism maintained a respect for the autonomy of individuals and a belief that relationships among citizens should not be governed by rigid social rules, but instead by a clear legal relationship—a rule of law that was rational and based on majority will and consent by the governed.

This emphasis of classical liberalism on the individual marked a sharp break from the prevailing social and political systems of the time. Classical liberalism believed that social progress depended not on social rules or aristocratic rulers but on the free and rational intelligence of the individual. In contrast with the older idea that truth could only be held by a privileged individual or class, liberalism proclaimed the ability of the individual to discover truth. Since they also saw the feudal system as holding back change, liberals welcomed a social system open to change and progress. Thus, an optimistic belief in change and in an individual's capacity for truth led liberals to espouse ideas like free speech, private enterprise, and self-representative government.

The political governance ideas of classical liberalism focused on representative government and on John Locke's idea of the social compact. According to John Stuart Mill, democratic government best provided for the full development of the individual, whereas paternal government was useful only when the people were not sufficiently educated or prepared to govern themselves. Under the social compact notion of government, individuals in a society agreed to be governed according to their self-made laws. They would give up some of their individual freedom in return for the ability to vote and participate in the political process and for the government's refraining from infringing on any areas of the individual's freedom not delegated to the government's sphere of power. The liberal political prescription was simple: majority rule with respect for minority rights. Liberals also believed that social mobility would preclude the establishment of rigid ruling classes and that fluctuating democratic majorities would serve as an additional protection for minorities.[6]

This eighteenth-century classical liberalism exerted a special influence in America. Colonial America had not experienced the feudal or aristocratic social system of Europe;[7] and colonial society was virtually classless in comparison with Europe. According to Louis Hartz, the absence of feudalism from America's past—along with the absence of a profound social passion to destroy the confining social order accompanying feudalism—contributed largely to an American political tradition based on a liberal consensus. American society, being far more middle-class oriented than Europe, quickly adopted liberalism as the accepted social and political philosophy, whereas in Europe liberalism was still just a philosophy held by dissenters. Furthermore, since Americans had no repressive feudal or social system against which to revolt, American liberal thought incorporated a strong belief in social harmony and mobility and an optimism about the future.

Although colonial society was a liberal society and had a more democratic political system than any existing in Europe, it was not yet a liberal political democracy. The American Revolution was a movement to establish such a liberal democracy.

Classical liberalism, with its belief in the individual and freedom from undemocratic rules, manifested itself in the American Revolution. When the Declaration of Independence was signed on 4 July 1776, America stood as the only country on earth to organize and govern itself according to eighteenth-century liberal political thought. The subsequent American Constitution reflected the beliefs of eighteenth-century liberals such as Jean-Jacques Rousseau, Mill, Locke, Alexis de Tocqueville, Jefferson, and Adam Smith, who espoused such "liberal" ideas as rational choice, capitalism, free trade, and representative democracy. These liberals effectively sought to abolish social barriers to citizenship status and rights.[8]

In the early years of the American republic, liberalism continued its prominent influence. Writing about his observations of the new nation, Tocqueville noticed how much Americans had incorporated liberalism into their political thinking. He believed in the liberal principles of his time—individual rights, constitutional restraints on state power, an abhorrence of socialism, and the value of liberty—yet deplored a politics dominated by self-interest and lamented the ill effects of commerce on political life.[9] Tocqueville saw the value and promise of a liberal democracy, but, in a prelude to the liberalism of Woodrow Wilson and Franklin Roosevelt, warned against a society of self-seekers practicing a narrow individualism and ignoring the common good. To Tocqueville, the conduct of democratic politics would draw individuals from their shell of private interests, sensitize them to common concerns, and form a new civic consciousness merging the public and private good. Thus, as Tocqueville noted, the liberal ideas influencing the founding of the American constitutional democracy included a respect for individual freedom, a belief in self-government, and a commitment to guide democratic rule in accordance with the common good and not in support of any privileged class or economic dogma.

## Liberals Who Shaped America

### James Otis and Samuel Adams: Liberals as Patriots and Fighters for Freedom

The liberal advocacy of individual freedom unified and strengthened America's movement for independence. The advocacy of these same freedoms today, however, attracts conservative attacks of "extremism" and "un-Americanism." Yet the fight for these freedoms defined the ideological essence of the American Revolution. Any move to weaken these freedoms, after 200 years of strength, would undoubtedly greatly disappoint eighteenth-century liberals like Sam Adams and James Otis.

In 1761, James Otis, a Boston lawyer, represented a group of American merchants challenging the legality of the British writs of assistance. These writs conferred broad power on the British tax collectors to not only search a colonial merchant's ship but to break into the merchant's home or warehouse to search for taxable commodities. In effect, the colonists were legally helpless in keeping these tax collectors out of their homes. Arguing in support of the writs, the Crown's attorney claimed that when the liberty of the individual came in conflict with the efficient collection of taxes, the latter must take precedence. Otis's arguments in opposition to the writs previewed the ideological foundations of the Declaration of Independence. He argued that the writs were an arbitrary use of the king's power that infringed on the natural rights of liberty and property. Citing English principles of liberty, Otis pronounced the now infamous principle that "a man's house is his castle," and argued that the freedom of the home could not be arbitrarily invaded. Otis, like other colonial liberals, believed that the writs represented the beginning of the Crown's attempt to impose complete control over the colonies.[10]

Although Otis received great praise for his courageous stand, Massachusetts conservatives sensed him to be "a dangerous new adversary."[11] Later, when he was a member of the colonial legislature in Massachusetts, Otis vehemently opposed the Crown's attempt to take away the legislature's power of revenue raising and to erode representative government in America. In response to his protest, conservatives charged him with treason.

Samuel Adams also was well known in Boston in the 1760s for his liberal politics and his passionate beliefs in liberty and justice.[12] He became involved in local politics to combat the growing abuse of power by the royal governor. One of Adams's first great achievements was to preserve the right of all Bostonians to hold town meetings for public business. Conservatives, as distrustful of the actions of the common colonial Bostonian as they were with the concept of democracy in general, had long wanted to do away with such meetings.

Adams and Otis joined forces in denouncing the Sugar Act in 1764. Britain, needing to increase its revenues following the Seven Years' War with France, looked to the colonies for income and decided to tax colonial shipping and trade. Otis published a pamphlet arguing that Parliament had no right to impose such taxes, which the colonists feared would kill commerce in Massachusetts. Adams agreed and formulated the now-famous slogan "No taxation without representation." He argued that Parliament could not tax the colonies without first giving them representation. To oppose these taxes and to fight British tyranny, Adams gathered fellow colonists who were determined to defend their freedom and who later came to be known as the Sons of Liberty.[13] The Sons of Liberty were instrumental in forcing repeals of the Sugar Act and the Stamp Act, which imposed a tax on all colonial newspapers, pamphlets, diplomas, and legal documents.

Adams and Otis, throughout the decade preceding the break with Britain, continued to oppose British attempts to control and curtail the colonists' freedoms. They saw each tax and each British intrusion as another step toward a larger British scheme to strip the colonial legislatures of their power and to regulate the freedoms of all the colonists. Adams and Otis argued that these British intrusions and controls violated the colonists' natural rights. Adams so forcefully opposed British rule that one conservative artist "said that if [he] wanted to draw the devil, he would get Sam Adams to sit for him." In fact, because of the ardent patriotism of Otis and Adams, some conservatives urged that they be brought to England where they could be tried and hanged for treason.[14] They were not taken to England for trial. Instead, Otis and Adams stayed in America and launched the move toward independence.

Although Otis and Adams strongly asserted the colonists' natural rights and opposed the arbitrary power of the Crown, it was quite another thing for them to argue against the legitimacy of the Crown's rule. What helped in this argument were the liberal doctrines of natural rights and individual sovereignty. These doctrines fostered an antiauthoritarian mood against government by the elite and asserted that individuals had a rightful place in civil government. This antiauthoritarian mood threw open all established rules, conventions, and institutions to question and reflected a condemnation of concentrated power.[15] Consequently, these liberal philosophies hastened the transformation of colonists from the king's subjects into self-made Americans. Colonial liberals came to see the people as the true source of political power and social virtue. The conservatives/monarchists, on the other hand, praised social hierarchy as divine, stressed centralized power, and believed that government was properly entrusted to the elite few occupying the higher status in society.[16]

Otis and Adams succeeded in their efforts to achieve independence and freedom. Their arguments in favor of the Americans' natural rights and against the tyranny of the British rule found expression in Thomas Jefferson's draft of the Declaration of Independence. Jefferson wrote that the rights of "life, liberty and the pursuit of happiness" were "unalienable rights"—rights which could not be violated by governments or laws. Jefferson also wrote that governments could only derive their power from the consent of the governed. In the Declaration, Jefferson enshrined forever America's commitment to liberal democratic principles. These principles, fought for by such patriots as Otis and Adams, articulated the values of equality, individual freedom, and a democratic government guided by the common good and based on the consent of all the governed.

### Thomas Jefferson and Andrew Jackson:
### The Liberal Performance of the Democratic Promise

The liberalism of Jefferson and Jackson, while protecting the freedoms won by patriots like Otis and Adams, sought to expand the American democracy and equip more Americans with political freedoms and power. Although the Declaration had expressed the value of democracy, conservative forces in society strove to limit and modify the democratic features of the new American government and hoped to implement a deferential political system in which the majority of average Americans would not participate in politics and would defer in all political decisions to the wealthy and educated elite. Jefferson and Jackson, however, opposed this limitation of democratic rights and this preference for government by the wealthy elite. In a preview to New Deal liberalism, Jacksonian liberalism also put government on the side of the common American. Government complicity with the privileged and wealthy elite was seen as anti-democratic and un-American.

The American Revolution achieved independence but did not automatically bring a democratic government to America. The movement for independence was not only aimed against British rule but against an old colonial elite that refused to abide by democratic rule and acknowledge the power of the colonial legislatures.[17] Indeed, the liberal spirit of democracy and independence infusing the struggle against Britain also spilled over to the domestic arena. No longer would Americans be content to recognize the "right" of the elite to control government. Thus, one of the most important consequences of the Revolution lay in the opportunity it provided for ordinary citizens to take part in governing themselves. Nonetheless, following ratification of the Constitution, forces in the new nation were working to restrict or constrain democratic processes.

During the early American Constitutional period, the Federalists succeeded in maintaining a political atmosphere of deference and limited suffrage—a system in which the wealthy elite effectively ran and controlled the political system. Fearful of the possible effects of the French Revolution on the young American nation, the Federalists and conservative elite distrusted the masses and any further extension of democracy. In their view, social order took precedence over popular government and democratic participation. The conservative outlook saw the liberty of civic participation as limited to the elite and that a legitimate social order was necessarily hierarchical in nature.

Jefferson and his fellow "Democrats" did not fear popular rule and welcomed public debate and political participation by "the masses."[18] He believed that only representative democracy is self-correcting, and that only "the people" can learn from their mistakes and correct them in the future. Jeffersonian liberals in the 1790s looked forward to the achievement in America of a classless society of free and independent individuals unrestrained by the dead hand of tradition, the operation of "privilege," or the chains of customs and outworn creeds. Conservatives, on the other hand, sought to create a "ruling class" and impose a political and economic order rather than letting one naturally develop through the free workings of democracy and a market economy.

Jefferson rose in popularity as the Federalists sought to impose control on society and passed a series of laws aimed at quashing any criticism of them or the government. These laws were just the kind of oppressive measures which had prompted Otis and Adams to promote independence. Uncomfortable with the pace of change in America and with the "noisy clamor" of democracy, the conservative Federalists sought not to direct change toward democratic goals but to repress it and muzzle debate. Jefferson, in keeping with his theory of natural rights and a government by consent of the governed, opposed these laws and later repealed them after winning the presidency. Many conservative Federalists, however, believed that Jefferson was an agent of the French Revolution and that his purpose was to destroy the federal government, reduce the nation to anarchy, and assume dictatorial powers.[19]

Contrary to Jefferson, Alexander Hamilton expressed the Tory view of democratic legislative bodies as dangerous and irritating obstructionists. He distrusted experimentation and sought to minimize any change not instigated by the wealthy elite, and debate and democratic action were seen as destructive at worst and unnecessary at best. As a Federalist, Hamilton favored a strong, centralized government that would support the commercial interests and dominate the popularly elected legislatures.

Jeffersonian ideology, on the other hand, opposed privileged monopolies and feared corruption resulting from a union between commercial interests and government. Jefferson, adopting the liberal suspicions of Otis and Adams toward centralized government, feared that Hamilton's proposed union between capitalists and the government would weaken the power of the legislatures and the people.[20]

The Federalists and Jeffersonians differed over the social and political context in which change would take place. The latter envisioned change through the natural harmony and interchange of free and autonomous individuals, therefore expanding the range of free expression and inquiry. This was the liberating alternative to the conservative Federalists' expectation of orderly growth within strict social limits.

In contrast to Jeffersonians, Federalists believed that the future would not be fundamentally different from the past and clung to traditional expectations about the role of authority in public life, the permanence of social classes, and the necessity for elite leadership and a passive citizenry. The Federalists, for instance, opposed the Jeffersonian attempt to widen and democratize public education. They saw it as a fatal permissiveness that would destroy society and eliminate the concept of education as devoted to the training of the elite.[21] The conservative Federalists in 1800, however, lacked the power to impose their vision of social order upon American society, and Jefferson was elected president.

Jefferson sought to open up American politics to a better fulfillment of the goals and values he set forth in the Declaration of Independence. Equality, in both opportunity and in political freedom and expression, became the guide for American democracy. Similarly, Jefferson's economics came from Adam Smith, who advocated free competition, open opportunity, and the absence of privileges or favors. To preserve America as a "land of opportunity," Jefferson opened westward expansion with the Louisiana Purchase. This westward movement, however, alarmed conservatives. The concept of wilderness contradicted their desire for social control and uniform civilized manners and conduct.[22] Though conservatives also feared such an expansion would compete with the status they achieved during the colonial period, Jefferson's purchase of the Louisiana Territory insured a future of opportunity for those Americans not already so secure.

The influx of immigrants from Continental European countries also troubled conservatives, who tried to tightly control and homogenize the manners and values of the European immigrant. Jefferson resisted the idea of controlling private morals and steadfastly believed in a separation of government and religion.[23] He wanted to ensure that the new immigrants would not suffer religious persecution for their beliefs. Religious freedom was more than mere toleration; it also meant the complete exclusion of religion from public life. He had too recently witnessed the threat of the Anglican Church establishing itself in America.

Jefferson initiated the democratization of the young American nation, but Andrew Jackson implemented that spirit. Arthur Schlesinger, Jr., has declared Jackson to be, along with Jefferson, the founder of American liberalism. As a liberal, Jackson believed in political equality and the expansion of democracy. He recognized that individuals might have different degrees of talent and economic success but should possess equal rights in the political arena. The Jacksonian system of political participation revolved around people, not property. To Jackson, a property-based right to vote foreshadowed the advent of separate classes and a denial of equality. Therefore, he advocated widening democracy and removing voting restrictions.

Jackson fought against a government dominated by the wealthy elite, excluding the majority of citizens. The Jacksonians strove to eliminate special privilege and to end the corruption that sprang from the cozy relationship between government and business. By contrast, Jackson's conservative Whig opponents distrusted the masses, placed a priority on social order over democratic participation, and believed that the protection of property was the primary function of society and the main component in social progress. Jackson's opponents argued that social and economic leadership, in addition to political leadership, should come from the leaders of finance and industry. Coinciding with a belief in social leadership by the elite, the conservative Whigs also believed in the moral supervision of private lives.[24] In response, Jacksonian liberals fought even harder to maintain separation of church and state.

Jacksonian liberalism recognized the political tensions between democratic ideals and the increasing concentration of economic power. Jacksonians saw that in the past the government had aided the wealthy class and protected their special privilege to the disadvantage of the common person. Just as liberals Otis and Adams had detected a threat to liberty in the power of the Crown, Jackson saw a similar threat in the power and dominance of concentrated wealth. Like Jefferson, Jackson distrusted all concentrations of power which could subvert the democratic process. The dominant economic power of the industrial corporations also jeopardized the independence of farmers and artisans and threatened to make them the "dependent laborers," an aspect of European society that Jefferson had so disliked. The primary aim of the Jacksonians, however, was not to redistribute property of the rich but to open the avenues of social advancement to all laborers.[25] They believed that the destruction of economic privilege would give free play to natural economic forces and lead to economic growth.

The Jacksonian support of farmers and artisans rested not only on the belief in the democratic necessity of independent citizens, but also on the Jacksonian views on work and wealth. The labor theory of value that pervaded this ideology was rooted in seventeenth-century Puritanism, eighteenth-century liberalism, and the Christian work ethic, which saw labor as creating value and idleness as waste.[26] Therefore, Jacksonian liberals resisted a society which conferred the privileges of wealth upon an elite class that had not labored for that wealth.

Jackson saw corruption in centralized economic power. Corporations and wealthy individuals sought government privileges of all types—charters, exemptions, tariffs, subsidies, and monopolies. Jacksonian liberalism opposed concentrated power not just for its threat to democratic liberties but for its manipulative use of government favor. Jackson worried that government was fostering an economic aristocracy and monopoly, thus risking the survival of a democratic society of independent and equal individuals. To Jackson, the ultimate power and ruler of society was democratic government. Within this framework, Jackson declared war on the Second Bank of the United States, claiming that it was a governmental tool of the wealthy used for personal gain. The bank's charter was in fact a monopoly grant given to private stockholders. Jackson's opposition to the bank followed Adam Smith's warning that banking was so inherently powerful and self-aggrandizing that the government should intervene. Moreover, Jackson saw that the bank's economic power translated into political power which could subvert the democratic process; it was known to advance funds to congressmen and keep key politicians on retainer.

Jacksonian liberalism valued a fluid society and fought for the common members of society who had no need or opportunity to gain government favors. Jacksonians were not opposed to economic development, only to a system that limited opportunity to a favored few. Jackson, unlike modern conservatives, did not oppose government involvement in the economy as a matter of principle; rather, he opposed the government making the rich richer and the potent more powerful. Without such government aid, Jackson believed, the passage of time would break up large fortunes and prevent the growth of a permanent upper class. Though individuals would always be free to gain wealth, aristocracy could never gain a foothold in America.

Jackson's view of liberty was thus broader than the mere absence of repressive laws; he saw liberty as freedom from monopolists and the holders of privilege. Jackson did not view democratic political power as a threat to liberty. To the contrary, he believed that the vast majority of Americans needed political power to ward off the predatory tendencies of the powerful monopolies. Articulating the liberal tradition initiated by liberals like Otis and Adams and later strengthened by liberals like Woodrow Wilson and Franklin Roosevelt, Jackson rejected the conservative defense of economic and property "rights" against the political decisions of democratic majorities.

### Abraham Lincoln and the Liberal Influence
### on the Birth of the Republican Party

The founders of the Republican party adhered to the general liberal thought of Jefferson. The first Republicans believed strongly in freedom, equality, and liberty. The liberal opposition to slavery also found a home in the Republican party. Throughout the Civil War and the postwar years, abolitionist Republicans campaigned for civil rights.[27] Republicans advocated giving blacks the vote, providing schools, and repealing segregationist laws. Ratification of the Fifteenth Amendment in 1870, making it illegal to deny the vote on grounds of race, resulted from Republican efforts.

Lincoln himself had a liberal view of freedom broader than merely an absence of restraint. Lincoln saw freedom in a social context—the preservation of an environment where individuals had the opportunity for self-realization. Consequently, Lincoln favored women's suffrage and endorsed labor's right to strike. He also believed strongly in minority rights and realized that majority rule and minority rights were interlocking parts of one structure of freedom.[28] Even though Lincoln had the power to suspend certain individual rights during wartime, he never contemplated a systematic effort to suppress dissent as the Federalists had six decades earlier.

In their economic outlook, liberal Republicans valued an economy which did not sustain a monopoly of the wealthy but which rewarded the common person. Indeed, there existed a certain suspicion of wealth within the Republican party. Charles Sumner, one of the most prominent first Republicans, frequently protested the indifference of the wealthy to social justice. One Republican newspaper stated that property "has frequently stood in the way of very necessary reforms"—like slavery.[29] The Republicans' free-labor ideology stressed equality of opportunity and reflected the view of the middle class. Their creed included a belief in government's role in improving the economy and healing public ills. For instance, the Republican platform of 1860 supported the homestead plan giving free land to western settlers.

The Republican party was the first political party in American history to build up and activate the national government as a powerful force in society. To conduct the Civil War, the Republicans had set out to strengthen a unified national community. They promoted a centralized national economy and encouraged manufacturing with a strong national government. Throughout and after the war, the Republican party approved of economic development sponsored by governmental assistance and supported social reforms such as public education. Their nationalizing spirit carried even beyond the economy; some even called for the creation of a national cultural authority.[30]

This government assistance to business, however, soon resulted in the occurrence of political corruption on an unprecedented scale. In 1872, a group of Republicans, upset over the corruption between the business community and the Ulysses S. Grant Republican administration, formed a Liberal Republican party. These liberals attributed the political corruption, as Jackson had, to the close ties between business and government. Though Jackson had fought the economic involvement of government on behalf of the wealthy and the corporations, government and big business in the 1870s continued to work together and support each other. The Republican party began supporting lavish aid to businesses, which went beyond just government leadership in the building of a national economy. At the same time, during the national depression of the 1870s, the Republicans also turned away from humanitarian concerns in favor of economic concerns. The Liberal Republicans protested this dramatic shift in focus away from general welfare concerns and toward complicity with business. They also deplored the fading of social moralism within the Republican party.[31]

Lincoln's views and those of the Liberal Republicans foreshadowed the liberal ideas that gave birth to the New Deal. The Liberal Republicans broadly interpreted the "general welfare" clause of the Constitution in human welfare terms. The emancipation of slaves, the granting of free farmland to the landless, and the establishment of public education were all acts of a welfare state—a government directed to promote the "general welfare." Lincoln's view of the legitimate role of government, as FDR's was to be, was "to do for a community of people whatever they need to have done, but cannot do at all, or cannot so well do for themselves, in their separate and individual capacities." Adhering to this view, the Republican party for many years sponsored legislation to police big business, build state universities, conserve natural resources, and improve working conditions. Even later, during FDR's administrations, Republican platforms increasingly recognized a governmental responsibility for the social welfare. The 1948 platform stated that the "tragic experience of Europe tells us that popular government disappears when it is ineffective and no longer can translate into action the aims and the aspirations of the people."[32] Forty years later, however, the Republican party, dominated by conservatives, repudiated this lesson from history.

*Woodrow Wilson—The Liberal as Defender*
*of Individual Freedom and Opportunity in a World*
*of Industrial Monopolies and International Autocracy*

America changed greatly from the post–Civil War period to the beginning of the twentieth century. The U.S. economy had grown at an unprecedented rate. Millions of immigrants had come to America to work in the busy factories. And America had become a world leader in science and technology, and its colleges and universities offered promise of continued progress.

With this fast-paced growth and rapid immigration, America also faced problems. The economic growth of the late nineteenth century had accompanied a dramatic transformation of the American economy from one made up of farmers and local competing businessmen—a free enterprise, competitive marketplace—to one dominated by large trusts and monopolies. Within this new environment of large national corporations, local communities experienced a loss of identity and control. No longer was economic production part of the community; it now emanated from far-away corporate boardrooms. Likewise, individuals who were once small businessmen and artisans now became dependent wage earners with no control over their lives. Furthermore, economic depressions frequently occurred in the boom-and-bust economy of the late nineteenth century. With each bust, which wiped out more and more independent local businesses, wage earners and local communities suffered an increasing loss of control over their economies and communities. The waves of immigrants also strained urban communities already suffering from a lack of jobs and overcrowded housing. The influx of immigrants heightened the urban slum problem, which in turn contributed to an increase in crime.

In response to these national problems, government offered little help. Bosses controlled urban political machines; and big business had almost complete support from government. With few existing alternatives and the increasing need for action, a Populist reform movement sprang up in the late nineteenth century in the Midwest, the West, and the South. A primary aim of populism focused on community self-determination and independence, and antimonopolism was populism's most common expression. Farmers saw the railroads and Eastern banking monopolies as threats to the existence of the local community, and they expressed a Jacksonian outrage at the increasing privileges and power given to corporations and financiers.[33]

The Populists' fierce individualism and belief in democratic values was in opposition to the nation's growing dependency on the monopolies and the corruption of the city and of Wall Street. Ignatious Donnelly, a Republican congressman from Minnesota, was one such Populist reformer. Donnelly and other Populists fought a battle for what they believed to be the Jeffersonian vision: independent communities of self-reliant individuals free from the corruption of the concentrated power of large corporations. To combat the power of the Eastern banks, Populists embraced the silver issue and called for the unlimited coinage of silver, which would end the currency monopoly of the Wall Street banks and open credit opportunities. However, the Populists faced powerful opponents and lost the battle of gold versus silver. By 1896, the movement had virtually died.[34]

Out of the ashes of Populism, and prompted by the increasing social problems now existing in the cities, arose a new reform movement in the early twentieth century called Progressivism. Progressives, like the Populists, sought individual and community control of social and economic forces. Progressives, however, tended to be middle-class urban dwellers. They accepted many of the changes that had occurred in America, such as economic and urban growth, but strove to direct those changes according to Progressive goals. Progressives sought to improve public education, separate the close ties between government and business, eradicate slums and dangerous factory conditions, conserve natural resources, revise archaic banking laws, and regulate the railroads and monopolies in the public interest. The central theme of humanitarian progressivism, however, was the child. Education, health, and child labor laws consistently attracted the progressives' attention.

Progressives held the Jacksonian view that government was not to be subservient to powerful private interests. Instead of a society directed by urban bosses and Wall Street bankers, Progressives envisioned a more open democratic society with an enlightened government responding to genuine public needs and encouraging social progress.

Woodrow Wilson was a Progressive and was elected president in 1912. Wilson's New Freedom program relied heavily on the values of democracy, equality, and individual freedom and opportunity. He called for a more open and mobile society, free of any barriers to individual advancement and accomplishment and free of any rigid economic and social status quo. While in office, he obtained passage of the Federal Reserve Act, engineered the enactment of child labor laws, and improved farmers' access to credit. Wilson geared his liberal philosophy to fulfilling the promise that America was the land of in-dividual opportunity. As he said in 1911, "The men who understand the life of the country are the men on the make, not the men who are already made."

The Wilsonian program aimed to return to the Jeffersonian liberal economic order of free competition and a competitive marketplace. In restoring political power to the individual, Wilson attempted to reverse the trend that had placed both economic and political power in large monopolized corporations. Monopolies in the early twenti-eth century exerted more power than the government—the source of law. Hence, in the Wilsonian view, these monopolies stood above and outside the rule of law. Recognizing that economic concentration threatened individual rights and freedom, Wilsonian liberalism also saw that the federal government needed to be strong enough and willful enough to check the new corporate power.

The liberal beliefs of Wilson followed in the Jefferson/Jackson tra-dition. Like Jefferson and Jackson, Wilson believed in the common person and in the right of that person to seek assistance and protec-tion from their government—what the corporate interests had been receiving for decades. He fought for democratically directed social change against the stubborn opposition of the wealthy and busi-ness elite. Not since Andrew Jackson had a national leader fought, as Wilson did, for individual freedom and equality of political and economic opportunity.

Niels Thorsen argues in *The Political Thought of Woodrow Wilson* that Wilson formulated a new brand of liberalism.[35] This liberalism emphasized the positive roles of political leadership in a twentieth-century democracy. However, its main focus continued to be on the individual. According to Thorsen, Wilson believed that the individ-ual's freedom depended on the welfare and progress of the nation, which in the increasingly industrialized and rapidly changing twen-tieth century required the positive contribution of modern gov-ernment. Wilson's patriotism, though still resting on American freedoms, departed from the traditionally exclusive liberal focus on the individual by emphasizing common interests. This emphasis paved the way for the New Deal liberalism.

Wilson grounded his liberal political philosophy on a belief in civic virtue and public morality. In his view, it was the duty of virtuous political leaders to encourage vigorous moral discussion. To Wilson, only individuals could provide the moral direction needed in a de-mocracy. He believed that society could be reformed by restoring the moral values weakened by monopolistic industrialization. Wilsonian liberals saw that industrial capitalism "had severed the relationship between the moral personality of those who earn money and those who merely come to possess it, between the ethic of work and the status of wealth."[36] Wilson also carried this moral message into the international arena and based his foreign policy on the moral values of democracy and freedom rather than on the compulsion of military might.

In many ways, Wilson sought to return to the world envisioned by Jefferson, where all individuals competed equally in the economic sphere and participated equally in the political sphere. Independent and equal individuals would then infuse democratic government with civic virtue. In such a world, no more than a limited government was needed. That world, however, had ceased to exist. Consequently, Wilson had to expand the activities and involvement of government so as to combat the growing dependency of Americans on the increasingly concentrated corporate economy. As FDR later did, Wilson acted out of necessity, not to abrogate individual freedom and democratic rule but to strengthen them against opposing forces.

### FDR and the Liberal Use of Government to Alleviate Misery, Achieve the Common Good, and Renew Individual Opportunity

Following the end of World War I, Wilson's unsuccessful attempt to bring the U.S. into the League of Nations, and almost two decades of progressive reforms, Americans retreated from the business of reform and relied almost strictly on business to manage and direct the nation's social and political well-being. Americans, disillusioned because the war had not produced the liberal international democratic order that Wilson had envisioned and ready to immerse themselves in the materialistic consumption promised by a new period of prosperity, elected conservative Republican Warren Harding as president in 1920. Harding promised to remove government from economic and social reforms and give free reign back to business.

Throughout the 1920s the conservative administrations of Harding, Coolidge, and Hoover increasingly dismantled the activist, progressive government and promised that support of big business and indulgence in private consumption would ensure peace and prosperity for the future. This prediction crashed along with the stock market in October of 1929.

The crash of 1929 made a mockery of conservative claims about prosperity and the power of business, left alone by government, to ensure social and economic progress for all.[37] Before the end of

Hoover's third year in office, the bottom had dropped out of the stock market and industrial production had decreased by more than half. By 1932 the unemployed numbered more than thirteen million: one out of every four who had held jobs in 1929 were unemployed.

During the Great Depression, many Americans lived in the primitive conditions of a preindustrial society and were stricken by famine. Twenty percent of New York City's schoolchildren suffered from malnutrition. In the Appalachian coal fields, families evicted from their homes spent the winter in tents and children went barefoot. It was estimated that during the Depression two million people wandered the country in a fruitless quest for work. On snowy days, hundreds of men huddled over fires at railway yards waiting for work. In empty lots in all the big cities, homeless men threw together makeshift shacks of boxes and scrap metal. St. Louis had the largest such "Hooverville" with more than a thousand people. In Chicago, a crowd of some fifty hungry men fought over a barrel of garbage set outside the back door of a restaurant; in Stockton, California, men scoured the city dump to retrieve half-rotted food.[38] Throughout the country, desperate, violent protests erupted in the cities.

In the face of all this misery, a stubborn Hoover held firm to conservative antigovernment principles and fumbled vainly for a voluntarist formula with which to combat the Depression. Hoover rejected direct relief, believing it would undermine individual character and the capitalist system. However, as the Depression intensified his opposition to federal action diminished, but only toward action aimed at traditional conservative interests and constituencies.

Hoover created the Reconstruction Finance Corporation (RFC) to make loans to banks, insurance companies, and railroads. The theory behind the RFC was that it would lend money to large entities at the top of the economic system and that benefits would trickle down to people at the bottom through a sort of percolation process. This "trickle-down" theory—like the trickle-down economics of a conservative president fifty years later—did not help the majority of Americans and did not solve the economic crisis. To finance this government aid to banks and insurance companies, Hoover appealed for an increase in taxes to be paid by those Americans lower on the trickle-down scale; but he never sought repeal of the loopholes that permitted the partners of J. P. Morgan and other wealthy Americans to escape paying any income taxes in 1931 and 1932.[39] In effect, Hoover prepared the way for the substantial federal activity of the New Deal by giving private enterprise the opportunity to solve the Depression—and to fail.

Through his inactivity and his promises of recovery "just around the corner," Hoover appeared unconcerned about the problems suffered by the nation. His proclamations of the country's economic health also diminished his credibility to the public. When accepting the Republican nomination in 1928, for instance, Hoover had declared that America had triumphed over poverty. Good times, he insisted, were not the result of good fortune, but of the wisdom of the Republican party and business leaders.[40]

The Great Depression similarly ruined the credibility of business leaders. As business had proclaimed throughout the 1920s that if left alone it could guarantee continued growth and prosperity, the Depression also caused the public to lose confidence in business. It was less their financial transgressions than their social irresponsibility, however, which caused the loss of faith in America's business leaders. At a time when millions lived close to starvation and some even had to scavenge for food, corporate executives continued to draw astronomical salaries and further manipulated the economy to their personal profit. The real responsibility for poverty, claimed businessmen, lay with the jobless themselves; there was no problem with the system, they argued.

The depth of the economic misery prompted large numbers of middle-class Americans, previously caught up in the obsession with self-indulgence in the 1920s, to adopt traditional working-class values centered on cooperation, work, fairness, and justice. These Americans looked to their government to express and implement these values. Franklin Roosevelt responded by promising a "New Deal" for the American people, who no longer wanted corporate domination of American life. The New Deal liberals drew on a storehouse of past political experiences.[41] From Jackson came a renewed commitment to democracy and the common person; from the Populists came a suspicion of monopolies and of the social wisdom of Wall Street; from Theodore Roosevelt's New Nationalism came a knowledge of regulation of the large corporations; from the mobilization of World War I came a knowledge of the use of government; and from urban social reformers of the Jane Addams tradition arose a sense of social compassion and justice. The New Dealers also shared John Dewey's conviction that rational social intelligence applied through government could shape and improve society. The novel and revolutionary aspect of the New Deal, however, was its significant expansion of the role and activities of the federal government.

However, this expansion also had its political precedents, particularly in reference to the changing U.S. economic marketplace.

During the pre–World War I decades, the American economy was transformed from a highly competitive, small producer system to a highly concentrated system dominated by large corporations. The rise of the monopolistic corporation threatened Americans' most basic political ideas inherited from Locke, Jefferson, and Jackson. According to these ideas, liberty and equality depended on the diffusion of small-property ownership, a free enterprise system of independent individuals, and an open democratic society of equal individuals.[42] However, this free-market model of Adam Smith, the New Dealers argued, had vanished forever.

In the early twentieth century, the corporate state stood more powerful than democratic government. Wilson sought to reverse this monopolization and return American society to the Jeffersonian ideal. Yet Wilson had stopped short of using the full power of government to achieve this ideal and had not altered the relationship between government and society, in which government had long occupied the same type of limited role. The continuing influence of the Jeffersonian model during Wilson's term prevented clear vision and debate of the relationship between government and society. Thus, the increasing government intervention under Wilson was not accompanied by an increasing awareness of the need for a more equal relationship between government and the economy, but by a dogged adherence to a nineteenth-century model of limited government and free enterprise economics that had ceased to exist in reality.

The change in economic life consequently forced a change in American political liberalism. Limited government no longer insured liberty, since the corporate state was now capable of unchecked power. The New Dealers therefore abandoned the Wilsonian attempt to recreate the classical society of small competitors and instead advocated structural reforms needed to stabilize the economy and bring it under democratic control. Although the expanded government of the New Deal conflicted with the somewhat obsolete small-government philosophy of Jeffersonian liberalism, an active government was necessary to oversee the giant corporate sector and ensure that it functioned in the public's interest. Thus, expansion of the state arose from the liberal "determination to enhance individualism against princes of plutocracy."[43]

The New Deal faith in government rested on the belief that democratic government, contrary to the monopolistic corporation, would not be alien or indifferent to the public. The New Deal envisioned using the federal government to put corporations to work for the nation, since the economy was largely in the corporations' hands.

The New Deal borrowed the idea from the New Nationalism that corporations should be able to fulfill their natural growth so long as federal powers were used to confine their activities to democratically established boundaries. The model was a partnership between business and government in which government had more than a passive role. Reviewing the history of the American economy, FDR pointed out that big business had often used a passive government to gain special privileges at the expense of the general public. Hoover's protective tariffs and government loans, for instance, had benefited big business at the expense of the individual.

Once elected, Roosevelt went to work addressing the economic crisis. One of his first programs, the National Recovery Administration (NRA), even though a temporary measure, boasted a considerable success: it gave jobs to some two million workers; helped stop the deflationary spiral that had almost wrecked the nation; improved business ethics; and wiped out child labor and the sweatshop. Roosevelt's farm program during his first term succeeded in raising farm income 50 percent and decreasing rural debt.[44]

The New Deal immediately roused the opposition of business. However, FDR insisted that the public interest was paramount to that of any private group. This approach put him in conflict with the banking and securities industry, which asserted that it was independent of government and should not be regulated. When Roosevelt asked Congress for legislation to regulate the stock exchange, financiers protested that the regulation would turn Wall Street into a "deserted village" and claimed that "the Exchange is a perfect institution."[45] Roosevelt persisted and secured passage of the Securities Exchange Act of 1933, which sought to prevent manipulation of the securities market by insiders and end misrepresentation in the sale of securities.

Besides regulating business, the New Deal strove to assist the starving and unemployed people. FDR set up the Civil Works Administration (CWA) as an emergency relief measure to get America through the winter of 1933. In its short life, the CWA built or improved some 500,000 miles of roads, 40,000 schools, 3,500 playgrounds, and 1,000 airports. Alarmed at how much the CWA was costing, however, Roosevelt ended it as quickly as he could. He had always believed in budget balancing.[46] And though he shunned massive deficit spending, FDR adopted it as a last measure to get the nation through the Depression.

Roosevelt also did not want to create a permanent class of "reliefers" who might never get off the government payroll. Yet despite these concerns, the need for relief on a massive scale still existed in 1935. Roosevelt proposed a comprehensive program of emergency public employment. The program would hire the jobless and pay them more than the relief dole but less than the prevailing wage so as to discourage idleness yet avoid competition with the private sector. Nonetheless, Roosevelt's proposal to spend almost five billion dollars on work relief alarmed conservatives who actually favored the less costly dole, notwithstanding Hoover's warnings of the effect of the dole on individual character. Despite this opposition, Roosevelt's proposal easily passed Congress and created the Works Progress Administration (WPA), which throughout its history built or improved more than 2,500 hospitals, 5,900 school buildings, 1,000 airport landing fields, and nearly 13,000 playgrounds.[47]

While the WPA addressed the needs of those who could be employed, it ignored the unemployable—the aged, the sick, the crippled. For these, Roosevelt proposed a social security program. Conservatives naturally opposed the program and charged that the social security idea violated traditional American values of self-help, self-denial, and individual responsibility. In the battle of values, however, the New Deal liberalism prevailed.

Traditional American political and religious values supported the New Deal social programs. For instance, Catholic religious beliefs provided a sense of social responsibility to government service.[48] During his 1932 campaign, FDR often quoted from the Encyclical of Pope Pius XI, which denounced the unchecked power and economic dictatorship consolidated in the hands of a few. The American Catholic cardinals and bishops had denounced Hoover's commitment to a socially irresponsible capitalism. For them, the Roosevelt plan making up the New Deal was the Catholic plan of assistance to the poor and unemployed.

In 1935, the New Deal began its "Second Hundred Days." In addition to the public works and social security programs, this period witnessed an assault on the power of large holding companies whose monopoly power was holding back the recovery. The liberal opposition to monopoly focused on the way the inflexible administered prices of industrial monopolies impeded recovery. Besides the launching of antitrust suits and the collection of taxes against big business, the FDR administration obtained major legislation, such as the Public Utilities Holding Company Act, regulating or counteracting corporate monopolization. Roosevelt sought to break up the huge holding companies because they had fleeced the consumer, corrupted legislatures, and, by their elusive operations, evaded state regulation.[49]

At no time, however, had Roosevelt considered the creation of a planned economy.[50] Even the most precedent-breaking New Deal projects reflected capitalist thinking and deferred to business sensibilities: social security was modeled on private insurance systems, and relief directors were forbidden to approve projects which interfered with private enterprise. Roosevelt's program rested on the assumption that a just society could be secured by imposing democratically determined social welfare measures on a capitalist foundation and by moving the economy closer to the freely competitive market model.

The New Deal addressed the questions of whether business or government was ultimately responsible for society's well-being and whether democratic government has the power to intercede when business fails in its economic or social mission. The immediate goal of the New Deal, however, was a fairly conservative goal—the survival of democratic society. Historians have claimed that Roosevelt saved the country from revolution; although he merely expanded on the Jacksonian and Wilsonian theme of using government on behalf of the individual. Roosevelt called the New Deal a "war for the survival of democracy," since the states were not capable of achieving the necessary reforms by themselves. He cast the New Deal as a campaign between the people and the "privileged princes" of the "new economic dynasties," and called for extending "American freedom and American peace by making them living facts in a living present."[51]

Roosevelt's liberal programs achieved so much popularity and success that even his 1936 Republican challenger, Alf Landon, endorsed many New Deal projects and favored the regulation of business. However, Roosevelt's style of politics deeply offended many conservatives. Like Jefferson, FDR was skeptical of orthodox opinions and uninterested in moralistic reforms. While Jefferson was thought to be the agent of revolutionary French radicalism, Roosevelt was said to take his orders from Moscow.

In his governing style, Roosevelt refused to be bound by the restraints that confined other leaders in the past. He believed in experimentation and in the use of new knowledge and tools to solve new problems—one such tool being government itself. Roosevelt used this tool with amazing success. The list of New Deal accomplishments is almost endless: Social Security; the TVA; the Federal Deposit Insurance Corporation (FDIC); the Civilian Conservation Corps for the youth; the regulation of the securities market through the SEC; progressive taxation; the National Labor Relations Board (NLRB); and farm legislation, which included the Commercial Credit Corporation and the soil conservation program. On an average day, the Farm Credit Administration saved three hundred farms from foreclosure.[52]

The New Deal liberalism expressed the spirit of the Constitution and grounded itself in the most fundamental of American values. It expressed the communal desire to solve social problems through democratic action; it sought to expand economic opportunity; and it strengthened political equality by attempting to give every individual an equal chance to govern. The New Deal followed the rule of government set down by John Quincy Adams in his first message to Congress:

> The great object of the institution of civil government is the improvement of the condition of those who are parties to the social compact, and no government, in whatever form constituted, can accomplish the lawful end of its institution but in proportion as it improves the condition of those over whom it is established.

In recent years, the shortcomings of New Deal liberalism have been greatly exaggerated. Conservatives have charged New Deal liberalism with deliberately bloating the federal bureaucracy at the expense of state and local governments and with creating a national government which panders to special interest groups to the disadvantage of the general interest. These critics ignore, however, that the New Deal focused on the public interest and included many groups and individuals previously left at the fringes of American politics, such as Catholics, Jews, blacks, and working men and women—not "special interests," but Americans deserving of participation in the American democracy. Contrary to conservatives who opposed any government response to the Great Depression because of the effect on special corporate or property interests, FDR made the government more responsive to the needs and wishes of the majority of Americans who did not fall within the select interest group made up of wealthy individuals and corporations.

In the tradition of Jefferson, Jackson, and Wilson, FDR empowered the individual American by reasserting the liberal rule that the sovereign will of the majority, rather than economic principles and interests, must form the basis of political government. Indeed, for FDR to have failed to take bold and assertive governmental action to fight economic depression would have been to ignore majority will and the very foundation of law in a democratic society. Furthermore, since local and state governments did not possess the resources to effectively respond to the crisis, FDR out of necessity resorted to the federal government. Thus, the New Deal was not based on a belief by liberals that American federalism should be replaced by an exclusive reliance on the federal government; rather, it simply recognized the reality that the magnitude of the Great Depression—like the waging of war—could only be addressed by the greater resources of the federal government.

### Harry Truman: A Liberal for a Fair and Just Democracy

By 1946, liberals had brought America through two world wars and a major economic depression. But in the quest to ensure economic survival and protect democracy abroad, liberals in the postwar era realized that further work remained at home. Since the post–Civil War period, little had been done to remedy the discrimination against blacks. In the late nineteenth and early twentieth centuries, the South had passed Jim Crow laws imposing a segregated society.

Truman became the first president of the twentieth century to commit to the elimination of racial discrimination. In 1946, he set up the President's Committee on Civil Rights, which later issued its historic report, *To Secure These Rights,* recommending a series of changes in racial practices. Truman quickly moved to implement the committee's report by issuing an executive order banning discrimination in federal employment, stepping up the pace of desegregation of the armed forces, and requesting the Supreme Court to act against racial discrimination. Truman also sent to Congress a ten-point civil rights message calling for a strengthening of civil rights laws, a law against lynching, an end to segregation in interstate transportation, and protection of the right to vote.

While FDR had been concerned with the economic survival of black Americans, Truman focused on achieving political equality and civil rights. So long as he remained in office, Truman wrote, he would continue the fight for equality of opportunity for all human beings. Truman summed up his cause with graphic examples:

> When the mob gangs can take four people out and shoot them in the back, and everybody in the country is acquainted with who did the shooting and nothing is done about it, that country is in a pretty bad fix from a law enforcement standpoint. When a mayor and a city marshal can take a negro sergeant off a bus in South Carolina, beat him up and put out one of his eyes, and nothing is done about it by the state authorities, something is radically wrong with the system.[53]

Truman termed his political program the Fair Deal, stating that "every segment of our population and every individual has the right to expect from our government a fair deal."[54] Truman's Fair Deal proposed a broadening of civil rights laws, more low-cost housing, increased coverage for social security, and federal aid to education. Truman's farm program also sought greater efficiency and fairness. Whereas previous farm programs had primarily assisted the big farmers, the Truman program proposed to eliminate that favoritism and to encourage more efficient production. The Republicans, however, criticized Truman's program as being too socialistic and wanted to continue giving the big farmers thousands of dollars in disguised subsidies. Today, ironically, conservative Republicans support a farm program modeled on the Truman proposal.

Truman saw the purpose of American politics to be the creation of opportunity for the common man: the blue-collar worker who wanted a job without having to buy a union card or pay off a labor leader in advance; the small businessman threatened by monopolistic practices; the minorities attempting to make their way against discrimination.[55] Yet Truman's liberalism, like FDR's, placed the public interest above all else, even above requests from constituent groups for special treatment. This focus on the general interest was reflected in the labor troubles of 1946. Labor had generally been friendly and supportive of Truman. However, Truman saw the labor strikes of 1946 as threatening a collapse of the economy and attempted to get the workers back to work, especially in the key industry of coal mining. Truman resolved the strike; but when the union later wanted to back out of its contract and go back on strike, Truman opposed it and sought an injunction against the miners. The union caved in and went back to work.

Truman also achieved remarkable success in foreign policy. The Truman Doctrine, the Marshall Plan, and the North Atlantic Treaty creating NATO were accomplishments of Truman. Through these plans and treaties Truman committed the United States to a strong role in world politics, to peace and democracy in the world, and to fighting communism. By 1948, Truman had successfully "contained" communism in Europe. The Truman and Marshall plans provided economic aid to Europe, which allowed it to prosper economically so that the seeds of Communist revolution would not take hold. NATO, on the other hand, created an allied military defense of Western Europe.

Despite Truman's success in containing communism, however, conservatives continued to lob charges of communist leanings against the Truman administration. Such charges by conservatives were nothing new to the Truman administration; they "were in fact a routine feature of right-wing rhetoric." Given their attack on liberals for being "soft on communism," however, the conservative foreign policy in the late 1940s seems oddly inconsistent.

Senator Robert Taft—a conservative known as "Mr. Republican"—argued against American involvement across the world to fight communism. He believed that America should not concern itself with Europe and initially opposed the Truman Doctrine, the Marshall Plan, and the North Atlantic Treaty. Although an enemy of communism and a critic of liberals for being soft on communism, Taft opposed a total offensive against communism, since such an offensive would require expensive foreign aid programs and heavy military spending. Thus, while pushing Truman to stand firm against communism, Taft opposed Truman for using the means to effectively do so. Moreover, this conservative opposition only served to lay the groundwork for Joseph McCarthy's witch-hunt of the 1950s. The routine accusations of communism directed against the Roosevelt and Truman administrations, even though made in rather general fashions, set the precedent for the irresponsible McCarthy attacks against individuals.[56]

Truman's Fair Deal ingrained in American politics the age-old liberal ideals of fairness and justice held so strongly by the early patriots. As did Roosevelt before him, Truman ardently advocated democratic values and made government the ultimate expression of the public interest. His belief in democracy also translated into a fight against the spread of totalitarian communism. And in the tradition of twentieth-century liberalism under Wilson and Roosevelt, Truman opposed the conservative tendency toward international isolationism. While the McCarthy hysteria expressed a conservative fear of communism and a desire for American isolation, it did nothing constructive to fight communism and only served to cause divisions within America. Truman's policy on communism—although accused of being soft—actively and rationally set out to strengthen American and European democracies against Communist erosion. As with so many previous periods of national crises, liberals attacked the roots of the problems while conservatives reacted to change with fear and by attacking liberals.

### John F. Kennedy: A Liberal Who Brought Pride and Purpose to American Politics

In 1988, America recognized the twenty-fifth anniversary of John Kennedy's death. The Kennedy dream and the hope he offered still attract and inspire a nation that remembers. Yet just as Americans in 1988 were celebrating the Kennedy dream, they were hearing that liberalism was un-American and irrelevant.

The Kennedy years offer a kind of promised land for liberals who have become disillusioned and frustrated throughout the decade of the eighties. It is as though liberalism somehow lost a sense of direction in Dallas back in November of 1963. Yet the long-standing meaning of the liberal tradition has endured; it is only the present awareness and direction of that tradition that has wandered. Indeed, John Kennedy was only one of many spokespersons of the liberal tradition initiated by Otis and Adams, sustained by Wilson, Roosevelt, and Truman, and still alive today.

Kennedy appealed to a nation needing to recover a sense of purpose, to renew its strength and refresh its idealism after a decade in which it was somewhat adrift and complacent in its outlook. Signs of fading national optimism became evident by the late 1950s. The slowing of economic growth, the Soviet launch of Sputnik, and demonstrations of hostility toward the U.S. in supposedly friendly Latin America and Japan spurred America toward a desire for activism and progress. Kennedy brought this activist spirit, a sense of purpose, and promise of progress to Washington. His spirited and idealistic liberalism expressed a refreshing conviction that the world could be changed, that intelligent public service could accomplish great things, and that the constructive potential of government remained scarcely tapped.

Perhaps the Peace Corps was Kennedy's most idealistic achievement. By channeling youthful ideals into constructive activity around the world, the Corps represented the best of American idealism. It also fulfilled his call to public service: "ask not what your country can do for you; ask what you can do for your country." In keeping with the liberal tradition, Kennedy saw that public service was a noble and worthwhile endeavor. Unlike modern conservatives, JFK did not think that private interest and the profit motive had exclusive holds on American ingenuity and accomplishment.

Though Kennedy's liberalism followed in the Roosevelt and Truman tradition, it adapted its policies to the challenges of the times. While Roosevelt and Truman had addressed "quantitative problems" of American life, such as economic depression and wide-scale poverty and unemployment, Kennedy addressed qualitative concerns, such as education and health care. By 1960, many of the quantitative needs—food, clothing, shelter, and employment—had been met for most Americans. Yet liberalism faced a great challenge, and Kennedy

realized that the "final lesson of the affluent society is surely that af-
fluence is not enough—that solving the quantitative problems of living only increases the importance of the quality of the life lived."[57]
Kennedy stood for civil rights, for assistance to the poor and the unemployed to give them the opportunity to better their condition, for
excellence in education as the only insurance for a sound future, for
confidence in our scientific and technical abilities and for an expansion of our vision through his space program, for economic growth,
for the nobility of public service, and for a foreign policy committed
to democracy and free trade. He stood for the public interest and for
causes that were in the best interest of all of society.

Kennedy was an innovator and optimist. This spirit was exemplified by his challenge to America's scientific and technological abilities with the launching of the space program. In a promise that
would come true, he vowed that America would land on the moon in
the 1960s. Kennedy's faith in experimentation echoed that of FDR
and of the framers. He believed that "no problem of human destiny
is beyond human beings," and he urged Americans to "go forward"
with an innovative spirit. In a 1962 commencement address at Yale,
with a speech that could be given today, he proclaimed that

> We cannot understand and attack our contemporary problems if we
> are bound by traditional labels and the slogans of an earlier era. The
> unfortunate fact of the matter is that our rhetoric had not kept pace
> with the speed of social and economic change. Our political de-
> bates . . . too often bear little or no relation to the actual problems the
> U.S. faces.

In economic matters, Kennedy's activist impulse aimed to "get the
economy moving again" and to achieve full employment. As a result, the economy was robust during his administration—economic
growth averaged 5.6 percent annually, unemployment dropped almost two percentage points, and inflation stood at 1.2 percent. His
tax-cut plan kept the economy growing, but his concern about inflation led to his showdown with U.S. Steel when it defied the national interest and unnecessarily raised prices. This confrontation
showed that Kennedy considered the government to be the boss in
matters of national interest and that he would assert the American
interest against a giant American corporation just as well as against
foreign adversaries.

Though the economy was strong during the Kennedy years, serious social problems and challenges faced the nation. The civil rights

issue was smoldering. Riots occurred at the all-white University of Mississippi when a black student named James Meredith tried to enroll; Kennedy was forced to call out federal troops. Eight days later he sent Congress a civil rights bill calling for equal access to public accommodations and ending discrimination in schools and jobs and at the polls. Kennedy died before his civil rights bill could become law, but already by 1963 Kennedy began to see civil rights as a moral rather than just a political issue. In June of 1963, in an idealistic speech calling for civil rights legislation, Kennedy proclaimed that "we are confronted primarily with a moral issue. It is as old as the scriptures and is as clear as the American Constitution."

Kennedy also had the strength and courage to defend democratic values and principles. In the area of foreign relations, FDR had insisted on the equality of all nations and the right of self-government by nationality groups.[58] Kennedy followed this approach and opposed those conservatives who wanted a more "imperial" foreign policy in which America would dictate the affairs of its allies. In his inaugural address he also affirmed his conviction to reach peaceful diplomatic solutions—"Let us never negotiate out of fear. But let us never fear to negotiate"—yet promised to never compromise our basic freedoms and values—"we shall . . . pay any price . . . to assure the survival . . . of liberty."

Kennedy was a committed anti-Communist, but he was equally committed to peaceful diplomatic solutions in favor of military standoffs. Indeed, in rejecting air strikes against Cuba during the missile crisis and in handling Khrushchev by firm negotiation, Kennedy set a new standard of statesmanship and prudence in dealing with the Soviet Union. But even during that crisis, Kennedy enlisted the support of the Organization of American States—a body which the Reagan administration has all but completely ignored in its Latin American policy.

Through the Peace Corps and the Alliance for Progress, Kennedy paid greater attention to the aspirations of the Third World, which had rejected the simple categorization of the world into two inherently incompatible blocks—communism and capitalism—and the reflective American opposition to any country not completely adopting the American view. What distinguished John Kennedy's foreign policy from Dwight Eisenhower's was the belief that Third World revolutions were progressive, democratic movements harmonious with the interests and traditions of the U.S. and that they could be redirected along the lines of the American Revolution. This assumption gave Kennedy's foreign policy a crusading, rather than reactionary, quality.

Kennedy moved away from the simple conservative outlook that saw every blowup in Latin America as Communist inspired and every anti-American expression the work of Communists. He was willing to give free reign to native democratic movements. Kennedy injected a positive spirit into his Latin American policy—trying to make the region safe for democracy and capable of economic independence. He advocated Wilsonian liberalism to promote democratic values and self-determination of nations and individuals. He also followed FDR's Good Neighbor Policy, which emphasized cooperative arrangements among allies rather than control by one. Kennedy's vision of an interdependent world "united by free trading arrangements was a recreation of the liberal vision of global unity and prosperity."[59]

Although Kennedy believed in international diplomacy, he infused an intense sense of purpose and tenacity into his foreign policy. For instance, in no area did JFK exhibit more determination than in the Berlin crisis. With the Berlin airlift, Kennedy showed his preparation to go to any lengths to defend the American commitment to the city. In 1963, as Berlin was still in need of reassurance, JFK visited the city and told an electrified crowd, "Ich bin ein Berliner."

When he died in November 1963, Kennedy was already moving America away from the Cold War. He had accomplished the limited Test Ban Treaty eliminating nuclear testing—a treaty unbroken to this day—and had made his eloquent American University speech in June of 1963 in which he said:

> If we cannot end now our differences, at least we can make the world safe for diversity. For, in the final analysis, our most basic common link is that we all inhabit this small planet, we all breathe the same air. We all cherish our children's future. And we are all mortal.

Kennedy offered both the hope and the tools for a peaceful world.

### The Liberal Tradition in the Republican Party

American liberalism revolves around three basic precepts. First, it advocates a fair and open democracy that includes all of society and that gives voice to all members without discrimination; it is a democracy that is not subservient to any other social or economic institution. Second, American liberalism respects the basic human rights and freedoms preserved in the Constitution and the integrity and moral will of the individual. Finally, liberalism espouses the constructive and innovative use of government as a positive force to remedy social ills and encourage social progress. Underlying these precepts is the belief in the sovereignty of the individual and the supremacy of the democratic order. All political power resides in the individual, and anything that weakens that power goes against the liberal strain. A democratic government made up of free and equal individuals constitutes the ultimate source of law and power in society. To the extent private conglomerations of power exceed the power of government, the political freedom and power of the individual is threatened.

These liberal beliefs have not been solely the beliefs of various members of the Democratic party. Throughout the Republican party's history, it has included men and women professing the liberal faith and calling themselves "liberal." Abraham Lincoln—the "father" of the Republican party—advocated the basic liberal beliefs. He believed in opening and expanding the democratic order to include blacks and women and in protecting black civil liberties. He believed in using the power of government as an active instrument of reform in society. Indeed, enough members of the party so believed in these principles that there existed a large contingent of professed Liberal Republicans in the 1860s and 1870s.

The Liberal Republicans came together in the 1860s in their vehement opposition to slavery. This opposition rested on moral and constitutional values—middle-class capitalist values, individual liberty and autonomy, and freedom of opportunity. Furthermore, they opposed the political corruption that occurred when strong private economic interests could control or influence government.[60] The Liberal Republicans also resisted the attachment of federal power to the upper-class interests.

To accomplish their reform goals, the Liberal Republicans endorsed positive government action and favored a strong central government. Charles Francis Adams, a member of the famous Adams family, was a Liberal Republican and was the founder and first chairman of the Massachusetts Board of Railroad Commissioners. He believed in railroad reform because the industry had become one of monopolists exercising unchecked, unscrupulous power at the expense of the general welfare. To combat corruption and dishonesty in government, Liberal Republicans also called for a thorough reform of the civil service.[61] In 1872, at the urging of liberals and celebrated women's suffrage leader Susan B. Anthony, the Republican party adopted the first women's plank in a national platform.

The Progressive reform movement of the early twentieth century first found a home in the Republican party. Theodore Roosevelt's program envisioned progressive reform through the federal government. The Republican administrations of Roosevelt and Taft began the twentieth-century trend toward an ever-stronger national government. But soon after assuming office, Roosevelt quickly encountered the opposition of big business, which was unaccustomed to such rivalry. Roosevelt saw that big business had become monopolized and had destroyed the reality of Adam Smith's and Thomas Jefferson's ideal of a market economy of freely competing, independent small producers. Roosevelt believed that government, concerned with the general welfare and controlled by democratic rule, must act to protect that welfare when it becomes threatened by big business. For instance, the discovery of unsanitary packing plants and stockyards led to Roosevelt's push for the 1906 Meat Inspection Act. He also regulated the railroads and the food and drug industries and established the first national large-scale conservation program.[62] Thus, to regulate the large corporations, Roosevelt had to create government commissions possessing enough power to combat the monopoly power of the industrial corporations.

Roosevelt was the most popular president since Jackson. His Square Deal liberal reforms included conservation of the nation's natural resources, regulation of big corporations in the public interest, and a cessation of hostility toward labor unions. Like Wilson, Roosevelt believed in individual freedom, equality of opportunity, fair wages, and social mobility. Nonetheless, as Roosevelt left office, conservatives announced that "sanity would now return to the government's affairs." When Roosevelt campaigned again in 1912, conservatives called his supporters "destructive radicals" and accused him of trying to change the Republican party from a party of "moderate liberalism" to a "radical party."[63]

Following the Progressive Era, the next major period of reform and government activism occurred during the New Deal. Many Republicans came to endorse and support the liberal foundations of the New Deal. Indeed, Republicans like Wendell Wilkie and Thomas E. Dewey—the party's presidential candidates in 1940, 1944, and 1948—accepted the welfare provisions of Roosevelt's New Deal. Liberal Republicans also later succeeded in denying the 1952 endorsement to conservative Ohio senator Taft and in nominating Eisenhower, who promised to preserve the framework of the New Deal and to continue Truman's foreign policy.[64]

Eisenhower's "new Republicanism," unlike Reagan's conservatism of the 1980s, did not advocate a return to the 1920s nor an abolishment of the role of the federal government. Eisenhower accepted broad government responsibility for the general welfare and warned conservatives that "should any political party attempt to abolish social security and eliminate labor laws and farm programs, you would not hear of that party again in our political history." Indeed, during his presidency Eisenhower extended the work started by the New Deal: he created the Department of Health, Education and Welfare; increased federal funding for education, housing, and health; allowed increases in minimum wage and in Social Security; and approved a program of medical care for the indigent elderly. Like FDR, Eisenhower resorted to deficit financing to buffer the impact of the three recessions that occurred during his presidency.[65] He also undertook huge government public works projects, like the St. Lawrence Seaway project and the interstate highway system. In contrast to his domestic spending, however, Eisenhower dramatically cut military spending and presided over an era of low defense spending.

Eisenhower "internationalized" his party by obtaining a ratification of many of the liberal foreign policy initiatives of the Roosevelt and Truman administrations.[66] Furthermore, Eisenhower opposed the Bricker amendment—an attempt by conservative Republicans to place strict limits on the authority of the president to negotiate treaties or enter into executive agreements with other nations. The conservative position in the 1950s on the Bricker amendment, incidentally, contrasts sharply with the conservative position in the Iran-Contra scandal of the Reagan administration.

The most liberal Supreme Court rulings of the century have come from a Republican-appointed Court. Earl Warren, appointed Chief Justice by Eisenhower, had been the Republican candidate for vice president in 1948. Some of the decisions of the Warren Court included *Brown v. Board of Education* condemning segregation, *Baker v. Carr* declaring the principle of "one person, one vote" and requiring fair reapportionment of state legislatures, and *Gideon v. Wainwright* ruling that a poor person charged with a felony had the right to a state-appointed lawyer. The Warren Court also banned prayer in public schools and upheld the Civil Rights Act of 1964 and the Voting Rights Act of 1965.

So while Republicans in 1988 derided the Democrats for their association with liberalism, they ignored their own historical tie with liberalism. Even as recent as 1980, with the presidential candidacy of John Anderson, the Republican party contained a clear strand of liberalism. Today there still exist some Republicans who are unafraid of professing their liberal values and are disappointed by the recent conservative attack on liberalism. Elmer Andersen, a former Republican governor of Minnesota and a founder of the Liberal Republican Club, recently commented that it is "unfortunate today that 'liberal' is used as a derogatory term."[67]

## CHAPTER FIVE

# Liberalism and Affirmative Government

## The Liberal Belief in a Positive Role
## for Democratic Government

The American liberal tradition reflects a consistent belief in the two basic concepts of liberalism—individual freedom and dignity and democratic rule of society. An outgrowth of these two concepts, and a feature of liberalism which has become increasingly apparent in the twentieth century, is the support of a positive or affirmative government. By affirmative government, liberals mean a government capable of acting in society when so directed by the democratic majority: a government which is not confined to inaction because of some constitutional mandate or principle.

Conservatives in the twentieth century have often opposed affirmative government with the argument that the American political system created by the constitutional framers envisions a limited government with little authority to affirmatively act in economic or social matters. Using this limited government model, conservatives have argued that the use of affirmative government—Wilson's Progressive reforms, FDR's New Deal, Truman's Fair Deal, and Kennedy's New Frontier—contradicts the true nature and scheme of the American constitutional system.

In opposing affirmative government, however, conservatives effectively oppose the democratic principles of the Constitution. The liberal use of affirmative government has resulted from the democratic demands of the American public for government action. For instance, the early New Deal programs received overwhelming support from Congress and the public. Conservatives, out of touch with popular opinion and reluctant to abide by democratic decisions, opposed those programs and defeated them by convincing the courts that the programs exceeded the power and authority of a limited government. This defeat of the New Deal programs was a denial of democracy, a denial based simply on the rejection of the power of democratic government to act when necessary.

The liberal support of affirmative government also results from the liberal belief in the individual. Clearing away the institutional roadblocks to the fulfillment of democratic decisions strengthens the political rights and freedoms of individuals in a democratic society. A belief in democratic rule cannot exist with a doctrinal opposition to affirmative government.

Conservatives, however, often accuse liberals of inconsistent and contradictory positions on the role of affirmative government. In support of their opposition to affirmative government, conservatives point out that a belief in limited government constituted a staple of eighteenth-century liberalism. Indeed, liberals in the eighteenth century developed their limited government notions from their experience with England. During the colonial and revolutionary periods, the only source of oppression and injustice perceived by Americans was English rule. In the feudal, aristocratic world of eighteenth-century Europe, the strongest institutions in society were the institutions of government. Likewise, in America, with its competitive small-scale producer economy, no social or economic organizations even approached the power and authority of the colonial governing bodies. Given this experience, the political leaders of the new American nation concluded that the way to protect freedom, liberty, and opportunity was to have a government of limited powers. Therefore, the American support of limited government arose not out of an inherent belief in limited government but from a desire to provide checks on the one institution most capable of eroding individual freedom and opportunity.

Throughout the nineteenth century, and finally by the Great Depression, liberals realized that many social and economic forces possessed the power to erode American individualism. The only check on the power of those forces lay with the political power of the individual to direct democratic government to channel those forces to support, not erode, American freedoms and opportunities. Thus, the liberal advocacy of affirmative government sprang from the same values and ideals that prompted the eighteenth-century belief in limited government.

The style of affirmative government by liberals in the twentieth century has focused on pressing social and economic problems not remedied by the private sector. True to form, conservatives have reacted to these problems not by proposing solutions but by attacking the "Americanness" of affirmative government. Conservatives make the illogical comparison between affirmative government and socialism or communism. It is as though, to conservatives, the only distinction between democracy and communism is whether the government possesses any active role in society. The democratic use of affirmative government, however, differs dramatically and fundamentally from the doctrines of socialism or communism. First, government in a democracy acts only upon the wishes of the democratic majority. Second, in a liberal democratic capitalist society, the center of economic activity is in the private sector, even though the government establishes some basic rules and guidelines for the economic activities of that private sector. Thus, the conservative's connection between a belief in affirmative government and a belief in socialism or communism is unfounded. Furthermore, the conservative labeling of affirmative government as "un-American" is equally baseless and historically false.

The willingness of liberals to use government affirmatively, conservatives claim, goes against the grain of the American spirit—a spirit built on the myth that this nation grew and developed without the involvement of government. The conservative antigovernment myth explains American history as the story of unfettered free enterprise left untouched by the hand of government, and this history of progress was threatened in the twentieth century when government took a more active role. This myth, however, contradicts reality. Throughout American history, government has taken an active role in the economy. A difference in this trend did occur in the twentieth century, however. The government switched from actively and primarily favoring business to focusing on the needs of the common American. Thus, when conservatives criticize liberals for their advocacy of activist government, they ignore the American historical experience with affirmative government and the role of affirmative government in the nation's economic development.

## The History of Affirmative Government

Throughout the eighteenth and nineteenth centuries, government was actively involved in economic affairs. The constitutional framers and early national leaders believed that government had a duty to foster the national interest and to actively shape the national economy. George Washington recommended a national economic policy in which the government was actively involved. Alexander Hamilton, Washington's chief economic advisor, called the notion that the economy could regulate itself a "wild speculative paradox."[1]

During the administrations of presidents Washington and Adams, government participation in and regulation of the economy was strongly supported. The states also routinely regulated economic activity. Passage of inspection laws to govern the quality of goods constituted one such use of government regulation. Thus, eighteenth-century American leaders had no doctrinal commitment to an unregulated marketplace. Rather, they built an economy blending public and private initiative. Although the economy was founded on private property, the legitimacy of government intervention was unquestioned.

In the early nineteenth century, government increased its role as an affirmative agent of economic development. Its subsidies to railroad construction amounted to some of the largest subsidies in American history. John Quincy Adams, the sixth president, favored an affirmative government role in encouraging diversified growth and restraining the wasteful use of national resources. Like Adams, many other public leaders supported government involvement out of a belief that the national interest was too important to entrust solely to the private sector.

The government involvement in the economy went beyond organizing public works and protecting industrial development; government even participated in and regulated individual corporations. Each corporation was chartered by the state and was granted various privileges enabling it to serve certain public needs. The corporate charter, however, also subjected the corporation to regulation of working conditions and inspection and licensing systems.[2] Nonetheless, the special privileges granted by the corporate charters brought a hostile reaction from Jacksonians.

Jacksonian liberals in the 1830s and 1840s criticized this type of government involvement in the economy. They saw corporations as monopolies receiving exclusive, and therefore undemocratic, privileges. The Jacksonians opposed government favoritism, although not necessarily government intervention in the economy. To combat the power and special privilege of the corporation, they pushed for economic regulation, even though such regulation also contradicted the American ideal of a limited government. Indeed, Jackson proposed to turn popular government from the servant into at least the rival of business. Yet to combat the power of concentrated wealth, to recapture government from business control, and to govern in the interests of the people, Jackson had to enlarge the power of the state.

Meanwhile, in the mid-nineteenth century, business interests began retreating from the Hamiltonian concept of active government involvement in the economy and adopted the Jeffersonian notion of limited government. Corporations had become strong and wealthy enough to make them less dependent on government. They had also obtained private corporation laws which transformed them from quasi-public entities to strictly private concentrations of wealth. Thus, business for the first time began adopting the doctrines of laissez-faire and limited government to guide economic affairs.

The victory of laissez-faire as a governing doctrine, however, did not come until after the Civil War. By that time, business had completely repudiated Hamiltonian notions about the economic leadership of the state. Laissez-faire was then sold as the true doctrine of American history, despite its relative absence during the first century. However, business interests only invoked laissez-faire when the government action was not to their liking. Surprisingly, the perceived compatibility of laissez-faire with government aid to business existed alongside the perceived contradiction between laissez-faire and certain rules of conduct for corporations. This one-sided probusiness application of laissez-faire, however, was not what Adam Smith had envisioned.

As laissez-faire gained ascendance, economic misery deepened. Depression occurred in 1873, lingered through the 1880s, and hit again in 1893. The government refused to act, as laissez-faire had replaced the general welfare as a guide for government action. Although government had aided the development of business corporations, it refused to act on behalf of the individuals who had suffered through those depressions.

Not only did conservatives use the laissez-faire doctrine to oppose any government regulation, they employed it to defeat the attempts of working Americans to collectively bargain. The conservative fear of unions, however, ignored the history of other democratic societies in which effective labor unions gave workers some assurance that economic justice could be gained by peaceful, gradual means. Where trade unionism was oppressed, democracy became unstable and extremist movements tended to prosper.

As a result of the often harsh conservative one-sided application of laissez-faire, public views began to change and to suspect the legitimacy of absolute laissez-faire. In the Jacksonian spirit, some saw the giant corporations as threatening democracy. As Henry Adams said in 1870, the Erie Railroad had "proved itself able to override and trample on law, custom, decency, and every restraint known to society, without scruple, and as yet without check. The belief is common in America that the day is at hand when corporations . . . will ultimately succeed in directing government itself."[3] Indeed, laissez-faire, once the supposed guarantor of equal opportunity, seemed increasingly the defender of inequality and exploitation.

During the period between the Civil War and the Great Depression, the public increasingly called upon the government to regulate and restrain big business. Monopolization of American business reflected to many Americans a moral crisis of civilization and resulted in a public outcry against trusts and monopolies. Liberals called on government to intervene so as to preserve free enterprise and individual initiative, and in 1890, Congress enacted the Sherman Antitrust Act.

Yet monopolization was not the only aspect of the industrialization subjected to regulation. Industrialization and mass production had brought miserable working conditions for laborers, especially women and children. Most female industrial workers earned as little as $1.56 for seventy hours of work. By 1900, 13 percent of all textile workers were below age sixteen. Industrial accidents rose steadily, killing or injuring hundreds of thousands every year. In the railroad industry alone, 72,000 workers were killed between 1900 and 1917.[4] These occurrences further eroded public adherence to strict laissez-faire and prompted safety laws and regulations limiting the working hours for women and children.

As the Jacksonians had done half a century earlier, Americans in the late nineteenth and early twentieth centuries sought to empower the national government to combat economic concentration and privilege. This movement proceeded from a deep belief in capitalism and a rejection of socialism. It was a movement to resurrect the competitive, individual-oriented capitalist society envisioned by Thomas Jefferson and Adam Smith. In earlier days, when private enterprise was competitive and not concentrated in powerful institutional trusts, laissez-faire was in the interests of the majority of Americans. But economic and industrial development had changed things. Americans at the turn of the century witnessed the curtailment of competition and individual opportunity. The industrial corporations were engaged in cannibalistic behavior, swallowing up one another in an effort to achieve a monopolistic position. To avoid this outcome and its harmful effects, liberals began to regulate the workings of the marketplace to bring it back into conformity with the capitalist ideal.

This liberal use of affirmative government followed the earlier liberal tradition. As Schlesinger has noted, common threads existed between eighteenth-century liberal laissez-faire and twentieth-century liberal affirmative government.

> When a laissez-faire policy seemed best calculated to achieve the liberal objective of equality of opportunity for all—as it did in the time of Jefferson—liberals believed, in the Jeffersonian phrase, that that government is best which governs least. But, when the growing complexity of industrial conditions required increasing government intervention in order to assure more equal opportunities, the liberal tradition, faithful to the goal rather than to the dogma, altered its view of the state.[5]

Under Republican president Theodore Roosevelt, the federal government for the first time took action against economic depression during the banking panic of 1907. Roosevelt was the first modern president to address the social and economic irresponsibility suffusing industrial society through the use of positive government to redress the balance.[6] Like Jackson, Roosevelt believed that democracy could not endure if private concentrations of wealth were permitted to become more powerful than the democratic state. He warned that capitalism had to be reformed or it would destroy itself. Roosevelt therefore contemplated a significant increase in the power of the state over an increasingly centralized and unaccountable economy.

To Woodrow Wilson, who still yearned for the Jeffersonian vision and the competitive era, the emergence of large corporations and the growing concentration of wealth had eroded the shared goals of capitalism and democracy. Wilson sought to restore the unity of the democratic principles of political equality and the capitalist principles of equal economic opportunity. He believed, as had Madison, that ownership of property gave a citizen some necessary independence and protection from corruption.[7] Madison and the other constitutional framers, however, had overlooked the danger that a large concentration of ownership might lead to the opposite result: the corruption of the government by the rich. This danger was not overlooked by Wilson, who used affirmative government to check big business and increase opportunities for the small entrepreneur. Yet Wilsonians did not envision otherwise enlarging government functions and activities, due to their Madisonian suspicion that an enlarged state could not be kept out of the hands of the interests it was supposed to control.

The merging of the concepts of affirmative government developed by Theodore Roosevelt and Woodrow Wilson occurred with Franklin Roosevelt's response to the Great Depression. Once again, conservatives argued against the propriety of government action, just as nineteenth-century conservatives who regarded depression as a "natural" occurrence beyond human control had done. Hoover maintained the conservative position: "The sole function of government is to bring about a condition of affairs favorable to the beneficial development of private enterprise." FDR asserted the opposite view: "Modern society, acting through its government, owes the definite obligation to prevent the starvation or the dire want of any of its [citizens] who try to maintain themselves but cannot."[8]

To FDR, the community of interests, and not just the business interests, should determine government action. The New Deal aim was to bring the gigantic economic and corporate forces under democratic guidance. Roosevelt, in designing the New Deal, articulated the liberal standard for affirmative government: "As new conditions arise beyond the power of men and women to meet as individuals, it becomes the duty of the government itself to find new remedies with which to meet them."[9] Conservatives, on the other hand, believed that individual initiative and private philanthropy could adequately address all situations and that government action on behalf of the general welfare need never be taken. In retrospect, it is fortunate that conservatives did not prevail in the 1930s. American life would have been far less comfortable and stable if the government had failed to face economic realities as dismally then as it had in the 1920s.

The liberal approach to affirmative government in the twentieth century did not develop in a historical vacuum. As it had since America's birth, affirmative government responded to events in society and the economy. The liberal conception of affirmative government achieved, in a sense, its greatest triumph in the election of 1952 when the Republican party, the conservative party, accepted the political changes made by a generation of liberal reform.[10] It essentially rejected the idea of the national government as adversary or intruder. Reagan's later attack on government as the cause of social ills marked a sharp break in the conception of government in the twentieth century. The attack also contrasted sharply with the conservative attitude toward government during America's first century. Thus, the recent conservative crusade against government ignored not only the history of government involvement in the economy, but the history of failures and inadequacies in the marketplace as well, which necessitated government action in the first place.

The conservative movement in the 1980s for a return to a policy of strict laissez-faire also ignored the changes in the American economy over the last century. The economic doctrine of laissez-faire presumes a perfectly competitive economic marketplace. With such a marketplace, under our economic theories, a policy of laissez-faire should work. Economics, however, has no proper theory for an oligopolistic market structure. Yet, according to economist Lester Thurow, oligopolies constitute the most prevalent form of industrial organization today.[11] Therefore, since laissez-faire is unworkable in an oligopolistic marketplace, and because of the absence of the economic "checks and balances" present in a competitive economy, affirmative government becomes necessary even for the proper functioning of the economy.

Some conservatives concede the fact that an affirmative government provides a useful and beneficial economic function. Even Chief Justice William Rehnquist, a staunch conservative, recognizes the historical necessity and desirability of affirmative government involvement. He affirms the belief of the "conservative wing" of the Court in the mid-twentieth century that the government had "considerable authority" in economic affairs. Looking back in history, Rehnquist concluded that the Court in the mid-nineteenth century wisely qualified commercial and property rights "in favor of the need for state regulation" in economic matters. He further recognizes the failure of post–Civil War laissez-faire for the staunchly independent midwestern farmers who, devastated by high monopolistic railroad freight rates, came to believe "in governmental intervention in economic affairs."[12]

## The Recognized Need for Affirmative Government in the Present Age

Despite Reagan's vociferous attack on government, most Americans have remained supportive of many government activities and programs. Indeed, George Bush has not only ceased the attack on government, but has come to realize the current need for affirmative government. President Bush, for instance, has activated the government on environmental issues which Reagan neglected—issues like acid rain and global warming. Furthermore, in his education position set forth to the nation's governors at the 1989 education conference, Mr. Bush called for a "Jeffersonian compact," an active federal-state partnership to achieve national education goals, and committed the financial resources of the federal government to this task. Moreover, the business agenda developed by Treasury Secretary Nicholas Brady takes "a sharp departure from Reaganism" in that it proposes curbs on corporate takeovers. This active government role results from the Bush administration's recognition that "deal mania is diverting America's resources and sapping U.S. competitiveness."[13]

In addition to increased stock market supervision, President Bush has actively involved the government in other areas of the economy. The Bush administration, by proposing to subsidize sunset industries, guard American technologies, and force other nations to open their markets to American products, has done what some liberals have long advocated: employ the power of government to rebuild America's industrial base. The trade proposals of President Bush, in fact, reflect the recommendations of President Reagan's Commission on Industrial Competitiveness, which called for establishment of a Department of Trade and a Department of Science and Technology to oversee changes in U.S. trade and industrial policies.

The integrated, complex world economy of today poses as great a challenge to laissez-faire as did the monopolization movement in the early part of this century. Trade barriers erected by countries like Japan have made "free trade" a myth. Since the late 1970s, for instance, every major steel-producing nation has subsidized steel production. The rest of the world obviously does not let laissez-faire dictate steel production. Indeed, the economies of America's foreign competitors incorporate an active governmental leadership. In *The Zero-Sum Solution,* Lester Thurow proposes a vast range of institutional and political changes needed to reform America's economic system and bring it in line with our foreign competitors.[14] Thurow notes that after World War II, Germany and Japan, with the help of the United States, thoroughly reformed their political economies. Consequently, the successful and growing economies in the present era are the result of active government involvement, not of dogged adherence to a doctrine of laissez-faire that was never even completely followed in America's history. Thus, with the growing complexity of the international economy, the debate increasingly will focus not on whether government should act, but on what role government takes and on the degree of its involvement.

The intense global competition and lagging American competitiveness in the international economy have recently prompted calls for a business-government "partnership" to meet this international challenge. In fact, such a partnership has already developed in the U.S. semiconductor industry, which fifteen years ago dominated the world market but which today is struggling for survival against Japanese competitors. American business has come to realize that it alone cannot compete against foreign competitors that combine the skills and resources of government and business to compete in the international economy. What makes this partnership approach novel in the United States is the historical stubbornness against acknowledging that government has a proper role in strategically addressing the fate of American industries. Nonetheless, it is becoming increasingly apparent that "government must provide the authority and business the competence to decide for the long run what we want our economy to look like—to define the national interest reliably."[15]

Government cooperation or partnership in economic matters is certainly not without precedence. Indeed, business and government *in partnership* best describes the historical dynamic of America's economy. In describing the New Deal economic role of the government, Franklin Roosevelt explained the nature of this government involvement and defended it from the exaggerated conservative attacks: "It is wholly wrong to call the measures that we have taken Government control of farming, industry and transportation. It is rather a partnership between Government and farming and industry and transportation . . . a partnership in planning."[16] Roosevelt's partnership theory of government involvement in the economy followed directly from the theories of George Washington, Alexander Hamilton, and John Quincy Adams.

The need for government action, however, is not confined to the economy. Throughout American life in the 1980s, from providing public investment in roads and education to combating a new generation of racism among teenagers who have little memory of the civil rights struggles of the sixties and seventies,[17] the need for affirmative government has become increasingly acute. Unfortunately, the occurrence of these needs does not neatly coincide with times of plentiful social resources to meet the needs. Nonetheless, although society might not be able to meet all its needs, it is only self-defeating to cover up that limitation, as conservatives did in 1988, by denouncing the value and use of affirmative government.

Economic hard times and record budget deficits have undoubtedly eroded support for certain governmental social programs targeted for the poor and minorities. But recognizing these realities is one thing; it is quite another to say, as many conservatives do, that all of the programs were ill conceived from the outset or that the need for those efforts no longer exists. For instance, conservatives have portrayed the food stamp program as symbolic of a federal program gone bad. Undoubtedly, some fraud and abuses exist in that program; yet those failures must be compared with its accomplishments. Indeed, because of its success many have forgotten the conditions that led to the creation of the food stamp program. In 1967, a team of physicians toured the rural South to study the prevalence of hunger. They found the conditions shocking, and they found children for whom hunger was a daily fact of life. Ten years later, another team of physicians visited the same areas. Although many of the outward signs of poverty still existed, the extent of malnutrition was appreciably reduced. The reason for this dramatic change, in the opinion of both the doctors and the people they visited, was the food stamp program. Today, many conservatives argue that the program is unnecessary and unaffordable. However, while the major nutritional worry for most Americans is being overweight, the opposite concern of hunger is the primary nutritional worry for many other Americans who depend on food stamps for their survival.

## The Modern Conservative Reaction to Affirmative Government

Affirmative government has existed throughout American history, and often with no objection from conservatives. The real issue, however, has been the object of affirmative government action. Depending on what interests are being served, conservatives may favor either strong or weak government. They denounce "as government meddling those policies that appear to move toward an equalization of life chances . . . or that attempt to make business more accountable to public authority."[8] Conservatives tend to favor a strong government that can restrict dissent, exert military power, and regulate private morals. Conservatives also favor reduced government spending, but the reductions they favor are selective. In boosting defense spending and in cutting taxes for the wealthy, Reagan, far from being frugal, regularly produced record budget deficits which were more than twice that of any liberal administration in American history.

Conservative business interests have opposed the use of affirmative government for public interest goals such as environmental protection and safety regulation on the grounds that such action poses a menace to the liberties of citizens. The "liberties" threatened by government action, however, have included the freedom to deny minorities their basic civil rights, the freedom to work young children in factories and immigrants in sweatshops, the freedom to permit squalid working conditions, the freedom to make misrepresentations in the sale of goods and securities, and the freedom to pollute the environment.[19] These freedoms find no protection in the Constitution and are not valuable to a civilized society. On the other hand, the agencies of big government, like the FBI and CIA, and practices such as censorship and book banning that do threaten basic individual liberties do not attract a similar level of suspicion by conservatives.

The conservative creed has consistently expressed a belief in the supremacy and omnipotence of business. According to the conservative argument, American business, if left alone, can solve all social problems. Surprisingly, conservatives have continued this argument in the face of historical contradiction. Business failed to achieve such grandiose goals in the 1910s, the 1930s, and the 1960s; and the American public each time called for some affirmative government to address the problems left by business. The American public is again making such demands in the 1990s. The public's confidence in business leadership and competence was dramatically shaken in the late 1980s by the Wall Street scandals and the fraud indictments on the Chicago Board of Trade and Chicago Mercantile Exchange. Consequently, across the country, a "new brand of citizen activism" is developing as part of what some call a "backlash against business."[20]

Despite the historical record, conservatives view the interests of business and the wealthy as identical to the interests of society in general. According to this view, while government regulation of business threatens the proper functioning of society, government favoritism toward business and the wealthy simply supports the "natural" order of society. The conservative opposition to affirmative government focuses only on the former kind of action, which is pejoratively characterized as the "taking" from the rightful possession of those fortunate enough to be wealthy.

In many instances, however, the real aim of government action is not one of "taking" from the rich, but of "giving" to the rich. With this latter type of government action, of course, conservatives have no objection. The conservative campaign in 1988 to cut the capital gains tax exemplifies such conservative-supported action. Despite the massive federal deficit for which all Americans must assume responsibility, and despite all the legislative effort and national consensus behind the 1986 Tax Reform Act, which did away with special loopholes and tax breaks, conservatives now want to dismantle the scheme of that act and give the wealthy a hefty tax break. Conservatives have no problem claiming that this tax break does not amount to government favoritism and that it will benefit all of society. This claim, however, contradicts public opinion. In fact, during the 1988 campaign, the capital gains tax cut was one of the few issues on which George Bush took a beating from Michael Dukakis.

Conservatives rarely recognize a positive or innovative capacity of government. Their buzzword of the 1980s was "privatization." While liberals want government to run better, conservatives do not want it to run at all. This intent to erode government authority makes conservatives inherently bad managers of government. Consequently, their misuse of government has resulted in a public suspicion of affirmative government. With the many scandals in the Reagan administration and the increasing power of influence peddlers in the government, it is hardly surprising that the public screams when new taxes are discussed. This public reaction, however, should not be confused with a basic opposition to governmental action of any kind, as the conservatives urge us to believe. Rather, the public reaction stems from a conviction that most of any new tax revenues will be squandered or misused. Thus, new and vital government programs raise public opposition not because the public disagrees with the program but because it fears that the endeavor will eventually result in a scandalously expensive bungle.

The historic conservative reaction during periods of political crises and social turmoil in America has often been an instinctive anti-government crusade. Yet the conservative position against government action just as often makes no sense. Government exists to act, to do something. No institution can live on inaction. Indeed, the conservative attitude conflicts with the longstanding public opinion calling "not for less government but for better government."[21] Unfortunately, the constant conservative harangue against government has fostered a government impotence, a "can't do government."[22]

The conservative attempt to deactivate and disarm government in the 1980s has not only brought an increase in social problems, but has also failed to rejuvenate America's economic foundations. Economic productivity growth and domestic investment in the 1980s were significantly lower than in the 1970s.[23] National savings plunged while the budget deficit and trade deficit skyrocketed. Indeed, conservatives replaced the reviled "tax and spend" motto of the seventies with a new motto of "borrow and spend." While in previous decades Americans had consumed less than 90 percent of their increase in production, during the 1980s the consumption rate hit 325 percent. In effect, the "feel good" decade of the 1980s occurred without the work of actually producing a decade to feel good about.

Not only did the economic foundations decline in the 1980s, but the cutback of governmental involvement in the economy threatens the economic foundations of the next decade. For instance, federal investment in the public infrastructure declined steeply during the 1980s. Roads, bridges, mass transit, and water and sewage systems are vital to economic health, and investment in these resources has dropped by 75 percent over the past two decades. In addition to the decline in infrastructure investment, federal investment in natural resources and human capital has also plummeted. From 1979 to 1986, federal spending on natural resources fell 24 percent, nondefense-related research and development by 25 percent, education by 14 percent, and energy conservation by 65 percent.[24] This failure to invest in the future marks another way in which Americans under conservative leadership in the 1980s did not meet their social contract with future generations.

As with their opposition to liberal principles and values in general, conservatives label affirmative government as "un-American" and as destructive of American institutions and business. Conservatives, for instance, have argued for decades that any regulation or intervention in the economy would ruin it. In the 1930s, for instance, as Congress was debating legislation establishing the SEC to oversee the stock market and to prevent fraudulent practices, conservatives claimed even in the wake of the Great Crash that the market was already perfect and that any government meddling would destroy the foundations of the economy. Contrary to these claims, the decades following the establishment of the SEC witnessed one of the stock market's highest growth periods ever. It is now widely acknowledged that the SEC has been extraordinarily successful in stabilizing the stock market and making it a fairer institution holding greater investor confidence. It has even been called "a model government agency."[25] Moreover, the Boesky scandal and "Black Monday" market crash in October of 1987 prompted investors to clamor for still more supervision of the stock market.

Despite the lessons of history, conservatives still seem to want to take the nation back to the 1870s, when government existed only to serve and support business interests. Their indictment of government rests on their chronicle of past governmental failures, even though past business failures are not seen as a permanent indictment on business. Notwithstanding this habit of conservatives to denounce government as incompetent and unnecessary, the truth is that government has been very successful in many of its undertakings. Rather than hindering the economy, government involvement has generally improved it. The success of the SEC provides just one example. Overall, the post–New Deal economy has been astonishingly healthy and productive with the government regulations and taxes introduced by the New Deal. Economic growth reached its highest rate during the sixties—the decade in which the supposed governmental burdens were most aggressively enlarged. Under the government farm programs, agricultural productivity has steadily increased 5 percent annually—more than three times as fast as productivity in nonagricultural business. Thus, measured by gains in efficiency and productivity, government intervention in agriculture has been a dazzling success.

Involvement of the government in the economy has greatly remedied some of the chronic difficulties of a market economy. Between 1819 and 1932, economic depression occurred approximately every other decade. With the government-installed stabilizers of the New Deal, however, America for the first time in its history has gone for almost sixty years without a major depression. Furthermore, government programs have succeeded in preventing the burdens of economic downturns from being placed on the poorest members of society. A recent Census Bureau study found that without government assistance programs an additional 6.3 percent of the population would have fallen below the poverty line in 1986.

Affirmative government has also succeeded in rectifying some of the negative effects of economic activity and in raising the quality of life in society. Government health and safety programs have succeeded in lowering infant mortality, providing better health care to more people, and decreasing the number of safety-related accidents in the workplace. As a result of the federal government education programs, high school graduation rates have increased from 50 percent to 85 percent over the past three decades. More than eleven million children have benefited from Head Start, the federally funded preschool program for children living in poverty. Its graduates are more likely to do better in school than other poor children; they have been found to have better attendance, to need less special education, and to drop out less often. Indeed, child advocates and business leaders regard the program as an essential component of any strategy to improve the American educational system.

In *America's Hidden Success: A Reassessment of Twenty Years of Public Policy,* John Schwarz credits the federal government with meeting, over the past generation, the two main domestic priorities of the time: the reduction of poverty and the control of environmental pollution. As a result of government programs, the proportion of people living in poverty declined from 18 percent in 1960 to less than 8 percent in the late 1970s; pollution fell by 30 percent in just five years; the proportion of those living in substandard housing declined from 49 percent in 1940 to 8 percent in 1976; and the mortality rate of black infants dramatically decreased after 1965. In *Hidden Success,* Schwarz suggests not only that we cannot rely on the private sector alone to meet every social problem and that the creation of a just society requires an active role for the national government, but also that our government has done much better than we sometimes realize and that it can continue to do so in the future.

## The Liberal Use of Affirmative Government

### Affirmative Government as an Expression of the Liberal View of Government and Society

History teaches that affirmative government is as much a part of America as is its capitalist system. Moreover, the American democratic form of government existed before the capitalist economic order developed. Affirmative government also occupies a greater part of American history than does the business corporation. Indeed, the corporation owes its birth to active government involvement in the economy. Far more than the concept of laissez-faire, the notion of a positive, activist government has influenced our political tradition. History demonstrates that the framers envisioned government directly leading and regulating the economy.

Complete laissez-faire has never been a true characteristic of the American economy. Instead, an interwoven relationship between business and government has existed. Each is dependent on and affected by the other. The achievement of political goals like increased social opportunities and improved public health depends greatly on economic performance. The economic system, in turn, depends on the government to protect private property, manage the monetary system, educate the future labor force, provide public services and infrastructure, and generally maintain social peace and an environment conducive to economic growth. According to economist Paul Samuelson, the American economy is a mixture of public and private initiative. Throughout its history, the American economy has never put up a "keep out" sign to government.

No historical precedent or principle exists, then, for citizens to prevent themselves from using government, in combination with the market economy, to achieve common goals. Indeed, a market economy will not necessarily provide those ingredients of the common good; and sometimes it even detracts from the common good. For instance, a federal study released in June of 1989 revealed that more than 200 industrial sites across the nation posed alarmingly high cancer risks for the public. And each year more than 2.7 billion tons of industrial toxins known to cause cancer and birth defects are released into the atmosphere. These problems, and their negative impact on the common good, require affirmative government. In addressing such problems, the public may even choose to sacrifice some economic rewards. Liberalism believes in the ability and power to so choose. Furthermore, the public has often called on government to deliver benefits, such as easier access to home ownership financing through FHA and college educations through the college loan program, that were not otherwise provided by the economy.

As demonstrated by Andrew Jackson, Woodrow Wilson, and Franklin Roosevelt, the liberal use of affirmative government reflects the liberal view of democratic society and the relationship between democratic government and a capitalist economy. In contrast, by opposing affirmative government and advocating greater power for economic and business interests, conservatives essentially favor a one-sided view of society. While liberals see government as concerned with the whole of society, conservatives measure government according to its effect on certain private interests. They seek freedom for the economic system to express economic values, yet they do not advocate the same freedom for the political system. To conservatives, the political system should not express democratically determined political values but should merely defer to economic values. This view imposes subservient status to the role of democratic government.

Society, however, is more than a capitalistic economy; it is organized under a democratic government capable of acting according to popular desire. Both exist in an ever-evolving relationship. Recognizing this relationship, liberalism does not envision a society driven by a single force—business or government—and does not exclusively emphasize either political or economic values. The capitalist economy is capable of great and efficient production of goods and services. But that is all. Its function does not also qualify it to educate our citizens nor to set the rules for political participation; the economy has also proved that it cannot regulate itself in such areas as environmental pollution. Furthermore, the market economy favors and rewards different groups in society. For instance, on 11 March 1989, the *New York Times* reported that the "Dow falls after report of drop in jobless rate." To most Americans a drop in unemployment was good news, but to stock market interests it was worrisome news.

The liberal need envisions affirmative government as a tool to help society better itself; just as families are to help individuals in their own lives. The notion that government should get out of certain public issues and leave them to private agencies is absurd as a general rule. By definition, the democratic government is the public and therefore can best represent and serve the public interests. Conservatives, however, proclaim that the private sector will somehow automatically satisfy the public interest. By ignoring the existence of a common good apart from the conglomeration of certain private interests, conservatives can then categorically deny any affirmative role to government.

Something is wrong with the conservative belief that the public interest cannot be served by the only true public body in society and can only be served by private institutions. This belief stems from the illogical premise that individuals acting together within economic organizations are capable of so much good and that individuals engaged in a public organization are capable of so little. Apparently conservatives believe that money is a more reliable and admirable motivator than is public service and social interests.

### Affirmative Government
### as the Expression of Democratic Values

A consistent theme throughout American liberalism has been the active use of the public sector to offset the inequalities and anomalies of a market economy dominated by large corporations.[26] While the free-market economy can achieve the most efficient production of goods and services, it necessarily produces certain negative side effects or anomalies and leaves pockets of poverty and unfulfilled social needs. A society based only on market or economic values ignores these shortcomings of the market economy. Most likely, the members of society adhering to such values are those who are immune from any adverse economic effects.

The economy has never been able to fulfill the American concerns for compassion, justice, and charity. Only through democratic government have those ideals found expression. The liberal belief in these ideals was perhaps best articulated in the 1939 film "Mr. Smith Goes to Washington" by an idealistic young U.S. senator played by Jimmy Stewart: "I wouldn't give you two cents for all your fancy rules," he harangues his fellow senators, "if behind them they didn't have a little bit of plain old ordinary kindness—and a little bit of looking out for the other fella, too." While conservatives have traditionally looked on government as a potential nuisance, liberals have sought to engage government in making America a first-class society. As Hubert Humphrey proclaimed in one of his last public appearances, "The moral test of government is how it treats those who are in the dawn of life, the children; those who are in the twilight of life, the aged; and those who are in the shadows of life; the sick, the needy, and the handicapped." And as Supreme Court Chief Justice Oliver Wendell Holmes stated, "Taxes are what we pay for civilized society."[27]

In the twentieth century, shortcomings of the marketplace have no longer been seen as inevitable. As the "sanctity" of the marketplace has lifted, social problems have come to light and have been addressed affirmatively by an institution committed to those concerns—the government. For instance, not until the New Deal did our society or economy commit to working with persons with disabilities. The liberal creed of affirmative government brought the disabled into the social contract and gave them the opportunity to contribute and overcome their disabilities. Liberals recognized that opportunities were not limited by disabilities, but by the conservative use of the laissez-faire doctrine to protect the freedom of employers to deny the disabled jobs and opportunities.[28]

The question posed by Andrew Jackson is relevant today: Why are we afraid to use democratic government to correct and address public problems produced by economic forces not otherwise accountable to the public? In other words, in a democratic society, citizenship values must have at least equal standing with economic values.[29] Do citizens have the right to use government to increase their economic interests—by, for example, obtaining an education or job retraining—or to achieve a result not produced by the market, like health and safety improvement? Or, as conservatives preach, do market values provide a trump over all other values and rights and thereby make the marketplace the ace of the social deck?

The liberal goal has been to balance democratic values and economic values, to make democracy and capitalism compatible. Through the political process, liberalism seeks to empower people and communities to shape their social, cultural, and economic values and environment. During the period of corporate mergers, takeovers, and relocations in the 1980s, for instance, local communities appeared more vulnerable than ever to outside economic forces. One resident said of his community's attempt to control its fate despite the continuing layoffs and relocations caused by the large multinational corporate employer in town: "We were always a pawn in some political or economic game. Now we've got a bad taste in our mouths from the big conglomerates. Now the community is starting to write its own history."[30]

The supremacy of economic values over democratic values would obviously place economic power over political power. But in a democracy, individuals cannot be deprived of political power by economic rules or doctrines. The American democratic order based on equality of political rights translates into the rule of "one person, one vote." However, the economic system rests on a concept of "one dollar, one vote." The more dollars a person has, the more economic power. Economically, all persons are not equal. Therefore, to deprive the political arena of setting rules for the economic arena would subvert the constitutional rule of "one person, one vote." Furthermore, since the economic status of individuals is dependent on the impersonal forces of the international economy and the large conglomerate corporations, the rule of economic power over political power would further alienate individuals.

The democratic values of liberalism have served as a guarantor of the social contract, imposing social responsibility along with the right to operate in the economic marketplace. Liberalism strives to create a sense of unity between economic and democratic values and a sense of mutual obligations among all Americans. In the liberal view, a nation in which shareholders believe they have no responsibility toward workers, in which workers believe they have no stake in the health of their companies, and in which consumers have no concern for how or where products are made, is a nation in trouble. The interdependency and mutual obligations of Americans has become increasingly obvious after a decade of denial. The Ford Foundation recently released a major report on social policy entitled *The Common Good: Social Welfare and the American Future*. In that report, the authors stressed the need to recognize our social interdependency:

> As taxpayers and as victims of a violent society, we end up paying for the social wreckage that results from a lack of earlier investments in other people and their children. We cannot build enough prisons or buy enough home security systems to protect our private worlds from the social decay that spreads when true opportunity is denied to large numbers of people. . . . Each and every one of us has a stake in providing infants and young children the nutrition and emotional nurturing that allow them a decent start in life, both because it is right and because if we don't, they may burden us for decades with the costs of illness, dependency and crime.

The Constitution and the political process set the rules of the social contract which both binds and governs society. Part of society is its economic system. In intervening in the economy and making it accountable to the social contract, the government aims at establishing conditions for economic decisions, not at making the decisions itself.[31] As the family is the part of society assigned the task of raising the young and instilling in them proper social values, the economy is the part of society assigned the task of production of goods and services. While both must be free to carry out the assignments, both remain subject to the broad rules and guidelines set by the entire society through the democratic process. Just as society has decided that economic players cannot freely pollute the environment, it has also determined that families must provide a certain degree of education for their children and cannot stretch child discipline into child abuse.

Despite conservative charges, the liberal use of affirmative government does not result from an antibusiness bias. Liberals tend, however, to take a broad society-wide view of business. Conservatives, on the other hand, by taking a narrow view of business divorced from its social setting, in some ways retard its future potential. For instance, business is coming to realize that the future labor force is being decimated by high dropout rates, crime, drugs, poor education, and illiteracy. This poses a great cost to business, far more threatening and uncertain than the cost of taxes. Conservatives, with their negative political message of low taxes, cannot see this threat to business and the role government can take in preventing it.

The competitiveness of American business in the 1990s hinges on the success of affirmative government in shaping a productive society. This reality was recognized in a statement addressed to Congress and signed by 327 American economists, including six Nobel laureates in economics:

> In addition to our trade and fiscal deficit, America faces a 'third deficit'—the deficiency of public investment in our people and our economic infrastructure. This deficit will have a crippling effect on America's future competitiveness. . . . If America is to succeed in an increasingly competitive world, we must expand efforts to equip our children with better education and our workers with more advanced skills. We must assure that disadvantaged children arrive at school age healthy and alert. We must prevent drug abuse and dropping out among teenagers. We must fix our bridges and expand our airports.[32]

To insure a quality labor force in the future, business needs the help of government. The future demand for better-educated workers, for instance, will be intense. Yet these workers will increasingly come from nontraditional sources. White men, who now make up 44 percent of the labor force, will number only eight of every 100 new workers during the 1990s. Minority groups will make up the majority of the new labor force: a third of the new entrants into the work force in the 1990s will be members of minority groups, which currently have the highest rates of poverty and illiteracy.[33] This demand for educated future workers and the need of future workers for education is of vital concern to liberals. Indeed, only liberals have consistently fought to better educate all members of society, an effort that will yield huge payoffs for the economy in the future.

Although conservatives have tried to depict liberals as antibusiness, the true aim of liberalism through affirmative government is simply to make the market economy work better for all Americans. This faith in affirmative government has been a distinctive trait of the liberal tradition. Unlike conservatives, liberals have not been content in standing idly by as social problems occur. The liberal creed believes that political leadership and action can improve society. Conservatives, on the other hand, believe that politics had little to do with the success of society.

## CHAPTER SIX

# Lessons from History:
# A Comparison of Liberalism and
# Conservatism

An examination of the American liberal tradition and of the impact of liberalism throughout the span of American history reveals far more about American liberalism than do the slurs voiced by its critics in the 1980s. Individual freedom and democratic rule, each dependent on the other in a free society, have formed the basic beliefs of the liberal political philosophy. The efforts of James Otis, Samuel Adams, and Thomas Jefferson focused on elevating the place of the individual in the political system and on guaranteeing that political sovereignty rest in the individual and not in any institution or privileged class of persons. To retain that sovereignty, each individual must be free to exercise the most fundamental of rights: through speech to influence public affairs; through the vote to participate in democratic rule; and through religious worship to practice moral and cultural values and beliefs outside the political arena. And to fulfill that sovereignty, individuals require the power to govern themselves through a democratic political process.

Jefferson and Jackson followed the liberal philosophy in widening democratic participation. Property requirements for voting were lowered; the political control of the wealthy elite was loosened; and legal obstacles to political participation facing large groups in society—women, immigrants, and racial minorities—came under attack. Exclusionary laws, however, were not the only barrier or threat to true democratic rule. The rise of business monopolies created powerful economic rulers of society and a dependent working class. The power of self-government, up against the awesome economic powers, was put to the test.

In facing that test, Woodrow Wilson believed in the founding principles of American democracy and that a democratic society required the voice of the people to count more than the voice of a small, corporate segment of society. The people, as Wilson believed, could end child labor through their democratic government even if they could not through their economic institutions—the corporations. The New Deal under Franklin Roosevelt gave even greater power and freedom to democratic government. The concept of laissez-faire no longer served as an absolute veto over the will of the people; and the economic arena was no longer off limits to government action, especially when the government could alleviate the misery occurring in the economic sector.

Robert Kelly argues that four basic ideologies have characterized and influenced American history—nationalism, moralism, libertarianism, and egalitarianism.[1] These ideological themes exist in both the liberal and conservative political philosophies, but the differing focus or emphasis of each theme within the two philosophies illustrates certain historical differences between liberalism and conservatism. Conservatives have been nationalistic in their military views and in their support of a strong, centralized economy; whereas the liberal nationalist focus has been on the power of democratic government to respond to the needs and desires of the majority and to check the political power of the increasingly centralized national economy. Conservative moralism has emphasized the imposition of private religious moral beliefs on the rest of society, whereas liberalism has followed the founders' belief in separation of church and state and has stressed civic morality and moral responsibility in the actions of business and government. Conservatives have advocated economic libertarianism while liberals have advocated the political libertarianism of the Declaration of Independence. And the conservative egalitarianism has shown itself in the effort to achieve equality (or homogeneity) in the moral beliefs of all individuals, whereas the liberal egalitarian impulse has focused on achieving equality of democratic political freedoms and of economic opportunity.

The conservative vision of society has always been rooted in tradition and in the experiences of the most affluent and comfortable members of society. Since this vision has not often been shared by the majority, democratic debate is unsettling to conservatives because the majority could form its own social and political vision and use governmental action to achieve that vision. Indeed, such democratic action took place during the Progressive and the New Deal eras when the people decided that absolute laissez-faire and deference to business were not in their best interests.

Periods of conservatism have normally witnessed the government faithfully and unquestioningly serving business interests. The administrations of Harding, Coolidge, and Hoover are such examples along with the Reagan administration, which faithfully followed the Wall Street agenda and at the same time allowed the ranks of the poor to expand by approximately 3.1 million people. Yet throughout American history the business community has not had an inspirational record in politics: it fought Jackson, Lincoln, Theodore Roosevelt, Woodrow Wilson, and Franklin Roosevelt.[2] Indeed, on most government reform issues that business opposed, Americans now believe the business position to have been wrong.

Twentieth-century conservatism has contained a strong antigovernment bias. Unlike Jefferson, who believed in the value of government endeavors and suspected the ability of private corporations to act in the public good, conservatives deride the value and worth of government as agent for the public good. Conservatives do not have the pride in government that JFK espoused; they instead look to the private sector to accomplish all public goals. The conservative vision of the ideal society, directed by the leadership of the market economy, sees "political leadership" as "unnecessary and even dangerous."[3] Thus, to conservatives the corporate headquarters more closely symbolize America than do our courthouses and other public buildings.

Given the conservative attitude toward government—the only good government is an inactive government—it is not surprising that government directed by conservatives is not only incompetent but often plagued with corruption. Persons who do not believe in government are less likely to treat it with respect and are less likely to practice democratic statesmanship. As George Will has said, "People who despise government should not be entrusted with it." Indeed, the Reagan administration has been one of the most corrupt administrations ever. Indictments for influence peddling abounded, along with revelations of fraud and corruption within several departments such as Labor and Housing and Urban Development (HUD). This pattern of corruption accompanied a similar pattern in private business. Scandals rocked Wall Street and the securities industry, and corrupt savings-and-loan practices led to a virtual bankruptcy of the industry. As Tocqueville warned, when the scramble for material wealth becomes the supreme quest and self-interest remains the only legitimate individual interest, society often suffers a decline in its ethical and moral standards.

Although conservatives react strongly to the presence of government action or power, they worry little about the tremendous concentrated power of corporations. Concentrated power in government is dangerous, but to conservatives such power in corporations is desirable and even benevolent. The privileged place of the corporation in America has been long justified by conservatives using the argument that corporations fuel economic growth and that what benefits shareholders necessarily benefits all Americans.[4] Yet all Americans are not corporate stockholders; and the vast majority of corporate shareholders receive only a minute fraction of their income from their stock holdings. At the same time, corporations can generate strong negative externalities—like pollution, unsafe products and working conditions, and monopolistic pricing structures—that can easily outweigh, even to their own shareholders, the income and profits earned. Finally, as the economy and individual corporations become increasingly internationalized, the link of corporations to the national economy becomes increasingly weakened. Therefore, the conservative faith in and reliance on the corporation as the institution most responsible for social progress and the well-being of all Americans appears both naive and misplaced.

In relying so heavily on the private sector for social progress, conservatives often hesitate to adopt changes needed to open up economic opportunity. Economic equality has two components: equality of access and opportunity (legal prohibitions against discrimination) and equality of outcome (income equalization). Conservatives tend to label the liberal advocacy of equality of opportunity as an attempt to impose on society massive income redistributions. According to conservative theory, the American laissez-faire economic system automatically provides for equal opportunity. By definition, conservatives claim, American capitalism insures equal access and opportunity to all citizens; yet most Americans know that this definition does not hold true in reality. While the economic system does provide freedom, access, and mobility, it is not perfect and often breaks down in the face of prejudices, discrimination, poverty, and inequality of economic and educational opportunities. The victims of discrimination, physical and mental handicaps, and inadequate education, for instance, do not always have an equal chance at economic success. Without assistance and opportunity, they sink lower on the economic ladder. The historical pattern shows that corporations have not come to the rescue; so without government action society would lose the benefits of the potential productivity of these individuals. This is why liberalism, according to FDR, "believes that, as new conditions and problems arise beyond the power of men and women to meet as individuals, it becomes the duty of the Government itself to find new remedies with which to meet them."[5]

The American economy of the 1980s, with an increasingly dormant government, demonstrated little ability to provide opportunities to the poor. Between 1978 and 1987, the poorest one-fifth of American families became 8 percent poorer, while the richest one-fifth became 13 percent richer. According to Robert Reich, the increase in inequality showed up most strikingly among Americans who have jobs. Between 1978 and 1987, as the real earnings of unskilled workers were declining, those of investment bankers and brokers rose 21 percent. The number of impoverished *working* Americans climbed by 23 percent between 1978 and 1987.[6] Therefore, as Reich claims, the real test of equal opportunity today is whether a talented American child, even if reared in the ghetto, can become an investment banker. Unfortunately, the economy has not met that test. As egalitarians, liberals espouse equality of economic opportunity and support changes and reforms that will make possible even the dreams of ghetto children to become investment bankers. As defenders of the status quo, however, conservatives forget that from the time of the pilgrims the chance to gain economic well-being has been tied to the power to change the status quo.

This belief in continuity, order, and stability is at the heart of conservative thought. It is a belief that handcuffed conservatives in their attempts to deal with economic crises like the Great Depression and social injustices like discrimination which obviously require change. In a healthy democracy, change must freely occur when it is the verdict of a democratic majority. The conservative resistance to change and discomfort with the constant flux of democracy contradicts even the political philosophy of George Washington. Unlike conservatives today, Washington tolerated the "unruliness and untidiness" of democracy. He understood, as did Jefferson, that a democracy must contain the breeze of a little rebellion in the air. In contrast to today's conservatives, Washington saw that autocratic societies resembled great ships that sailed majestically until they struck a reef and sank forever, whereas democracy was like a raft that never sinks but always has a little water in the bottom.

Conservatives not only resist change, but they often ignore even the need for and inevitability of it. In doing so, they ignore history. Indeed, conservatives today would do well to heed the warning Woodrow Wilson gave nearly a century ago:

> America is now sauntering through her resources and through the mazes of her politics with easy nonchalance; but presently there will come a time when she . . . will be obliged . . . to pull herself together, adopt a new regimen of life, husband her resources, concentrate her strength, steady her methods, sober her views, restrict her vagaries, trust her best, not her average, members. That will be a time of change.[7]

Similar to their attitude toward change, history shows that conservatives are uncomfortable with robust debate, which must also occur in a healthy democracy and which the constitutional framers sought to encourage and protect. Conservatives have never been advocates for First Amendment freedoms. Perhaps it is because questions arise from debate, and from questions come possible change and experimentation. Likewise, conservatives have tended to avoid debate and change in their foreign policy. Their isolationist approach, in contrast to the liberal drive for a world community organized around liberal democratic values, puts up strong barriers to change and to a commitment to "democratic" dialogue with foreign allies. For instance, the frequent use of covert military operations during conservative administrations ignores international law as well as the democratic requirement of an informed public at home.

By resisting change and striving to protect the status quo, conservatives also fail to grasp the changing world around them, the diversity of nations and peoples, and the increasing impact of this diverse world on America. Their outlook tends to be strictly two-dimensional, split between the mutually exclusive spheres of "American" and "un-American." For instance, conservatives interpreted most Third World tensions as manifestations of the Soviet-American conflict. This rigid outlook prevents appreciation of the complex and interrelated developments rapidly occurring on the international scene and recognition of America's place in a transformed world.

The world has changed greatly since World War II. Asia has risen out of the cinders of war to attain power as a world region, and the Third World has struggled to enter the modern world and throw off its colonial past. Furthermore, the American economy is now subject to the movements and developments in the international economy. The conservative philosophy has not fully comprehended the scope of these global economic changes, their effect on American national goals and policies, and America's new role in a transformed world.[8] This conservative resistance to change, and its focus on maintaining the status quo of the past, differs markedly from the democratic dynamics of liberalism.

As Franklin Roosevelt demonstrated, the liberal creed advocates experimentation to solve social and political problems. This liberal approach parallels the scientific method: human intelligence applied to a process of experimentation will produce knowledge and scientific progress. The scientist trusts the rational mind and the outcome of experimentation and knows that no progress will occur without experimentation. This faith in progress, through experimentation and positive change, also marks the political liberal. Without liberal experimentation, farmers would still be growing crops in a dust-bowl, children would still be suffering from malnutrition, higher education would be a luxury afforded only by the wealthy, the elderly would not have adequate health care, and the pace of environmental degradation would not have been arrested.

Conservatives have often opposed such experimentation and throughout history have resisted liberal changes and reforms such as universal suffrage, public education, women's suffrage, abolition of child labor, and safety and health regulation of the food and drug industries, even when these changes were supported by a democratic majority. Despite their past opposition to these reforms, however, conservatives have now come to accept and defend them. The conservative, as Schlesinger notes, eventually protects what liberals achieved. Even during the 1988 campaign, the Republicans most adamantly defended Social Security, which liberals first enacted.

The differing attitudes among liberals and conservatives regarding experimentation and democratic government also reflect a difference in views on the political relationship between individual self-interest and the public interest. Tocqueville long ago described the unique principle of self-interest in the American system as a sort of refined selfishness prompting Americans to help one another and to willingly sacrifice a portion of their property to the general welfare. This "enlightened" American self-interest contrasted with the European brand of narrow selfishness. Tocqueville, however, also foresaw problems with the acquisitive scramble for wealth and the love of money, which would blind Americans to their enlightened sense of self-interest. In what seems an insightful prediction, Tocqueville feared that a time would come when individuals, in their intense anxiety to make a fortune, would lose sight of the close connection that exists between the private fortune of each and the prosperity of all. Tocqueville's distinction, made in 1840, between different understandings of political self-interest reflects an important distinction between liberal and conservative philosophies.

American conservatism has tended toward Tocqueville's "European-style" self-interest. To conservatives, the accumulation and use of economic wealth defines self-interest, and the public interest—apart from the accumulated desires of individuals for wealth—is rarely recognized or considered. Thus, the "interest" focus of conservatives is narrow and one-dimensional, focusing only on the economic interests of the individual in isolation. As Tocqueville warned, during conservative periods acquisitiveness and consumption of wealth crowd out public service and concern for social welfare. Even so, during the Reagan era of "European-style" selfishness and of business supremacy, the economy faltered. The standard of living declined, as did the rate of savings, domestic investment, and growth in national output. At the same time, stock speculation, mergers, takeovers, and leveraged buyouts mushroomed and further shook an already precarious economy. As stock speculation went wild and corporate takeovers dominoed, the public suffered. Even takeover artist Irwin Jacobs, known for his conservative, laissez-faire corporate views, admitted that there were legitimate corporate takeover areas in which government should intervene to protect the public interest.

The liberal sense of self-interest, contrary to the conservative philosophy, coincides more with Tocqueville's "enlightened self-interest." Even Adam Smith, one of the founders of free enterprise, recognized that "all for ourselves, and nothing for other people, seems in every age . . . to have been the vile maxim of the masters of mankind." Within the liberal creed, American political self-interest includes both a private interest and public interest: the quest to build a political order in which individuals can maximize their own private interests while enjoying a just and peaceful society that protects those interests. Liberals, unlike conservatives, do not arrive at a common or public interest simply as a derivative or by-product of private interests. They envision a society in which economic interests, social interests, political interests, and private interests intermingle to make up the public interest. While the capitalist economy focuses primarily on private interests, the liberal democratic political system focuses on the public interest and health of society. Thus, while the conservative simply presumes that the individual-oriented market economy produces the best possible social goods, the liberal looks at the economy from the standpoint of the whole society and evaluates how well it produces certain social goals—like a well-integrated, socially mobile, and educated society.

In The Common Interest, Leslie Dunbar demonstrates the importance of public service and of incorporating the common interest into each individual's sense of self-interest. He urges Americans, as did Tocqueville, to recognize the common national interest in attacking poverty: namely, that an alleviation of poverty will decrease crime and stop urban decay and, hence, increase the wealth and well-being of society in general. Frank Levy, in Dollars and Dreams: The Changing American Income Distribution, also notes that poverty tends to perpetuate itself and that children brought up in poverty are more likely to remain poor as adults. He claims that a person may be permanently damaged economically by being raised in poverty. And, since the greatest victims of poverty today are children, the issue raised by our increasing income disparity is not just inequality itself but the quality of the future labor force.[9]

In addition to this economic interest, a social or moral interest also exists in the alleviation of poverty. Because all Americans possess a shared national identity with mutual obligations as citizens, we have a moral or "American" stake in the well-being of all citizens. The existence of extreme poverty detracts from the value of communities and the pride we all place in them. For centuries, American pride has rested on the promise of opportunity, which offered a beacon of hope to its citizens and to the rest of the world. Indeed, in the not-too-distant past, being born poor usually meant dying poor almost everywhere in the world but the United States. The thought that this no longer may be true in a country which believes in equality of opportunity is troublesome. Yet social solidarity or concern is difficult to achieve under the conservative recognition of a relatively narrow concept of self-interest.

As with their view on self-interest, conservatives have tended to take a more narrow, limited view of the social compact. Though voicing support for the charity obligations of private individuals, conservatives often ignore the civic and social obligations of individuals as citizens. While focusing on what the compact does not require, conservatives rarely address what the compact does require. For instance, conservatives claim that government should not regulate the environmental effects of business nor implement educational programs funded by tax dollars. Conservatives apparently deny that through the social compact corporations are responsible for any damage they cause to the environment or that poor youths, who may some day be called to serve in the military, are entitled to a basic education. This narrow conception of the social contract results from the equally narrow group of people or interests with which conservative philosophy is primarily concerned. Conservative parties in American history have not included a diverse cross section of the population, and they have tended to exclude minority groups and recent immigrants.

In contrast, the liberal view of the social contract looks to the health of society. In this view schools are seen not as a drain on tax dollars but as an investment for a healthy and productive society. Unlike the conservative view, the liberal interpretation of the social contract spans vertically across generations past and present as well as horizontally along class and ethnic lines. It imposes on the present generation an obligation to pass on a healthy environment, society, and government to future generations.

The conservative philosophy does not incorporate such a broad generational view of the social contract. This more narrow view revealed itself during the Reagan era. Just as pollution destroys the environment for the future, the deliberate budget deficits under Reagan left a legacy of debt and social instability. During the 1980s, conservatives tried to obtain prosperity and popularity with borrowed money and loaded America with a burden of debt that will wipe away years of gains. As Benjamin Friedman argues in *Day of Reckoning*, Reagan put America on a course of overconsuming and underinvesting and of borrowing from future generations without their consent. The Reagan economic plan of "now-ism" advocated immediate increased consumption with no corresponding payment of taxes and with no investment for the future.

In the 1980s, conservatives deliberately broke the social contract with future generations—deliberately because they drastically cut taxes in an effort to destroy certain social programs, all the while increasing spending on conservative pet programs, like the military. In running up the deficit, conservatives said that they were no longer going to pay their share of taxes and that future generations would pay for this breach. To break this "covenant with future generations is a social decision of the gravest import."[10] On the other hand, concern for future generations has been a staple of modern liberalism. Even the liberal spending programs of the present focus on investing for the future: job training, education, child-care programs, as well as building and maintenance of roads and bridges.

A discussion of the differences between liberalism and conservatism would be unfinished without a discourse on individual rights and sovereignty. While conservatives have long espoused property rights for the individual, they have not accepted full exercise of individual liberties. Conservative thought glorifies the unhindered economic activities of the individual, but it mistrusts the unregulated social and political activities of the individual. This conservative tendency contradicts the American movement for independence and natural rights in the eighteenth century. The heart of this movement, as reflected by James Otis, Samuel Adams, and Thomas Jefferson, was the call for civil liberties such as freedom of speech and religion, freedom from arbitrary search and seizure of one's home, and freedom for a trial by jury.

The conservative suspicion toward civil liberties reflects a lack of faith in open debate and in individual action. Individual action is unpredictable and, hence, uncontrollable. Conservatives have attempted to lessen this area of uncontrollable action, and stave off change, by curtailing individual liberties. Yet, these individual freedoms and liberties form the cornerstone of our democratic system. Individual sovereignty and freedom, according to the constitutional framers, provide the only true guard against tyranny. Indeed, in the twentieth century, totalitarian societies exist only by denying individual freedom. However, in a striking paradox, modern conservatives seem to fear individual freedoms more than they fear totalitarianism. During most of the significant national crises of this century, conservatives have reacted not to the crisis itself but have sought to impose order and to silence debate by curtailing American civil liberties. Yet, as Justice Thurgood Marshall warned, "History teaches that grave threats to liberty often come in times of urgency, when constitutional rights seem too extravagant to endure. When we allow fundamental freedoms to be sacrificed in the name of real or perceived exigency, we invariably come to regret it."[11]

This conservative fear of the freedoms of speech and press completely contradicts the ideological tenets of American history. If Samuel Adams and Thomas Jefferson were alive today, they would tell us how vitally "American" our freedoms are and would listen in shock to the conservative attacks on individual liberties. Indeed, where a reassertion of the freedom and ultimate integrity of the individual is occurring, as in Eastern Europe and South Africa, so also an opening up and democratization of the political system is taking place. During the 1989 democratic protests in China, the *World Economic Herald* in Shanghai proclaimed that "political democracy is closely related to freedom of the press."

The differences between liberalism and conservatism in the area of civil liberties and individual freedoms are clear. However, another recently cited difference regarding the espousal of values has been greatly exaggerated and distorted. Conservatives claim that liberalism is void of any moral, social, or political values. This deficiency, according to conservative critics of the 1980s, puts liberalism outside America's historical development and national identity. The religious Right has been extremely forceful in attacking liberalism, and through the sharpness of its attacks has convinced many Americans that the liberal philosophy has no concern for, and even rejects, values long cherished by democratic society. This attack has misrepresented liberalism. Indeed, the liberal tradition owes its greatness, its vitality, and its timelessness to the values it has espoused.

## CHAPTER SEVEN

# The Recognition and Role of
# Values in the Liberal Tradition

## The History of the Conservative
## Reactionary Politics of "Morals and Virtue"

A frequent conservative criticism claims that the liberal philosophy is devoid of any values. In his biography of leading conservative William F. Buckley, John Judis discusses Buckley's similar criticism of liberalism.[1] To Buckley, the problem with liberals is not so much that their beliefs are wrong, but that they lack any real beliefs at all. This lack of beliefs and values in the liberal creed contrasts, of course, with Buckley's conservatism. He argues that the political arena must foster and enforce individual virtue and religious morality. Buckley's argument is not new. Conservatives have long used it not to bring about a more decent, virtuous, and progressive society, but simply to oppose change and to enforce rigid moral codes.

Conservatives have been preaching civic virtue and religious morality for nearly two centuries. They used the argument during the Jefferson/Jackson era to oppose the widening of democracy. According to conservatives, the common American lacked the proper education and property ownership to instill within him the necessary "virtue," and therefore should not be entrusted with the vote. Conservatives again used this argument in the mid-nineteenth century to justify excluding the Irish from the political process. According to conservatives, the social activities and Catholic beliefs of the Irish disqualified them from the "virtuous" Protestant class and marked them as members of the "pope's army" and, hence, as a dangerous heretic class. The Irish Catholics even had to start their own school system because no other education was available to them.

Conservatives continued the "morals and virtue" argument in the late nineteenth and early twentieth centuries, this time to support

Prohibition. Conservatives hoped that Prohibition would tame and discipline the new immigrants who lacked proper virtue, social behavior, and religious morality. This argument has also been used to exclude women and African-Americans from the right to vote. Women did not have the individual character and strength necessary for political virtue, and blacks had neither economic independence nor proper cultural and religious training. Conservatives have even used the virtue argument as a justification for not acting in the public interest and for thwarting majority will. For instance, during the Depression, conservatives argued that any government relief or public works would destroy the "virtue" of the working class.

Arguments for virtue and morality made by conservatives follow a one-way track. The "lessons" for morality and virtue, which throughout history have been preached by the upper-class elite to the common person, deal primarily with cultural and sexual behavior. Yet the same calls for public virtue and morality seem to disappear in connection with Wall Street securities fraud, tax evasion, corporate bribery schemes, and environmental waste. Conservatives tend to focus only on religious morality and not on a larger concept of morality that includes political and social morality. Consequently, conservative administrations have historically been plagued with a disproportionate share of ethics scandals.[2]

Although conservatives have always preached virtue and religious morality, it was not until recently in the twentieth century that conservatives directed this preaching toward liberals. The social turmoil of the 1960s led to this indictment against liberals, for, to conservatives, the liberal political philosophy was the cause for everything that went wrong during that decade. Conservatives blame liberals for the social permissiveness that led to an increased level of countercultural activities like drug use. However, even by the late 1970s the inaccuracy of the conservative diagnosis was clear. The mindless hedonism that ruined individual character and independence was not confined solely to the 1960s counterculture, as any observer of the 1970s scene of disco and cocaine could see. Indeed, the most severe and long-lasting problems brought to light in the 1960s were caused and aggravated by the marketplace, not by "permissive" liberal intellectuals. The multibillion-dollar cocaine industry, for instance, is not the creation of "permissive" liberalism; it is the work of profit-seeking individuals, many of whom ardently support conservative causes and politicians. The effects of "permissive" conservatism, on the other hand, can be directly traced in 1989 to Wall Street, to the savings and loan industry, and to the Department of

Housing and Urban Development. Nonetheless, when conservatives blame liberals for all that went wrong during the sixties, they fail to see the distinction between the political liberalism of the sixties and the "cultural radicalism" that protested certain social or cultural rules and customs.

## The Distinction Between Political Liberalism and the Cultural Radicalism of the 1960s

Political liberalism in the sixties and seventies was responsible for slowing pollution, sponsoring alternative energy exploration, regulating nuclear power, ending the Vietnam War, prohibiting racial discrimination, and initiating clean-ups of city slums. These accomplishments are not mentioned when conservatives trace America's present problems to "those sixties liberals." Instead, conservatives cast the liberalism of the 1960s as a philosophy promoting unrestrained sexual behavior, condoning drug use, encouraging destruction of private property, and attacking religious institutions and values. However, the great majority of the radicals and activists espousing these positions were "cultural radicals" rather than political liberals, and their radicalism was "primarily cultural rather than political or economic."[3]

Conservatives are correct in claiming that the "cultural liberalism" of the 1960s had few beliefs or values; it was a rebellious movement primarily of middle-class youths against the social and cultural values of their parents. This "offspring rebellion" resulted in no real and lasting political philosophy. The counterculture radicals of the 1960s called not for social unity and progress based on an extension of the liberal consensus, but for revolution. The objects of their protests were not real social problems, but rather the "personal complaints of a bored and pampered middle class." By the end of the decade, the schism between political liberals and cultural radicals had grown wide. The "counterculture" had degenerated into a mere youth cult motivated not "by the aspiration to build a free society so much as by an Oedipal hostility to the older generation." Middle-class youths had "turned to the lifestyle of the counterculture for all the things they had missed in the sheltered, affluent suburbs where they grew up: excitement, purpose, a feeling of community, and some measure of individual worth."[4]

Two such student radicals of the sixties who subsequently turned conservative in the eighties base their present criticism of liberalism on a criticism of the sixties. In *Destructive Generation: Second Thoughts about the '60s,* Peter Collier and David Horowitz claim that by attacking all authority the young leftists of the 1960s destroyed the American consensus of values and the institutions based on them. For the adverse effects of this generational rebellion, Collier and Horowitz, like most conservatives, blame not the individuals involved but an impersonal social force called the New Left, which also gets blamed for contemporary problems like drug addiction, drug crime, and AIDS. Also like most conservatives, Collier and Horowitz equate the New Left with American liberalism. Contrary to the conservative creed of individual responsibility, Collier and Horowitz look not to the moral culpability of the participants in the sixties' drug culture but to the larger social force of the New Left.

The history and roots of American liberalism demonstrate that the conservative judgment of "empty values" is itself empty of truth. Furthermore, in their exaggerated criticism of liberalism, as with their criticism based upon the sixties' cultural radicalism, conservatives greatly expand the ranks of liberals to include any unpopular or different causes. Yet it is important to keep in mind that liberalism means political liberalism in the tradition of American political history. Unfortunately, the liberal label is often used to describe anyone who wants to change anything. For instance, persons seeking to lower the barriers to public-supported gambling claim they are seeking a "liberalization" of the gambling laws. They are not liberals, especially since liberals oppose such changes. Instead, they only want a change for their own advantage. Liberals believe in the value of change and in its necessity when certain social conditions change, but they do not automatically favor any change at any time. The liberal philosophy and its values provide a guide as to what changes are necessary and how to accomplish those changes.

## Liberalism and the Civic Virtue Ideal

American liberal values gave birth to the movement for independence and the formation of our constitutional democracy. One of the values recognized by the liberal eighteenth-century political theories on self-government was the concept of the "virtuous citizenry." The framers, in setting up a representative democracy or, as it was termed, a republic, believed that such a republic required the presence of public virtue. This virtue resided in the capacity of each citizen to adopt as a civic duty the pursuit of the public good.

Historians like Bernard Bailyn and Gordon Wood have found that civic virtue ideals contributed to the liberal ideological origins of the American republic. However, this concept of public virtue has been greatly distorted by conservatives in recent years. The framers did not intend public virtue to be the conveyance of religious beliefs or morals. Indeed, the framers believed strongly in a separation of church and state. Contrary to present-day conservative thought, the framers believed that such separation protected religion and served to strengthen religious institutions and practices.

According to John Diggins in *The Lost Soul of American Politics: Virtue, Self-Interest, and the Foundations of Modern Liberalism,* the framers of the Constitution did not believe that government should be an agent of moral education and improvement. Even George Washington did not think it was government's business to supervise or guide the private lives or morals of his countrymen. Washington's idea of the virtuous citizenry applied only to the individual's capacity as a citizen—exercising his political freedoms and accepting his obligations to the political order that guaranteed them. Therefore, to Washington, public virtue went hand-in-hand with political democracy.

The public virtue Washington and Jefferson spoke of was not the same virtue a minister preached about from the pulpit. It was similar to Tocqueville's "enlightened self-interest"—it meant the duty of each citizen to consider the public good, not just his or her private interest. To the contrary, it is the present-day conservatives who equate virtue with moral values dictated by religious beliefs.

The civic virtue ideal and its concern with the public good has infused American liberalism throughout history. Jefferson and Madison extolled the common American farmer—not the wealthy nor the corporation—as the repository of civic virtue. Jackson's expansion of democratic participation and advocacy of the common good, as opposed to the interests of the wealthy elite, reflected this ideal. The public virtue ideal also found expression in Wilson's and Roosevelt's liberal reforms as well as in Truman's campaign for civil rights and his Fair Deal. Kennedy's "ask not what your country can do for you" is a modern expression of the classical civic virtue ethic. To elevate private interest over the public good in the political process—as conservatives do—is to deny the ideal of civic virtue.

The ideal of civic virtue, which orients citizens to the common good, differs entirely from a religious ideal of spiritual laws and codes of morality. It is this latter ideal that conservatives seek to enforce through the state. Yet, as Harold Macmillan once said, "If people want a sense of purpose, they should get it from their archbishops." Moral meaning and absolute truths come from philosophy and religion, not from politics. In a democratic state, as created by the Constitution, politics exists to implement values, not to form and dictate them.

The conservative advocacy of a moralistically rigid Christian America is not consistent with America's founding principles and does not stem from the civic virtue ideal. Indeed, in a parody of the civic virtue ethic, the Reagan administration, perhaps the most enthusiastic administration of this century for state enforcement of Christian morals, was one of the most corrupt administrations in modern American history. Furthermore, many officials and members of the administration used public service as a means to further their private interests. This decline in the ethics in political leaders and businesspersons, according to 76 percent of the respondents to a *Time* poll, contributed to declining moral standards in the 1980s.[5] Instead of creating a morally upright America, the Reagan era witnessed a widespread sense of moral confusion.

The eighteenth-century political tension between "virtue" and "commerce" reveals the danger of exclusive emphasis on the virtue of wealth and private interest prevalent in the Reagan era. The early liberal thinkers warned of placing wealth too high on the scale of civic virtue traits. Thomas Jefferson and John Adams feared that selfishness and "luxury" would corrupt civic virtue. They saw danger in the "cultural authority of wealth " and opposed Hamilton's prediction that wealth "would replace virtue as a political ideal."[6] Jefferson's admiration of wealth hinged on the connection between wealth, work, and productivity. This connection was expressed by the Protestant work ethic. However, while Jefferson valued the earning and saving of wealth and the connection between work and wealth, conservatives in the Reagan era praised the having and spending of wealth—the mere status of being wealthy.

The worship of wealth not only undermined civic virtue, it was also seen to weaken religious values. In a critique of American culture and the frenzied drive for wealth at the turn of the century, Walter Rauschenbusch, in *Christianity and the Social Crisis,* argued that the unchecked pursuit of wealth encouraged envy, rivalry, pride, and indulgence. For this reason, Protestantism and liberalism joined as allies in the early part of the twentieth century. Continuing to adhere to the eighteenth-century principle connecting work and wealth, liberals throughout the twentieth century have placed "the man before the dollar," as had Lincoln a century earlier.[7] When pursuit of the dollar and obsessive consumption preempt all other social concerns, the influence and power of other values suffers. As Rauschenbusch recognized during the materialistic period earlier this century, Lawrence Shames, in *The Hunger for More: Searching for Values in an Age of Greed,* demonstrates how the conservative emphasis on material wealth in the 1980s prompted a decline in ethics and values and fostered an increasingly narcissistic society.

The decline in ethics and civic virtue during the 1980s has been forcefully argued by Barbara Ehrenreich in *The Worst Years of Our Lives: Irreverent Notes from a Decade of Greed.* Ehrenreich criticizes the culture of narcissism, materialism, and selfishness bred during the eighties. She argues that Americans lost their capacity for collective moral discourse. Lacking a civic moral vision, America came to ignore the hunger of the world's majority, the draining misery of the increasing poverty at home and abroad, and the torture and repression occurring in many totalitarian regimes supported by the U.S. According to Ehrenreich, while Americans during the Reagan era indulged in moral panic over welfare-cheaters and flag-burners, they dismissed any moral commitment to such concerns as health care, decent housing, child care, and quality schools. These concerns, and the public morality that addresses them, have traditionally been part of the value system of liberalism.

## The Values of Liberalism

When conservatives try drafting laws from the pulpit, they repudiate the civic virtue ethic and American Constitutional principles. Yet conservatives mask this contradiction by claiming that liberals believe in no substantive values. This claim, however, ignores the distinction between political values—with which a political philosophy is concerned—and other values, religious values.

The liberal tradition reflects a clear and dedicated commitment to political and civic values. In addition to the civic virtue ethic, liberalism values justice, fairness, and equality. It was the liberal America of fairness and equal opportunity that attracted the great waves of immigrants. It was the liberal America of justice that remained a beacon of hope in a world of Hitler, Mussolini, and Stalin. And it is a liberal America of equality which, unlike any other country in the world, has attempted, and even succeeded in many ways, to integrate its minorities as full-fledged citizens into society.

Liberalism places a high value on freedom—not just individual freedom but political and social freedom. The liberalism of Woodrow Wilson and Franklin Roosevelt defended American freedom in two world wars when the conservative creed at that time favored isolation and withdrawal from the international world. Liberalism provided the vision and strength for America to join and lead the United Nations, where it could defend and advocate its principles and values to the rest of the world. Indeed, the liberal mixture of individual and democratic freedoms has protected America from the hatred and oppression so prevalent in other societies. It is widely recognized that the pervasive liberal individualism in America is the reason for the lack of extremism in American society and for the absence of any socialist party on the Left and religious party on the Right in the American political system.

Liberalism has brought moral honesty to government, as it did under Wilson, Roosevelt, Truman, and Carter, and has also stood for the human intellectual ability to end mediocrity in government. John Kennedy reaffirmed the American pride in its democracy and in public service. He stood for a country that strove to be leaner and nobler, less self-indulgent, more courageous in its willingness to sacrifice, and more patriotic in its commitment to American democratic ideals. He advocated excellence in everything, including education, science, the arts, and business. Kennedy espoused the traditional liberal belief in the vital connection between education and democracy and that liberal studies are crucial for fostering the ideals and civic virtue that democracy requires.[8]

Consistent with a belief in the values of education, the pursuit of truth constitutes a core value of liberalism. The protection of a free press and free speech has historically rested largely on the liberal belief that such protections are necessary for attaining truth. The lessons of the past, the potential of the human intellect, and the challenges of the future all become useless and unattainable without freedom of knowledge and communication. Because of this freedom, America remains the higher-education capital of the world.

Committed to truth, liberals espouse openness in all public matters, even those which might cause embarrassment or some remorse. Compare with this liberal approach the opposite approach. In East Germany, a memorial was built to the World War II Buchenwald concentration camp, where more than a quarter of a million people had been imprisoned. The East German government made no mention of anti-Semitism, of the suffering of Jews, or of the fact that America liberated Buchenwald. Instead, the government used the site for propaganda and stated that the perpetrators were all fascists who existed only in West Germany and that the monument paid tribute only to the camp prisoners whose countries later became allies of

East Germany. Perhaps the government thought this propaganda helped East Germany retain national pride, but it was a lie about history that was eventually told, just as the terrors of Stalin are now being told in the Soviet Union.

Another traditional belief of American liberalism is that of the value of work. The liberal belief in this value has historically aligned liberalism with the working and middle-class consciousness. Liberals have consistently endeavored to expand and equalize the opportunities for work. Full employment, and the opportunity to work, has been more than an economic goal of liberalism—it has also been a social and individual goal. Liberals have long recognized that a working society is a healthy society and that the opportunity to work gives dignity to the individual. Conservatives, on the other hand, have traditionally looked to merely expand the accumulation of wealth. During the 1980s, for instance, those who benefited economically under the Reagan policies achieved wealth not through work but through privileges—tax breaks and windfalls. Thus, the connection between wealth and its achievement was severed.

The liberal value which conservatives have most recently distorted is tolerance. To conservatives, tolerance implies an absence of beliefs and values and a failure to choose. To the contrary, however, toleration implies the freedom of each individual, each generation, and each democratic majority to choose its values. While they may throw off traditional rules and constraints, they also may reassume them.

Political democracy cannot exist without compromise and tolerance. Indeed, tolerance plays a special political role different from the role it may play in other institutions, such as religious organizations and even business corporations. Those institutions are obviously more hierarchical than our political institution, which professes absolute political equality for each member. So while tolerance might erode the authority and decrease the effectiveness of these other institutions, it is vitally necessary for the proper functioning of a democracy in which each member must tolerate the equality of the other and the decisions of the majority. Today, the danger to democratic society is not social tolerance, but the growing influence of intolerant minorities like the Moral Majority.

The necessity of tolerance also results from the diverse American society. There are no true ethnic or religious Americans. America is populated by practically every ethnic and religious group in the world. No other nation possesses such diversity. While America as a nation and society must have some unified sense of identity and national purpose, it must also practice tolerance, unless it aims to completely wipe away all vestiges of diversity. Tolerance of diversity in turn increases social cohesion and community bonds. Church groups, ethnic groups, and cultural pride bring people together and unite them in a social setting.

Tolerance of diversity and a recognition of the pluralistic society that in fact characterizes America does not pose a destructive or divisive force. Indeed, history has demonstrated that tolerance affords better protection against totalitarianism than does military might. Though conservatives denounced liberals in 1988 for their defense of pluralism in America, George Bush after the election recognized the value of pluralism in a foreign policy speech at Texas A & M University when he called for the Soviets to "achieve a lasting political pluralism and respect for human rights." Indeed, as the Eastern European countries allowed more freedom and pluralism, conservatives increasingly praised pluralism. James Laney, president of Emory University, stressed the importance and value of pluralism and warned that "moral preachments and demands for a return to the old ways should not cause us to be less appreciative of a decreasingly homogeneous society." Even conservative John Silber, the president of Boston University, supports tolerance as a distinctive feature of American life.[9]

The value of tolerance becomes obvious when compared to intolerant societies, such as Iran. When an author published a book critical of their society and religion, Iranian leaders issued death threats against that author. Because of our more tolerant society, such a drastic retaliation would not occur in America. Yet the book-burning campaigns of the conservative fundamentalists do not signal a healthy development for society. For instance, recent occurrences of intolerance have led to sporadic outbursts of violence against unpopular groups. It was recently reported that seventy homosexuals were killed and 885 assaulted in 1988 "as part of an alarmingly widespread pattern of violence and harassment against gay people."[10] Such violence stems in part from the conservative attacks on tolerance. Indeed, what ultimately results from conservative attacks on tolerance is not a society more harmonious in its sexual mores, but a society more violent toward minorities and dissenters.

Intolerance causes many negative ripple effects throughout society, beyond just that of increasing violence in society.[11] Freedom of speech and religion are threatened; hysteria and herdlike mentalities increase; individuality suffers; and respect for the democratic process diminishes. A sobering distinction between tolerant and intolerant, free and unfree societies comes to light from simply glancing at the newspaper headlines of one relatively ordinary day, April 10, 1989. On that day, while one of the largest demonstrations ever in Washington, D.C., peacefully took place in connection with the Supreme Court's emotion-charged abortion decision, sixteen people were killed in a political protest in the Soviet Union.

Most of the large-scale social violence and terrorism in the world today results from absolutism and intolerance. Muslims and Jews are locked in violence in the Middle East, Sunnites and Shiites are fighting in the Persian Gulf, and Hindus and Sikhs in India are killing each other all in the name of religious, ideological, or racial absolutism. Indeed, the great majority of wars occurring around the world in the 1980s possessed a significant religious dimension. It seems true that, as Jonathan Swift said, "We have just enough religion to make us hate, but not enough to make us love." And because we cannot always love, liberalism reminds us to at least tolerate.

The conservative critics of liberalism frequently blame the practice of tolerance for the absence of a uniform and enforceable system of moral rules in America. Currently, in many parts of the world, zealous religious movements seek to impose rigid, intolerant rules on their societies. America, however, was founded on the principle of religious tolerance, which enables all religions to exist freely without interference by the state. When Roger Williams went to Rhode Island in the seventeenth century to escape the dictates of the Puritan leaders and to practice his own religion, he marked America as a land of religious tolerance. Indeed, the American belief that freedom is better than despotism and that legally established religious beliefs are unjust requires a belief in and practice of tolerance.

The American commitment to individual dignity also requires social tolerance. For without tolerance, persons are locked into conformity, and the exercise of freedom becomes impossible. James Madison typified the Constitution's framers in his passionate crusade against religious intolerance.[12] They were acutely aware of the dangers of intolerance, not just because of their political theories of separation of church and state, but also because of the great eighteenth-century Enlightenment movement, which struggled against religious intolerance, superstitions, and the uncritical compliance with tradition.

Amazingly, modern conservatives have condemned tolerance as "un-American" and as a destructive belief of present-day liberals. The entire American experience, however, has been just the contrary. Our national origins, our respected national heroes, our great national documents, and our costly national wars have all rejected absolutism and intolerance. America is a nation dedicated to the right of each individual to life, liberty, and the pursuit of happiness as he or she sees fit. And while absolutism is traditional, hierarchical, and deferential to authority, tolerance is consistent with equality, experimentation, and democratic rule.

Reinhold Niebuhr warned of the dangers of an absolutism based on perceived divine purposes. While the divine is necessarily absolute, the human is finite, imperfect, and incapable of the divine. To enforce absolutism in secular politics based on a divine absolutism is to ignore the fundamental difference between the divine and the human. As Abraham Lincoln stated in his Second Inaugural Address, both sides in the Civil War "read the same Bible and pray to the same God; and each invokes His aid against the other." Human beings have many inherent frailties, but intolerance is a self-imposed condition that will block the human quest for knowledge, truth, and peace.

## The Religious Influence on American Liberalism

Even with its belief in religious tolerance, liberalism is not completely neutral in matters concerning religious values. It certainly is not oblivious or hostile to the presence of religion or basic religious values. Yet in their criticism of liberals, conservatives confuse toleration with indifference.

Political liberals historically have had close connections with religion and have gleaned many of their political values from religious values. Throughout history, liberal reform movements in America have grown from two sets of ideas: the individual freedom ideals articulated in the Declaration and the concern for humane conditions and the general welfare found in the Judeo-Christian heritage. Religious ideals and denominational diversity greatly influenced the political ideas of the patriots during the revolutionary period and at the same time encouraged toleration.[13] According to Patricia Bonomi, the Great Awakening of the eighteenth century fostered a strong individualism in spiritual matters and had a spill-over effect in the political world by inspiring individuals to throw off corrupt, traditional forms of authority and to attack the doctrines of divine right and passive obedience to rulers that had propped up despotic bishops as well as tyrannous kings. Thus, by encouraging liberal colonial leaders to rebel against traditional hierarchical rulers in the name of individual freedom, the American colonial churches exerted a strong and vital hand in forming the American liberal political tradition.

The great reform movements of the nineteenth century, including the abolition crusade, were also inspired by liberal religious leaders. Protestant-driven social reform in the nineteenth century energized liberalism; at the same time, Christianity in America turned increasingly liberal.[14] The progressive movement of the early twentieth century also received strength and direction from Protestant churches and religious values. Both the egalitarian ideals of the Declaration of Independence and the vision of the Protestant faith were used by labor leaders to fight in the name of Christian social justice the horrible working conditions accompanying industrialization.

The Social Darwinism advocated by conservatives had made Christian morality and a sense of humanity in the economic arena a thing of the past. However, Woodrow Wilson, son of a Presbyterian minister, injected liberalism with a sense of public morality and the social gospel message. This message exerted even stronger influence in the New Deal reforms.

Religious values and the social gospel message once again provided leadership and vitality to the civil rights movement of the 1960s. The same moral and religious spirit that infused the abolition movement energized the civil rights movement. Martin Luther King, Jr., and his nonviolent campaign for civil rights followed in the American tradition of religious-political movements. He vehemently castigated the spiritual collapse of America, evident in its racism and its tendency toward violence. In his "Letter from a Birmingham Jail," King expressed the religious tenor of his mission and its attack on un-Christian institutions. Moreover, he patterned the nonviolent civil rights campaign after the missionary spirit of the early Christians; the driving force of King's campaign arose from his religious values and commitments. In addition to the civil rights movement, the antiwar and arms limitations movements also drew heavily from religious values. Indeed, up until the "moral majority" fundamentalist movement of recent years, religion has most often been associated with liberalism in America.

Besides the influence of religious ideas and values upon liberalism, the acceptance and support of "civil religion" also characterizes American liberalism. The concept of civil religion refers to the political recognition of the influence and tradition of religion in America's public life. Civil religion recognizes the strong influence on American liberal democratic principles of the Judeo-Christian values and heritage and expresses the correlation between religious and political behavior that has always prevailed.[15]

Civil religion arose from the founders' belief in America's transcendent purpose. Its tenets include a belief in justice, civic virtue, and tolerance. The Declaration of Independence is the bible of American civil religion; and symbols of America's civil religion include public holidays like Thanksgiving, public logos like "In God We Trust," and the use of the Bible in ceremonies such as an inaugural swearing-in. The Constitution, ever since its ratification, has stood at the center of America's civil religion.

In *Constitutional Faith,* Sanford Levinson outlines the parallels between political dialogue and history and the American civil religion. Although civil religion recognizes America's belief in religion and a Supreme Being, it is not sectarian.[16] American civil religion establishes a critical distinction in American public life between sectarianism and religion. It forbids the former, but encourages the latter—the opposite approach of modern conservatives. The conservative demand for school prayer, for instance, would make Jefferson and Madison reach in opposition for Article 16 of the Virginia Declaration of Rights calling for the "free exercise of religion, according to the dictates of conscience." Yet both Jefferson and Madison practiced civil religion.

The American civil religion of Jefferson and Madison accommodates pluralism—a pluralism that says in public life religion is proper, but only if all denominations are respected equally. It is meant to infuse American life with a sense of transcendent values, not to impose a religious sect on individuals. Civil religion, through its articulation of a higher law, also serves as a bridge between political law and a more secure, permanent natural law. It is part of the liberal tradition in America. Political liberalism and civil religion have existed and developed together from the time of America's birth. Moreover, American civil religion continues to live on and flourish in modern liberalism. John Kennedy articulated the ideals of American civil religion in his inaugural address, in which he proclaimed:

> We observe today not a victory of party but a celebration of freedom. . . . For I have sworn before you and Almighty God the same solemn oath our forebears prescribed nearly a century and three quarters ago.
>
> The world is very different now. . . . Yet the same revolutionary beliefs for which our forebears fought are still at issue around the globe—the belief that the rights of man come not from the generosity of the state but from the hand of God. . . .

With a good conscience our only sure reward, with history the final judge of our deeds, let us go forth to lead the land we love, asking His blessing and His keep, but knowing that here on earth God's work must truly be our own.

As John Kennedy did, present-day liberals actively strive to strengthen the role of civil religion in society. For instance, liberals support the teaching of religious diversity and the basic ideas of the major religions in public schools.[17] Learning about the importance of religion in American social and political history helps sustain civil religion.

Even among those who claim that the conservative political philosophy incorporates aspects of American civil religion, the connection between liberalism and civil religion is still recognized. In *The Restructuring of American Religion,* Robert Wuthrow outlines two strands of American civil religion, each with its own set of values and ideals. The conservative civil religion claims a divine blessing on the economic system and on militant foreign policy. The liberal civil religion, according to Wuthrow, emphasizes social responsibilities to promote freedom, peace, and justice and speaks more of human rights and of what will benefit humanity.

American liberalism, therefore, has clearly not been devoid of or antagonistic to religious values. Contrary to conservatism, it harmonizes religious values with democratic political values that recognize and tolerate the diversity of religious sects and moral teachings. While the liberal use of religion aims at inspiring the ideals of justice and fairness and at providing people with a source of comfort and sense of communal identification, the conservative religious tendency fuels a passionate resentment toward change and modernity. Rather than intertwine basic American political and religious values, conservatives attempt to circumscribe politics with moral rules to govern society. While liberals form political beliefs by asking what religious values apply to the political world, conservatives command that a particular set of private moral beliefs be imposed upon the public through the political process. They in effect ask the state to assume the role and duties of particular religious denominations.

America is the only nation consciously founded on a set of political values. Those values combine a commitment to inalienable rights with the Calvinist belief in a moral duty to do good, and they are embodied in the Declaration of Independence and the Constitution. Indeed, the elements for an enduring national moral consensus are at hand not in rigid religious rules but in the Constitution and Declaration, with their combination of Locke's natural rights and Calvin's moral right.

In addition to religious and civic virtue values and the ideals of freedom and democracy expressed in the Declaration of Independence, liberalism recognizes and encourages community values. These values reflect the American desire to live and work in a safe, supportive, and cooperative community. Indeed, the individualism of the American character has always existed alongside a strong concern for the well-being of neighbor and community. And since the days of Andrew Jackson, the liberal philosophy has most often served the concerns of the community.

## CHAPTER EIGHT

# Liberalism and Community

## The Liberal Democratic Community in American History

America's constitutional democracy stands for two areas of individual freedom. The first is freedom from abridgment of such fundamental natural rights as speech and religion. The second is freedom to form, through self-determination, a free and democratic community. In a democratic society, community exists in the common interests and bonds of its members. Only free individuals with respect for others' freedom and dignity can join together in a social contract to form such a community. By insuring individual freedom, liberalism gives the individual members of communities greater security, since they need not fear that membership in their communities will somehow in the future compromise their liberties. Thus, the history of American liberalism is a history of advocacy not only for individual freedoms but for survival and prosperity of the American community. Liberalism has combined its individual and community values by seeking to empower all individuals to participate freely and equally in their community.

Martin Luther King's leadership of the civil rights movement focused on building community bonds and on injecting liberal community values into the movement. He succeeded in revealing how segregation embittered blacks of all classes. In fighting segregation, King drew the entire black community together and "gave every person in it a chance to become actively involved in a way that would not have been possible if the battle had been exclusively a courtroom affair."[1] Thus, in the Jeffersonian and Jacksonian tradition, King chose the democratic and the communal process over a more formal legalistic process involving only a small minority of those concerned.

Throughout the twentieth century, liberalism prospered largely because of its support of community. Liberals like Woodrow Wilson and Franklin Roosevelt addressed the people's communal values and their fear, both individually and collectively, of losing control over the forces that governed their lives. This liberalism did not leave the individual alone to confront the impersonal forces of the economy without the resources of local and national communities. FDR proclaimed his commitment to "community rugged individualism": a political ideology encouraging each individual "to use his individualism in cooperation with his neighbors' individualism so that he and his neighbors may improve their lot in life." Long before Reagan ever did, Wilson and Roosevelt evoked the communal themes of family, neighborhood, and patriotism and sought to empower the community to survive and prosper in the face of powerful outside forces.

The difference between Reagan and the liberal view of community is that the latter infuses community with an activist spirit of moving forward and of becoming a better community, one which is more inclusive and more just. Reagan, on the other hand, saw community as a way to enforce conformity with certain traditional, individual moral values. Reagan wanted to instill individuals with conservative moral beliefs, not to strengthen and improve the social community of individuals.

During the Reagan years, the conservative espousal of communal values coincided with a further breakdown of many traditional communities. As the national and international economies became more fluid, local communities had less power to control their destiny. With the torrent of corporate takeovers, factories and businesses in communities dependent upon them closed or moved practically overnight. And as corporations became more international, American workers lost jobs because of remote corporate decisions to transfer a particular production function to another country.

Yet Reagan did not address this assault on community. Instead, he lambasted liberals for their emphasis on individual rights and claimed that community could be resurrected with public school prayer and a mandatory Pledge of Allegiance. Oddly enough, liberalism was also denounced by Reagan conservatives as akin to socialism or communism. The problem with socialism, according to conservatives, is that it sacrifices individual freedom for the collective interest. Therefore, conservatives simultaneously attacked liberalism both for being too individualistic and too communitarian. Furthermore, the conservative criticism also confused liberals with libertarians, who believe that community concerns or values only interfere with complete individual freedom.

In the name of communal values, Reagan sought to shift power from the federal government to states and localities. But, as Michael Sandel points out, this approach was bound to fail "because it ignored the conditions that led to the growth of federal power in the first place."[2] As Sandel argues, the federalism of the Constitutional framers presupposed the continuation of the decentralized economy existing at the time. The increased political power of the federal government in the twentieth century has resulted from the increased concentration of economic power. Therefore, decentralizing government without decentralizing the economy, as Reagan proposed, constitutes only partial federalism. Leaving local communities to the mercy of corporate decisions made in distant places does not empower them; if anything, it diminishes a community's ability to shape its destiny.

As Wilson and Roosevelt recognized long ago, the greatest corrosion of community comes not from individual freedoms but from features of the modern economy ignored by conservatives. These features include the unrestrained corporate takeovers and acquisitions with their disruptive effects on neighborhoods and cities; the concentration of power in large corporations unaccountable to the communities they serve; and an inflexible workplace that forces working men and women to choose between advancing their careers and caring for their children. Throughout the twentieth century, liberals have asserted communal values to counteract these dislocating changes and have advocated economic arrangements most amenable to self-government and the prosperity of community.

The historic liberal belief in political democracy demonstrates its commitment to community. Self-government and democratic rule contribute more to community building than mandatory prayers or pledges recited by our schoolchildren. In a democratic society like America, community flourishes only where democratic conditions and participation prevail. And political democracy, as John Dewey pointed out, can exist only where the social conditions for democracy exist. According to Gregory Fossedal in The Democratic Imperative, the way to greater democracy is to strengthen the social forces behind democracy, such as a free press, political parties, unions, business groups, and independent churches or religious organizations. These are forces which liberals support. Indeed, when liberals recognize the right of citizens to assemble, for instance, they encourage and enable the communal assembly of citizens.

The lesson of the power of democratic social forces received renewed vitality from the example of the Chinese democratic protests during the summer of 1989. In their protest for greater democratic freedoms, the Chinese studied and followed the American civil rights movement of the 1960s. The protestors, recognizing that totalitarianism requires control of the flow of information, called for freedom of speech and press and for greater access to public education. These conditions, they knew, were essential for democracy. Yet these same conditions have never received the full support of conservatives in America, the longest-lasting democracy in the world. Furthermore, and what should be an embarrassment and disappointment to Americans after a decade of conservative leadership, the personal hero and model of the Chinese protestors was Mikhail Gorbachev, who was declared "an emissary of democracy."[3]

In a democracy, the act of self-governance mirrors the act of community building. Liberals have understood this relationship. Their belief in community democracy has encouraged the proliferation of grass-roots organizations committed to social progress. Liberals have widened democratic participation, encouraged local political and social action, and opened the community to persons previously excluded. And throughout the twentieth century, liberals have attempted to bring some democratic control over the economic life of society. Such democratic activism enables citizens, according to Tocqueville, to practice the conduct of government in the small sphere of local communities.

Perhaps the clearest distinction between the liberal and conservative visions of community is that the former values community from the standpoint of the individual, while the conservative desires community from the standpoint of social order. Individuals become secondary in a conservative model of society. Within the liberal view of community, however, is the recognition of social nature and needs of the individual.

The liberal view of community also recognizes, as Michael Walzer argues, the "Four Mobilities" possessed by free individuals: geographic mobility, social mobility, marital mobility, and political mobility.[4] These mobilities have historically characterized American society and political beliefs, even though they may at times counteract the apparent stability of community. Yet to deliberately restrict these mobilities in the name of community, as the conservative agenda occasionally proposes, would be to destroy the unique characteristics of American society and would require a harsh application of state power. In the liberal view, these mobilities represent the fruits of liberty and freedom and the pursuit of individual happiness. Consequently, the liberal community is based on communal bonds that do not repress the Four Mobilities. And indeed, as history has demonstrated, the ties and bonds of place, relationships, and politics have successfully survived the Four Mobilities. Because of the liberal bonds of social tolerance, concern for social justice, and respect for individual freedom, individual freedom and mobility has not fragmented American society nor escalated social conflict.

### The Liberal Community: One That Inspires Allegiance

Liberals, in addition to addressing the political and economic forces affecting community, have also sought to improve the quality of life within communities. The liberal support of public education, improved health care, and a cleaner environment result in a more educated, prosperous, and healthy community in an environment safe and habitable for the future. Liberalism also envisions a more just community. The civil rights movement, for instance, represented a liberal communal movement for justice and strove to bring African Americans into the broader American community.

Contrary to conservatives who seek an imposition of traditional values as a sign of community, liberals seek to strengthen communal bonds by making voluntary association an everyday fact of life. Indeed, the liberal theory of relationship and community has voluntary association at its center. According to Nancy Rosenblum in *Romanticism and the Reconstruction of Liberal Thought,* real community is linked to human freedom; and liberalism provides for both a private life and a public life by creating an area of freedom in which individuals can form community bonds.

A difference between the liberal and conservative visions of community is that the former is a qualitative vision and the latter a quantitative vision. Conservatives appear satisfied simply that the signs of community exist: if everyone is reciting the Pledge, they must have communal bonds and feel good about their community. Conservatives do not favor an activist community, which could interfere with the economic freedom of business in that community. Liberals, on the other hand, look to the nature or quality of the community. For instance, a community can be a bad place to live if that community breeds violence, racism, or prejudice. In fact, the greatest threat to social cohesion arises not from individualism, but from "collective passions, ideological conflict, and inherited rivalries between hostile factions."[5] If a community is prejudiced and vindictive, like the Ku Klux Klan communities, communal solidarity is a problem. It would be better, in that case, to have no community at all than to have such a community where the children recite the Pledge but are taught values contrary to the American ideals of freedom and justice.

The conservative view of community is an inconsistent one. While it refuses any kind of communal values or activities in the economic sphere on the grounds that any interference with laissez-faire is "un-American," the conservative support of community focuses mainly on enforcing traditional individual moral and religious beliefs, which the framers constitutionally insulated from the political process. Individual morals, however, hardly forge communal bonds or develop common public interests. Because they fear government involvement in the economy, conservatives shy away from actually admitting or addressing the common interests of society. If, however, conservatives truly understood their society as a community with its survival and prosperity dependent on the well-being of all its members, they would strive to give everyone an equal opportunity and a helping hand when needed. Even George Will, a Reagan conservative, admits to the existence of our collective soul. In *Statecraft as Soulcraft* he concludes that a true conservative should support a stronger, more effective welfare state.

A strong community philosophy requires an identification of the community and of the problems it faces. If neighborhoods, churches, and school boards exemplify community, what political institutions or actions will support those communities? In the 1988 campaign, however, conservatives rejected political actions aimed at improving the housing stock of neighborhoods or at requiring businesses intending on closing to notify its employees so as to give them a chance to find new employment in the community. In calling for a return to communal values, conservatives simply advocated mandatory recitation of the Pledge of Allegiance. Yet it is highly questionable as to what community-binding power the Pledge has. After all, the Pledge was commonly recited in schoolrooms in the 1950s by the children who later, in the 1960s, threw off all communal values.

The issue behind the Pledge is not whether we must recite it, but whether it stands for the kind of community or society we have freely chosen. Conservatives in the 1980s showed little interest in describing to what they would have us pledge allegiance. The reality, rather than just the symbol, of patriotism is what concerns liberals. For example, in the nineteenth and early twentieth centuries, schools encouraged patriotism not because the Pledge was recited but because they tried to confer a real benefit on all classes of society, as well as new immigrants, and did so as an expression of the society's commitment to its people. Neither exhortation nor moralism will reinvigorate the American community or civic consciousness today. What is needed is a strong sense of public purpose and social action to build a community capable of providing jobs, security against crime, public education, and a belief in the future that will encourage saving and investment. Success in fulfilling these common interests will inspire loyalty and patriotism.

In America, individual consent—the social contract—must underlie community bonds. According to Sanford Levinson in *Constitutional Faith,* America has been a contracting community since the pilgrims disembarked. A community based on the social contract stresses the mutual obligations of all citizens and a sense of social and communal solidarity. John Rawls has described a liberal society as a pluralism of groups bonded by shared ideas of toleration and democracy.[6] Patriotism and community, therefore, must rest upon the communal values chosen by the members of society.

The American liberal political tradition has been an endeavor to build a just society on the consent of all citizens and fashioned according to the common good. Yet, during the 1980s, conservatives criticized liberals for failing to incorporate within their political agenda a vision of the common good. This, however, was not the conservative position throughout the previous century and a half, from the Jackson to the Roosevelt eras. During those periods, conservatives argued that the liberal vision of the common good violated the property and economic rights of the wealthy.

The common good has rarely been a communal vision of conservatives. Instead, their vision appears to express more a yearning for a symbolic moral community rather than for the reality of community. Conservatives have not yet accurately assessed the reasons for communal and patriotic breakdown in America. The reason fewer people recite the Pledge today is not because of the prevalence of "liberal philosophies" but because of public and political failures that symbolized a loss of collective confidence—like those that took place in Vietnam, a war we could not win; in Watergate, a scandal we could not believe; in Iran, a hostage-taking we could not remedy; in the stock market in 1987, a crash not even the experts could explain; in Lebanon, the needless and tragic deaths of the Marines; and in the Iran-Contra affair, another scandal which seemed only to repeat the trauma and failures of Watergate. These events, along with a continuing concentration and impersonalization of economic power through corporate mergers and takeovers, left the public with a loss of faith in community. Thus, the conservative response of seeking governmental enforcement of certain moral and religious values is not relevant to the causes of the decline in patriotic and communal bonds during the last several decades.

## Liberalism and the Family in a Changing Community

The nature of American community has greatly changed over the last three centuries. From the Puritan theocracy to the immigrant section of the city to the midwestern small town to the restored inner city of the yuppies, communities have adapted to changing times. They will continue to change, just as will the family. The large, economically independent farm family led to the small, suburban "Ozzie and Harriet" family of the 1950s. Today "fewer and fewer American families conform to traditional stereotypes," according to Peter Morrison, the director of Rand Corporation's Population Research Center.[7] Only drastic changes like a significant rise in fertility, a large exit of women from the labor force, or a big decrease in divorce would bring a return to the model family of the 1950s.

The political role in society is not to force these changes on individuals and families, but to help solve any social problems caused by the changes made by individuals in their own family lives. The conservative vision, however, seeks not to help strengthen a modern community, but only to force, against the practices of the members of society, a traditional model of family and community. Thus, while conservatives ignored the needs of the changing American family, liberals in 1989 obtained passage of a child-care bill aimed at improving the quality and supply of day-care services and at providing health insurance for thirteen million children previously without health coverage.

Community and family are closely related; each depends on the strength and support of the other. No political philosophy can neatly separate the two nor value one without the other. Given this connection, the conservative attack on liberalism in the 1980s naturally included criticism of liberal views on family. Of course, if being pro-family in the 1980s meant only that one strove to bring back the model family of the 1950s, liberals did not qualify. However, if pro-family means supporting the families existing in society, liberals have a long tradition of ardent advocacy for family and community values.

In *Family and Nation*, Daniel Moynihan outlines his idea of a liberal family policy. His policy does not seek to punish mothers or children whose lives do not conform to a traditional ideal; rather, he seeks to find remedies for the actual problems which affect many families today. Moynihan particularly looks at the increasing povertization of families and children. He recognizes that many factors—social, economic, and political—affect the health, prosperity, and stability of families. With the family subject to so many social forces, Moynihan argues for society to place a high political priority on the family and set out to actively promote its health, rather than merely wishing for a return to the mythical family of the past. He warns that the future of society may be determined by how it cares for its children. Caring for America's children may be the most important challenge to the nation in the decades ahead. During the last several years, we have devoted incredible energy to defining our society in terms of its economic competitiveness and corporate activity. But perhaps we have left behind the most vulnerable, and yet the most valuable, members of our society. As Paul Simon said on withdrawing from the 1988 campaign, "Americans instinctively know that we are one nation, one family, and when anyone in that family hurts, all of us hurt." Sadly, this has come to be less and less true for today's American children.

As the family is an indispensable component of the American community, the individual is a basic and vital member of both the family and the community. The liberal emphasis on individualism, therefore, does not contradict or diminish its support of community and family. While participation in communal life helps give meaning to individual lives, the ties of community and of family depend on individual choice and commitment. Furthermore, given the social nature of human beings, community and social identity are extremely important to individual identity. Indeed, a new recognition of this social nature of the individual has energized the communal values of liberalism.[8]

Mario Cuomo offers a communal vision of liberalism: the "America as family" message. As a community, Cuomo proclaims, we are bound to one another and to our social community. The heart of the liberal constituency and the community is the middle class—"the people not rich enough to be worry free but not poor enough to be on welfare."[9] To Cuomo, conservatives do not see America as a family and community; they instead have divided the nation into the rich and non-rich. Cuomo's community and family message, on the other hand, embodies the immigrant experience of people coming to America with nothing and seeking opportunity. According to the liberal promise, having the freedom to make a home, to live in a free community, and to decide about one's future is the American promise.

The concerns of Cuomo reflect an underlying "communitarian" movement which has recently emerged within the liberal ranks and has advocated strengthening communal values within the liberal philosophy. Communitarians argue that a person's social and communal roles—as citizens of a country or members of a community—partly make up the individual identity of that person. As Alasdair MacIntyre suggests in *After Virtue,* if individuals are partly defined by the communities they inhabit, then they must also be involved in the purposes and values of those communities. Such involvement, communitarians argue, would bring communal values to the heart of political concerns, would balance the communal and individual strains of liberalism, and would raise social and communal interests to a more explicit level in our political discourse. A strengthened community also gives greater power to the individuals inhabiting it. Communitarians consequently oppose the concentration of power in both the corporate economy and the bureaucratic government. The plant-closing law enacted by Congress reflects the communitarian strain of liberalism in its effort to protect communities from the disruptive effects of sudden corporate changes.

According to communitarians, the various intermediate forms of community sustain a vital public life, without which our sense of the common good diminishes. Indeed, a wide array of nongovernmental communal groups give shape and purpose to the social lives of most individuals. The challenge is to advance social and community interests while creating the atmosphere through individual freedom for the genuinely free associations of community. Contrary to the claims of conservatives that community values cannot be reconciled with traditional liberal concerns, communitarians argue that a communal philosophy complements individualism and pluralism, since intolerance flourishes most where individuals are dislocated, isolated, and unsettled.[10]

The historic contribution of liberalism has been in its accommodation of the shared goals of individual freedom and advancement of the community's common interest. Too great an emphasis on community creates a tendency to downgrade the unique worth and integrity of each individual. Indeed, the belief that human beings are entirely society-made has several alarming consequences. With individuals defined in terms of social relationships, notions of responsibility and sovereignty pass from the individual to an abstract "society." Individuals become important only in terms of their social participation. The erosion of a distinction between the personal and social sides of individual life also leaves a society conceptually defenseless in the face of totalitarian doctrines. European history in the twentieth century demonstrates that, without a high respect for the dignity of the individual, even democracies cannot assure protection of freedom and defeat of totalitarianism. The totalitarian and Communist movements of the 1930s gained power by justifying a sacrifice of individual freedom and autonomy for the "higher purposes" of social commitment and collective action. Consequently, the liberal campaign for greater individual rights in the 1950s and 1960s resulted largely from the lessons of totalitarianism learned during World War II.

## CHAPTER NINE

# A Liberal Approach to
# Four Contemporary Issues

During a political campaign, parties or candidates rarely have the time or opportunity to engage in lengthy discourse about the fundamental tenets and history of their political philosophy. Instead, the philosophy comes out in fragments through the candidates' responses to contemporary issues. In the 1988 campaign, the conservative attack on liberalism centered on four general contemporary issues: defense, crime, abortion, and welfare. Conservatives painted liberals as far out of the mainstream on these issues. Free of the confines of communicating in brief television news bites, a broader discussion of the liberal position on these issues demonstrates the slantedness of the conservative attack and the public misperceptions of liberal philosophies.

## National Defense and the Liberal Tradition

For most of the twentieth century prior to the 1980s, conservatives have criticized liberal foreign policy as being too interventionist. As early as the Wilson administration, liberals recognized that American interests were too intermingled with the rest of the world for the U.S. to ignore international developments and problems that threatened world peace. However, as late as the 1950s, conservatives under the leadership of Senator Robert Taft opposed American involvement in international peace-keeping efforts and adopted a head-in-the-sand isolationist foreign policy. Throughout the twentieth century, the differences between the liberal and conservative positions on foreign policy have reflected the American quarrel between internationalism and isolationism and between international extroversion and introversion.

The simplistic division of foreign policy views between "hawks" and "doves" has revealed the conservative isolationist thinking that the only two ways to conduct international affairs are by military action or by wimpish acquiescence. Diplomacy according to American democratic values apparently fell into the latter category. Indeed, the conservative isolationist approach has often put America on a "go it alone" course in international affairs. This approach clearly contradicts the liberal-inspired Western alliance which succeeded in World War II and in the postwar revitalization of Europe. Another area which illustrates the differences between the liberal and conservative foreign policy views is the U.S. Latin American policy. Kennedy's Alliance for Progress created a system with America as ally and partner, while Reagan's "go it alone" policy ignored such a system of alliances and instead dictated to Latin America as if it were a helpless child.

The isolationist impulse is also reflected in the conservative determination to act in world affairs without regard for alliances or international institutions. Reagan's covert and unilateral actions in the Middle East and Central America have ignored America's allies and proceeded on the assumption that they had no choice but to approve. The Reagan doctrine, which asserted a unilateral right to intervene through covert action and "low intensity warfare" in any nation's affairs in order to combat communism, is the most dangerous expression of conservative isolationism. The doctrine completely ignored the sovereignty of nations and demonstrated disrespect for international law. When the Soviet Union claimed a similar right of global intervention in support of "wars of national liberation," Americans forcefully protested. Yet the Reagan doctrine also rejected all constraints on international behavior that have developed under international law during the last two centuries. Not only did the doctrine weaken the international reputation of America as a nation conducting itself according to its constitutional ideals, it also was unrealistic and destructive to American interests. The doctrine did not formulate a clear notion of U.S. vital interests abroad and overextended America's resources in an era when the U.S. budget deficit was the largest in its history. As a result, the Reagan doctrine failed in countries like Nicaragua despite siphoning off billions from the U.S. national treasury.

To defend the Reagan doctrine in the 1988 campaign, conservatives detoured the focus and instead lambasted liberalism for advocating military restraint and multilateral diplomacy and for failing to isolate and weaken the Soviet Union in the international community.

However, the actions of George Bush shortly after the election demonstrate not only the fallacy and emptiness of the conservative attack but the lack of belief even by conservatives in their denunciation of the liberal position. For instance, in a 12 May 1989 speech Bush proposed as a foreign policy goal not the isolation of the Soviet Union but the "integration of the Soviet Union into the community of nations." Bush also proposed more arms cuts in an effort to wind down, rather than escalate, the military standoff between NATO and the Warsaw Pact.

Most importantly, however, Bush's handling of the Iraqi invasion of Kuwait reflected a rejection of the philosophical foundations of the Reagan doctrine. Instead of acting in isolation and with disregard for the vital interests of America's allies, Bush carefully forged a strong alliance with Middle Eastern partners. This alliance, at least according to government spokespersons, then participated in and consented to the diplomatic and military response to Iraq. Furthermore, Bush's conduct of the war greatly differed from the military actions waged by the Reagan administration, insofar as President Bush followed the rule of law by obtaining congressional approval and by complying with resolutions passed by the United Nations. Thus, Bush's actions in his first term illustrate not only the shallowness of the 1980s conservative criticisms against liberal foreign policy, but also the wisdom of a policy based on the liberal respect for international law and its recognition of international alliances and America's need for them.

During the 1970s and 1980s, the conservative fixation with military conflict produced a foreign policy without logical direction or consistent aims. For instance, while conservatives favored dumping billions of dollars into military support of the contras, who did not even have a clear majority of popular support in Nicaragua, Bush waffled on an opportunity to quicken the progress of democracy when he promised to give the democratically reformed Poland only 1 percent of the foreign aid they needed to continue their democratic progress. Such aid would have been a far better investment for international democracy than all the covert military actions conducted under Reagan.

The conservative foreign policy fixation on military actions hinders the ability of conservatives in the 1990s to deal with the monumental democratic changes taking place in the world. Indeed, during the democratic movements in Eastern Europe, the Bush administration was noticeably silent and inactive. This silence indicated that conservatives are not ready to define the purpose of American foreign policy in a post–Cold War era, because, to conservatives, American foreign policy has become simply a reaction against Soviet communism and an automatic support of corporate interests abroad. President Bush, for instance, was more worried about offending Deng Xiaoping than he was eager to champion the democratic protests in Tiananmen Square.

Contrary to the conservative approach, liberalism holds a broader and more timeless view of American foreign policy: to assist the peaceful spread of democracy around the world. Indeed, the democratic leadership in the world during most of the twentieth century was exerted by American liberals. They have led the fight against communism and totalitarianism around the world. Wilson committed America to the war effort in World War I in the hope of bringing a more stable democratic order to a world characterized by autocratic feudal remnants and revolutionary communism. Employing his liberal principles, Wilson tried to guide the world away from militant imperialism and revolutionary socialism toward an international liberal system of peaceful commercial and political order based on rational diplomacy and the rule of law. To the degree he succeeded, free trade and foreign markets were opened to United States businesses, and Europe briefly set aside its autocratic regimes for democratic governments. Yet conservatives saw little value in getting America involved in foreign affairs and opposed the League of Nations. Diplomacy soon broke down, as did the European democracies.

Franklin Roosevelt saw a world, and an America, threatened by fascist dictators. He recognized that the postwar world would greatly affect America, and by committing America to the allied war effort he once again bucked the conservative call for isolation. Roosevelt continued to oppose conservative isolationism when he guided America toward membership in the United Nations. For the first time, America belonged to a world political organization which could attempt to solve international problems peacefully and diplomatically and which also injected a dose of American democracy into the world community.

Harry Truman presided during the tumultuous postwar period. The enemy was still totalitarianism, only now its carrier had changed identity. To prevent Soviet communism from taking hold in war-ravaged Europe, Truman did not rely just on military might; he saw that the only true defense to communism lay in a free, prosperous, and just society. Through the Truman and Marshall plans, he funneled American assistance into rebuilding Western Europe into a region of democratic governments and strong economies.

John Kennedy and Lyndon Johnson kept up the anti-Communist spirit of American foreign policy. Both presidents built up the military after a fairly quiet Eisenhower administration, and unfortunately both committed America to a disastrous military involvement in Vietnam. By doing so, Johnson and Kennedy favored too much the anti-Communist strain in American foreign policy and ignored too much the democratic foundations and national sovereignty principles of the liberal tradition. Vietnam was a costly concession to the conservative paranoia of the Communist threat. Liberals have long paid the political price for this concession, and they have during the last several decades wisely opposed American military involvements in national civil wars in Nicaragua, El Salvador, and Lebanon. Moreover, those regions have since stabilized not because of any military action advocated by the conservatives but because of negotiated national settlements advocated by liberals.

Despite his involvement in Vietnam, Kennedy achieved significant diplomatic successes and provided valuable long-term lessons for American foreign policy in the future. First, he realized that an arms race itself would, at some point, threaten world peace and stability. Unlike many conservatives, Kennedy did not place his entire trust for the defense of America in the military. He applied in the foreign policy arena the principles for which America has so long been known—democracy and diplomacy. Kennedy negotiated the Test Ban Treaty and ended the Cuban missile crisis through strong diplomacy, not through bombardment. He launched his Alliance for Progress in Latin America, which aimed at developing a partnership between the United States and its Latin American neighbors and at fostering democracy and economic opportunity within the characteristically authoritarian and elitist region. Consequently, the great mass of Latin Americans looked optimistically to America to bring progress and democracy. Conservatives in the Reagan era, unfortunately, took the opposite approach to Latin America, with the result that many of our "neighbors" to the south wish they were in a different neighborhood. The difference between the Kennedy policy toward Latin America and the Reagan policy was that the former inspired the majority of Latin Americans to look to the U.S. with hope for the future, while the latter pandered to the desire of a wealthy minority to return to the past.

Jimmy Carter applied this important lesson and carried forward a foreign policy modeled after Kennedy's Alliance for Progress. Carter committed American support not to authoritarian regimes doomed to popular uprisings, but to countries following the principles of democracy and respecting human rights. The United States, Carter believed, had to get on the right side of international change by promoting human rights and supporting progressive movements that would deal with the root cause of the Third World revolutions. Because Third World conflicts were said to have indigenous causes and were not part of the East-West struggle, American military power would be ineffective in resolving them. Carter's policy was the natural expression of America's commitment to the rule of law and to the notion that America is a nation of laws, not of rulers. He tried to make America's foreign policy more stable by tying it to the political and legal structure of a country, not to whatever personality happened to be accepting American money.

Indeed, the liberal approach to foreign policy throughout the 1970s and 1980s followed the Kennedy and Truman approach to make America known abroad, as we know it here, as a defender of democracy rather than as a supporter of undemocratic regimes. Liberalism has tried to export America's most precious commodity—democracy and freedom. And it has been amazingly successful in doing so, according to Joshua Muravchik in *Exporting Democracy: Fulfilling America's Destiny.* Muravchik argues that most of the world's democracies have looked to import at least a part of the American example and that, consequently, the U.S. should make promotion of democracy the central theme of its foreign policy. The liberal outlook sees American democracy, rather than American military, as the beacon of hope to the rest of the world for two centuries. Consistent with its isolationist impulse, however, conservatives tend toward a militaristic foreign policy, which encourages not long-term peaceful international development toward American values but reactive military actions when all order has finally broken down. But, as Vietnam demonstrated, successful military commitments can only follow the democratic commitments made by the American people and the national intentions of other countries involved.

The conservative criticism in the 1980s of liberal foreign policy has ignored the fact that liberals have defended America through two world wars and during the most dangerous military confrontation with the Soviet Union. The criticism also has to ignore the great pride in American values like freedom and democracy that liberals have reflected in their foreign policy. Conservatives unfortunately have seemingly lost faith in the power of these ideals and have criticized those who advocate them over a foreign policy resting primarily on military might as "soft." Such a position would greatly disappoint Thomas Jefferson if he were alive today. As did Jefferson, liberals believe in the power of principles and values in the international arena. Indeed, liberal support goes where American principles of democracy and freedom are welcome. It believes that America's real strength and defense rest on its commitment to living by democratic principles.

## The Liberal Fight against Crime

The conservatives' most emotional attack in the 1988 campaign accused liberals of being soft on crime and of coddling convicted criminals. Surprisingly, and with so little historical awareness, conservatives try to equate liberalism with increases in crime. No president or attorney general has yet acted so forcefully against organized crime as did the Kennedys. They saw organized crime as a direct and dangerous violation of the social contract. The mafia not only deliberately engages in a purposeful career of crime but is responsible for the serious drug problem today. Furthermore, Kennedy and all liberals since have taken an active role against "white-collar" crime traditionally ignored by conservatives—a type of crime that costs our society far more than all the petty burglaries committed.

For most of this century, liberals and conservatives have had slightly different views on crime. Conservatives have been more concerned with stopping crimes against property; liberals have looked to ending crimes against the person. Yet the conservative "law and order" attack against liberals did not take shape until the Supreme Court's criminal law decisions in the sixties and seventies, in which the Court granted various procedural safeguards to persons accused of criminal activity. Liberals supporting these decisions were accused of pandering to criminals, but they were only upholding the principles which inspired the colonists to revolt in 1776.

The framers so believed in trial by jury and in the sanctity of one's home from police intrusion that they codified these principles in the Constitution. Contrary to what they had witnessed under British rule, colonial Americans wanted to preserve for each individual the right to defend himself or herself against criminal charges. This belief resulted from the colonists having often witnessed the state act out of a sense of reprisal rather than a sense of justice. Thomas Jefferson so fervently believed in the notion of "innocent until proven guilty" that he preferred a political system which set one innocent person free even if it meant also setting ten guilty ones free. Jefferson's belief in the sanctity of trial by jury reflected his democratic principles. Individuals lived in a society run not by "the state" or by an elite, but by the individual and his or her peers.

Crime has unquestionably changed since the time of Jefferson, and its existence poses a grave threat to society. Conservatives respond with a reactionary hysteria. Right-wing ideologues even call for an end to jury trials and for immediate punishment of suspected criminals. Talk-show host Morton Downey, Jr., received rousing applause when he suggested "trial-by-lynching." However, conservatives take a surprisingly unrealistic and simplistic approach to ending crime in a society where organized crime and sophisticated criminals exist: take away the right to an attorney from a poor man suspected of stealing a car, and we will stop crime; cease requiring the police to briefly inform suspects of their constitutional rights, and we will put all the criminals away. Such simplistic remedies would have no significant impact on crime; they would only serve to curtail constitutional freedoms of individuals. Those who think that constitutional protections produce no justice and promote criminal activity delude themselves. Indeed, organized crime had invested millions of dollars in the drug trade long before the Supreme Court decisions granted to individual defendants various due process rights.

While conservatives are willing to sacrifice our constitutional integrity and freedom in an illusory attempt to stop crime, liberals believe that crime can best be stopped by following constitutional principles. Throughout history, liberalism has opposed conservative hysteria in times of public crises. Liberals stood up to the fanatic Joseph McCarthy and his bogus campaign against imaginary Communists. Likewise, liberals have opposed conservative hysteria in the field of criminal law. Standing up for everyone's constitutional rights means insuring them for those most in need of them—the innocent. Nothing is more tragic for our society than when someone is accused, convicted, and sentenced for a crime he or she did not commit. Clearly, crime is not deterred by punishing the innocent or least responsible. The average American cannot afford a battery of legal power to ward off criminal accusations; therefore, to make the legal system credible, the individual must have faith in the system to provide him or her with a fair chance to defend against such accusations, regardless of the individual's material wealth.

In the present decade, the primary crime concerns are drug related. It is no answer to carve away rights available to our children who may be picked up by the police simply because they are young and driving old cars. The Constitution aims at preserving our rights in just such a period—when public uneasiness over social problems could translate into an arbitrary reaction against innocent citizens. The true answer to the drug problem is to stop both the supply and the consumption. It is not a constitutional problem; it is a political problem.

Liberals seek to fight crime not from hysterical reaction but from realistic assessment of its causes. They have led the way in remedying some underlying causes of crime, such as urban decay, unemployment, and racism. The conservative position on crime, on the other hand, has always been simplistically singular—to "get tough on" criminals.

Liberals have also taken the lead in finding ways to rehabilitate criminals and end recidivism. But liberals do not, as conservatives charge, believe in softly treating persons convicted of crimes. Liberals advocate punishment and penalties for crime, but only when a person is convicted *after* a fair trial. The liberal tradition has never claimed that punishment is not a morally legitimate or socially useful response to crime. Indeed, Walter Mondale, "way too liberal" according to Reagan, opposed plea bargaining for those accused of violent offenses and favored the construction of new prisons. Although conservatives blame liberals for the release of convicted felons from overcrowded prisons, they oppose allocating the funds to build new prisons and remedy the problem.

An underlying factor in the attack on liberalism for the crime problem lies in the race riots and urban violence of the sixties and seventies. Such wide-scale violence across the country had an especially sharp effect on the middle class. For the first time, middle-class Americans sat in front of a television set and viewed violence and unrest as it was occurring. Witnessing such events made Americans especially sensitive, even panicky, about crime issues; and conservatives succeeded in associating liberals with the riots and unrest of the sixties and seventies. As discussed previously, conservatives tend to attribute any change or new occurrence to liberalism; but in fact there was no connection whatsoever between liberals and the urban violence. Political liberals deplored the violence as much as, if not more than, anyone else. The difference, however, occurred in the response to that violence. Conservatives played on the sense of public panic and advocated a cutback in constitutional freedoms enjoyed by every American. Liberals, on the other hand, sought to address the social roots of the violence and remedy the causes.

Another curious aspect of the crime issue is the perception that liberals are antipolice. Conservatives claim that the Court's *Miranda* rulings have hamstrung police in their law enforcement duties. All

*Miranda* requires is a short recitation of rights which practically any average American can recite from watching "cops-and-robbers" television. On the other hand, liberals have supported police in their attempt to ban armor-piercing bullets and unrestricted public access to automatic weapons like the AK-47. Conservatives oppose such efforts and argue that the individual's right to own and use a gun precludes any laws which aim at protecting the lives of police officers. To conservatives, requiring the police to inform a suspect of his rights must pose a greater hindrance to law enforcement than a criminal's use of bullets which can pierce even the bullet-proof vests worn by police to protect their lives.

## Abortion and the Liberal Respect for the Individual

Few issues have been so socially divisive as abortion. The Supreme Court could not adequately resolve the issue back in 1973; according to Kristin Luker in *Abortion and the Politics of Motherhood,* little chance exists for a national consensus to resolve the dispute in the near future. The continued social tension and conflict have forced and will once again force the Court to reconsider the issue.[1] The reasons for the failure of the judiciary to resolve the dispute lie in the nature of the issue itself and in how the two approaches—liberal and conservative—narrowly view the issue.

The "liberal" position on abortion supports the freedom of choice of the woman. Consistent with the liberal belief in individual freedom, freedom of choice on abortion gives maximum freedom to the woman. Yet the "conservative" position on abortion may also arguably be consistent with liberal beliefs in individual freedom. Since conservatives strive to defend the right of the fetus to live, they are advocating the rights, as they see it, of a vulnerable individual.

The conflict arises in how the two different sides view the issue, which then determines whose rights they are defending. Liberals treat the abortion issue as a women's issue, involving the right of privacy and reproductive freedom. Conservatives see the issue from the standpoint of the unborn fetus, involving the basic right to life guaranteed by our constitutional and basic philosophical beliefs. Because the two positions define the issue differently, and because it has become a "moral" issue, compromise has become nearly impossible.

If a purely "moral" issue, abortion should not be regulated by the state, according to the views of George Washington and Thomas Jefferson. The liberal position on abortion expresses this view and attempts to guarantee that human reproduction remain a personal decision. The libertarian argument is that individuals, not politicians, should make the decision on whether a woman should have an abortion. Indeed, polls indicate that substantial majorities believe that the decision on whether to have an abortion should be left to a woman and her doctor.

The liberal position also seeks to prevent the whole area of sexuality and reproductive freedom from falling under a repressive "Victorian veil" woven by rigid religious fundamentalists. Moreover, liberals want to avoid bringing unwanted babies into a world where conservative fundamentalists discriminate against them for being "illegitimate" or fail to provide adequate guarantees of health care and education. Indeed, a cause of many abortions in the U.S. is the social and religious stigma attached to unwed mothers. Nonetheless, the current abortion issue is not just a purely moral issue; it involves a fundamental view of society and of individual life.

Philosophically, the core proposition of the pro-life view is that personhood is an inborn and inalienable right and that abortion threatens this right in the most fundamental way. This philosophical view resembles the liberal view on abolition a century and a half ago and on the civil rights movement of this century. Indeed, there are other consistencies between the pro-life position and the liberal tradition. Liberals have always spoken for the downtrodden and the voiceless. Although many contend that a fetus is not a "person," what if that belief is wrong? Political philosophies cannot answer the question of when life begins; only physicians and philosophers can provide such answers. Liberalism, however, has not encouraged a rational debate on this issue, and has in fact prevented such a debate by quickly labeling the pro-choice position as the liberal position. Meanwhile, by 48 percent to 40 percent, Americans regard abortion as murder; and a *Boston Globe* poll found that substantial majorities would ban over 90 percent of the abortions now being performed.[2]

In an apparent contradiction to their tradition, many liberals seem afraid of wide-open debate and of the prospect of thrashing out the issue in the give-and-take of the democratic process. Liberals have taken an undemocratic stance and have outrightly dismissed even the thought of speaking for the unborn. By having one value—the right of privacy—trump all others, liberals, according to Mary Ann Glendon in *Abortion and Divorce in Western Law,* have not encouraged the full interaction of American values and have not done justice to the complexity of American attitudes toward life and death. Furthermore, their focus on equality has sidetracked many liberals from the fundamental issue of the conflict between the right of privacy and the potential of life. Liberals have opposed restrictions on abortion, arguing that they discriminate against poor women. This equality issue, however, is secondary to the basic question of whether society should even regulate abortion in the first place.

For a generation, liberals have been hooked on the judiciary, have counted on courts to enact their agenda for them through broad readings of the Constitution, the civil rights laws, and the common law of torts. The liberal federal judiciary of the 1960s and 1970s, however, was a historical aberration. Hence, liberals should be especially wary of grounding important social rules on a judicially created privacy right. In the late nineteenth and early twentieth centuries, for instance, the Supreme Court struck down much of the social legislation sponsored by the Progressives and New Dealers. The Court's rejection of reform legislation arose from its conclusion that the laws, in effect, violated the economic privacy of the wealthy. Throughout American constitutional history preceding the Warren Court era, and once again with the Rehnquist era, the Court has consistently followed and exerted a conservative influence on political life. Therefore, it is historically unwise for liberals to rely on a judicially created privacy right, for such a right is indeed a "double-edged sword."

The abortion issue involves many liberal values other than an individual freedom of privacy. A fundamental value—individual life—has always been sacred to liberals. The question posed by the abortion issue, of course, is the status and rights of the unborn fetus. The liberal position here is somewhat contradictory. Currently, society imposes restrictions and regulations on prenatal care of the fetus. These restrictions receive liberal support, but they also show that society does not consider a woman to be totally free from responsibility to other life. Even if the other life—the fetus—is only potential life, it is clearly more than "no life." The importance of this distinction has been lost in the liberal dialogue.

The abortion debate cannot proceed constructively without confronting the life issue. While this issue might not be one which can be objectively and finally resolved, the risks or implications of a resolution either way must be considered, for the abortion issue fundamentally invokes society's deepest concerns of freedom and life, and issues involving these concerns touch on the vital decisions in a society's history. For instance, if Southern slave owners would have contemplated the idea that blacks were free human beings, an ugly side of American history may been avoided; if Hitler or his high command would have considered that Jews were not inferior to the

Aryan race, the Holocaust might never have occurred. Likewise, to-day Americans should not be afraid to ask whether we have failed to grasp the full implications of the abortion issue.

The exclusive focus on reproductive rights in the abortion debate has also distracted liberals from other related problems and from traditional liberal humanitarian concerns. The needs of unwanted children is one such concern. Since adoption has been used by pro-lifers as an alternative to abortion, many liberals have reacted by avoiding the whole area of adoption. Yet it is an area acutely ripe for liberal concern. Hundreds of thousands of unwanted "special-needs" children are unable to find permanent homes. These children, including minorities, the physically or mentally handicapped, and any group of siblings who must be adopted together, account for the majority of all the children available for adoption.[3] Liberals should renew their focus on these vulnerable members of society. By combining an advocacy of adoption programs for unwanted children with their abortion position, liberals can return to a more "pro-life," pro-individual position traditionally characteristic of liberalism.

Although the abortion issue involves many different and perhaps contradictory values, it is the liberal creed which is best equipped to reach a resolution. Liberals advocate women's equality, freedom of the individual to make religious and moral choices, and social support of single mothers and orphaned children. As these considerations all relate to the abortion debate, liberals can better find a humane solution than can conservatives. Indeed, the conservative position on abortion derives simply from religious beliefs and rules, which cannot be debated in a democracy. The conservative tradition has not included an advocacy for women's equality nor a concern for children who are not members of traditional families. This absence makes conservatives suspect in any decision that touches on women's freedoms and child welfare.

## Welfare, Individual Responsibility, and the Liberal Social Contract

In the area of welfare and social programs for the poor and disadvantaged, liberalism has taken a beating in the last decade. Twenty years earlier, however, the mere fact of continued poverty in a wealthy society provoked outrage and more than justified the government programs aimed at alleviating poverty. Thus, although the political reaction to liberal social programs and the social commitment to fight poverty may have changed during the last two decades, the existence of poverty has not. The poor now constitute 14 percent of the population, yet only a fraction of the social spending is targeted for the poor, and welfare benefits have been steadily declining. In many ways the problems have worsened, even though political concern and compassion have seemingly dissipated.

Income inequality in America grew in the 1980s and continues to grow. In 1966, 45 percent of the public thought America was a place where the rich get richer and the poor get poorer. By the late 1980s, the proportion of people agreeing with that description had jumped to 81 percent. The working poor are making no progress, and the future looks no better. Children, however, are the hardest hit by poverty and constitute the poorest segment of society. The poverty rate for the under-six age group is seven times that of the over-sixty age group. The increasing rate of poverty for children may also indicate a declining social respect for children.[4] In addition to the increasing poverty, other subjective evidence also suggests this decline: the increase in child pornography, child abuse, drug sales to children, and youth suicide. Additional signs of America's fading social commitment to its children are cutbacks in funds for education and an increase in present consumption and debt at the expense of investment for the future.

During the 1980s, the causes of poverty became more complex and less visible, especially in the case of the working poor. The technological revolution, international competition, and the transfer of manufacturing functions abroad have increased chronic unemployment at home and have decreased real wages. These factors are increasing the chances that those persons on the brink of poverty will slide into its grasp. For instance, according to Michael Harrington in *The New American Poverty,* many workers have been recently unemployed and then reemployed in a different kind of work and at a lower wage. Harrington points out that the once-great middle class is declining and that workers are slowly dropping out of the middle class because of structural changes in the economy. This trend increases the chances that poverty will become an even worse problem in the future. In addition to the declining economic security of working Americans, a permanent "underclass" is developing in American society. In *The Truly Disadvantaged: The Inner City, the Underclass, and Public Policy,* William Wilson traces this growing inner-city underclass. Wilson argues that demographic changes and structural changes in the economy are placing more young people in this underclass and keeping them there.

This rise in poverty has not escaped the attention of the American public. Public opinion has recognized the increasing percentage of Americans in poverty and has favored government assistance to help the poor.[5] The conservative opposition to governmental involvement, however, focuses on the alleged failures in the past of certain government programs.

Charles Murray, author of *Losing Ground* and more recently of *In Pursuit: of Happiness and Good Government,* states with force the conservative criticism that government has failed in the social programs it has conducted. Murray lays the blame for the increase in poverty and the rise of the underclass squarely on government welfare programs. Those programs, he claims, have sapped individual initiative, removed responsibility from the individual, and broken up communities. He ignores, however, the role government has taken in opening up individual opportunities and providing the chance to get an education, to find work, and to earn one's way in the world. Curiously enough, Murray also takes a very optimistic view of human nature—namely, that people are naturally benevolent and cooperative. Yet it is difficult to reconcile this belief with the assumption that if a welfare program exists people will flock to it, quitting their jobs and living off the work of others. Furthermore, despite his faith in human nature, Murray claims that people acting politically through their government are inherently destructive of rights, freedoms, and individual values. Consequently, Murray seeks to dismantle the whole framework of the modern state and return to a Jeffersonian world of minimal government and maximum human freedom. This position ignores the entire political history of the last century and the fact that government's role has increased because of the public need and demand for it. Furthermore, ever since the Jackson presidency, successive American presidents have come to realize that a return to a Jeffersonian model was impossible because the rest of society— particularly the economic system—had moved so far away from the Jeffersonian vision.

Nathan Glazer, in *The Limits of Social Policy,* joins Murray in condemning social policy and in expressing a deep pessimism about the capabilities of government. Glazer also claims, like Murray, that social policies have weakened traditional community structures such as neighborhoods, churches, and families and that the decline of these communities directly caused the occurrence of poverty and other social programs. Many liberals may agree with this last conclusion— that the breakdown of local communities contributes to many of our social problems; however, liberals recognize that this breakdown has resulted from a complex set of social forces, including the concentration and impersonalization of our economic system.

Both Murray and Glazer resort to the "thesis of the perverse effect" in their criticism of social programs.[6] This asserts that not only will a policy fall short of its goal, but it will bring about exactly the opposite result than the one intended. This is a purely argumentative opposition to government programs. An example is Murray's claim that government programs not only fail to relieve poverty but actually increase it. We can examine factually whether a particular program works or does not work, but to argue that the attempt to improve society actually weakens it is to engage in unfounded rhetoric. Such rhetoric completely ignores the complex causes of poverty in our rapidly changing economic and social world, preferring a simple condemnation of government, blaming it for all ills.

One answer to the conservative attack is to defend the value and accomplishments of government programs. This defense has been briefly stated in an earlier chapter, as well as in many other works. American history shows how government social action has enhanced democratic institutions, increased individual opportunity, and expanded the civic and political role of its citizens. However, besides the issue of government competence, conservatives rest much of their criticism on an ideological indictment of liberalism: the liberal creed divorces individual freedom from individual responsibility and individual rights from individual duties.[7] The liberal concept of freedom, according to conservatives, releases the individual from either a recognition of necessary restraints or an assumption of responsibility for actions.

Contrary to the conservative claim, the founding principles of political liberalism reflect a profound emphasis on responsibility. The liberal concept of a social contract, upon which democratic society rests, implies that each citizen is entitled to the rights and benefits of citizenship as well as obligated to the duties and responsibilities of citizenship. The social contract incorporates both a private responsibility and a public responsibility, which conservatives seem to completely ignore.

The conservative view of the social contract is somewhat one sided. While criticizing liberals for not enforcing the individual responsibility side of the social contract—in terms of welfare policy—conservatives have long ignored the public duties and responsibilities inherent in the social contract. Conservatives favor an allegiance of the individual to the state, but not a reciprocal one from the state to the individual. Conservatives also interpret the social contract without a sense of historical responsibility. They do not see the present generation of society as responsible for actions of past generations (i.e., racial discrimination), nor do they accept responsibility to future generations (i.e., burdening future generations with a mammoth budget deficit incurred not to fund emergencies like economic depressions, but simply to fund present consumption).

The liberal interpretation of the social contract combines private and public responsibility and is revealed in the recent welfare reform movements. These result from years of liberal efforts to address the problem of poverty. It is not as though the conservatives have disagreed with the liberal cause; they instead have simply closed their eyes to the problems. It has been a long time, according to Jack Kemp, since conservatives have "gotten real" about poverty. However, because liberalism has kept pushing the need to recognize and work at social problems, conservatives have now finally begun to join in the welfare reform. Kemp, the hard-hitting conservative among Republican candidates in 1988, admits that government has a legitimate role to help those in poverty and to remove barriers to equal opportunity.

Having finally won conservative cooperation on welfare, liberals have implemented welfare-to-work schemes. These programs, designed to move people from welfare to meaningful employment, have been termed "workfare." The workfare approach essentially places a safety net (public responsibility) into a social contract with the individual (private responsibility). It couples government payments with requirements that recipients take part in job-training programs. Workfare also recognizes that states must address a nest of social ills—like adult illiteracy, teen pregnancy, school dropouts, and alcohol and drug abuse—if welfare is to be reduced. The remedy for the welfare problem is not as simple as conservatives have argued in the past, namely that lazy individuals would go to work if the public dole were taken away.

Workfare is not a new idea with liberals. In 1934, Roosevelt decided to replace a system of cash relief for the able-bodied with the Works Project Administration (WPA). FDR's antidole and pro-WPA programs favored work welfare over cash welfare. Throughout the Great Depression, conservatives, on the other hand, often supported the dole to work relief programs simply because the former was less expensive than the latter. To conservatives, the values of self-dignity and freedom from dependency took a lower priority than did budget considerations.

Workfare reflects the liberal adherence to the social contract. A contract between citizens and government, it requires both individual and social responsibilities. Liberalism, the philosophy of individualism, does not question that individuals must accept responsibility for their lives and their actions. However, when children grow up in poor, single-parent households, with no available jobs, and with inadequate education, they often need a helping hand to get a fair chance at improving their lot in life. Under the social contract, government has a duty to help give these children a fair chance in life if the same children are to be held responsible to society for the actions and decisions they make later in life. The old welfare system did not so closely reflect a social contract as does workfare; and conservatives often criticized it as excessively permissive and as encouraging dependency. This criticism, as recognized by liberal workfare proponents, was in some ways justified. Yet liberals stood by the old system in part because of the conservatives' relentless attack on any public programs for the poor and their avoidance of any recognition of social responsibility for the effects of poverty in our society. By agreeing to workfare programs, some conservatives have finally recognized the many causes of poverty in our society and realize that government can help break up the culture of poverty. Thus, workfare became a possibility when conservatives no longer believed that the sole response to poverty was to do nothing at all. This gave liberals freedom to reform welfare without abandoning the fight against poverty altogether.

Aside from social contract considerations, workfare also promotes the work ethic—a value liberalism has always encouraged. Throughout American history, liberalism has protected the freedom and rewards of human labor. The independent working American living off his or her own labor stood at the heart of the liberalism of Jefferson and Jackson, who mistrusted the virtue of speculators and financiers not living by the nineteenth-century work ethic. Liberals later fought for abolition, arguing that the fruits of one's labor belonged only to that person. Liberalism believed that to enslave one's work was to enslave the person. In the late nineteenth and early twentieth centuries, liberals advocated freedom to work in dignity and in safety, as well as freedom of opportunity to work at all. Liberals sought to open up opportunities for work and for the exercise of the work ethic. The New Deal carried this ideal even further when liberals fought against the devastating effect of the Great Depression on the American work ethic. Thus, the liberal advocacy of the work ethic reflects more than just lip service to a traditional value.

A "work ethic" society proclaims the equal dignity of all who work. It strives to make work available to all and to infuse each citizen with the work ethic. Workfare helps achieve this "work ethic" dream. Despite their seeming adherence to this ethic, conservatives who oppose workfare refuse to have the government assist in strengthening the work ethic in America. They would rather criticize its absence than work to achieve its fulfillment. The conservative opposition comes back to their rigid ideological opposition to government: solving the poverty or welfare problem takes more government than they can stand, because to reform welfare means to require work, and to require work initially means to provide public works projects.

This discussion on contemporary issues illustrates the influence of the liberal tradition in modern politics. It also illustrates the degree of distortion and exaggeration in the conservative attacks on liberalism during the 1980s. However, some of the recent criticisms of liberalism provide insight into the challenges ahead for liberals. As with any philosophy or set of beliefs, liberalism must continually strive to remain true to its fundamental and historical values, to reevaluate its political mission, and to fashion its policy prescriptions to the current needs and problems of society.

## CHAPTER TEN

# The Crisis of Liberalism and the Challenges for the Future

## The 1960s and the Roots of the Decline of Liberalism in the 1980s

The conservative attack on liberalism in the 1980s did not occur without the help of liberals themselves. Since the 1960s, liberals have been opening the door wider and wider to public reaction and suspicion. They have weakened the liberal philosophy and opened it to the attacks that have taken place. The criticisms of liberalism made in the 1988 campaign exploited an identity crisis within liberalism that developed in the 1960s and intensified throughout the 1970s and 1980s. Since the decade of the sixties, liberals have departed in some important ways from the historical traditions and basic beliefs of liberalism. Thus, it is no coincidence that the last great liberal "hero" invoked by present politicians is John Kennedy.

The modern crisis of liberalism has resulted largely from the failure of liberals to remain true to the basic spirit and historical beliefs of the American liberal philosophy. This liberal "loss of identity" has correspondingly caused a loss of public faith in liberalism. It was not the failure of liberalism in America that brought about the decline in public esteem over the last two decades; rather, it was the deviation of self-proclaimed liberals from the liberal tradition of American history. Thus, the failure of Dukakis to define liberalism in the 1988 campaign essentially reflected the failure of liberals during the last twenty years to abide by the historic definition of liberalism.

Since the late 1960s, political analysts have increasingly characterized the type of contemporary liberalism being practiced as "interest-group liberalism." Indeed, the modern crisis of liberalism has resulted from the deviation of interest-group liberalism from historic liberalism. This interest-group liberalism has taken the liberal tradition of FDR to a breaking point and created a "politics of excess." According to Alonzo Hamby, the problem of excess was the most obvious of all problems with liberalism in the 1960s and 1970s and first emerged in the policies of Lyndon Johnson. Government entitlement programs, for instance, did not hinge on actual need and were "indifferent to the need for limits on any activity."[1] Without any limits or boundaries, government programs created stifling bureaucratic requirements, waste, and ineffectiveness. Instead of opposing the harmful effects of big business, interest-group liberalism supported big government and abandoned completely the Jeffersonian distrust of conglomerations of power and belief in the virtue of an independent individual.

### The Negative Influences of Interest-Group Liberalism

Two decades ago, Theodore Lowi wrote about the crisis of political authority caused by an emerging "interest-group liberalism." According to Lowi, interest-group liberalism sought to solve the problems of public authority by "parceling out to private parties the power to make public policy."[2] This parceling out of policy-making power to the most interested groups, according to Lowi, destroyed political responsibility. Government served primarily to satisfy the wants of organized groups within society. The traditional, historic notion of liberalism was displaced and no longer governed public philosophy.

Interest-group liberalism incorporated the "liberalism" label simply because it envisioned an active role for government; but important inconsistencies with traditional political liberalism existed. Interest-group liberalism presumed that organized interests were easily defined and adequately represented all of society. Liberalism, however, advocated government by democratic participation and aimed at ensuring individuals access to the democratic process, not just to organized interest groups. It saw political authority resting in the individual, not in social groups. Interest-group liberalism, unlike traditional liberalism, saw the political chain of authority as going from groups to the government and that the spokesperson for the group spoke for each and every member. The guiding principle behind interest-group liberalism was the pure power of the group— a principle which in effect replaced the rule of law as the standard for political action. The connection between political law and any timeless constitutional or moral values weakened. Interest-group liberalism also weakened the notions of popular government and majority rule.

The liberal demand for a greater, more flexible participatory democracy conflicts with the workings of interest-group politics. Interest-group liberalism is essentially conservative, in that its policies and programs create privileges for certain groups and discourages political competition. Weakening of popular government and support of privilege are two historical aspects of conservatism. Critics of interest-group politics also charge that government no longer regards people as individuals but as members of interest groups. The groups, in turn, are awarded specific benefits *as a group,* and the rights of citizenship and political sovereignty depend more on the group than on the individual. Under interest-group liberalism, politicians are not identified with the political philosophy they advocate but with the interest groups which they represent.[3] Interest-group liberalism, therefore, creates a nation of insulated and even exclusive groups competing with one another with no notion of the public interest or the common good. Indeed, the most serious defect in liberal thought in the 1980s was perceived as its denial of the existence of "a public interest apart from the sum of private, individual interests."[4]

Interest-group liberalism caused a political crisis in the 1980s not only because of its failure to consider the public interest, but because even the groups could not command loyalty of their assigned members. In the Reagan elections, the majority of women and working Americans did not vote according to the political alignment of the feminist and labor organizations. This divergence of people and organizations shows that it is too simplistic to think that in our complex society people's interests can be assigned to one single-interest group.

Many political observers argue that interest-group liberalism is a natural outgrowth of the New Deal liberalism. Critics claim that the ultimate effect of the New Deal politics was to legitimize groups' demands on government and to define the public interest as the total of group claims. Yet this interpretation of New Deal liberalism is inaccurate. The New Deal brought a vast collection of new voters and supporters into the liberal philosophy, but those individuals did not become entrenched in organizations whose agendas automatically became the liberal agenda until the late 1960s and early 1970s. Moreover, interest-group liberals have distorted FDR's New Deal legacy and attempted to govern the easy way—by protecting established client groups rather than by offering a workable vision for the country as a whole.

Interest-group politics has become solely a constituent-oriented political creed; and its vision looks only to the agendas of client groups. Roosevelt's New Deal, on the other hand, stood for the supremacy of the general welfare over factional or group interests. FDR believed that the public interest was more than just an aggregation of private claims, and sought to democratize American politics just as Jackson had—by eliminating special privileges created or sanctioned by government. Since FDR did open up the resources of an activist government, however, the potential for interest-group politics existed. Writing in 1950, Arthur Schlesinger warned of those who would "use liberalism as an outlet for private grievances and frustrations."[5] Schlesinger termed these persons "wailers," in contrast to the New Deal liberals he characterized as pragmatists and "doers." For the doer, democracy carries the burden of civic responsibility; for the wailer, politics is a process by which the individual relieves herself of responsibility for government's behavior. Unfortunately, interest-group politics has revolved more around the wailer than the doer.

The practice of interest-group liberalism has also adversely affected the ability to openly debate and address social problems identified with a particular interest group. While conservatives may use a litmus test for the candidates, interest-group liberals use a litmus test for issues—if you are for education, support teachers' unions; if you are for women's rights, support the feminist groups. Because interest-group liberalism's chosen path to political governance is paved by the loyalty of its groups and their members, liberals are unable, or lack the courage, to speak frankly about the issues facing these groups when the logical remedies may not coincide with the agendas of the groups' leadership. For instance, if the union leadership decides that protectionism favors the working person, liberals take up that cause even in the face of evidence that such measures— although in the short-term interests of the union leadership—will actually work against the long-term interests of the average working person. Thus, liberals are frozen in their ability to address and solve certain national problems with which liberalism is greatly concerned—such as public education, the black family, and the plight of the single working mother—and which may need to be handled differently than dictated by certain groups like teachers' unions, certain civil rights organizations, and feminist groups. The ultimate responsibility for a political resolution of the issues on behalf of all concerned lies with the democratic process, not with self-appointed groups.

### Interest-Group Liberalism and a Politics of Rights

Interest-group liberalism has created a politics of "rights" and "entitlements." Government has become a broker of benefits rather than an expression of the democratic process and an enforcer of the rule of law. As the primary constituents of the broker state, interest groups seek not to participate in the democratic process on an equal basis with other individuals and groups but to actually bypass the democratic process by establishing a system of rights and entitlements which will guarantee fulfillment of their interests regardless of popular opinion. As a result, rights and entitlements have increasingly come to have no solid constitutional or democratic basis; they are simply demands of a group. However, without the objective guide of the general interest, group politics cannot arbitrate the various conflicting claims to rights. Thus, for more and more Americans, the doctrine of rights has become alienating and confusing.

A focus on rights has also led interest-group liberals to favor the courts over the legislatures as the "political forums." Under the guise of public-law litigation, they increasingly passed their public agenda through the courts. Litigation has become more integrated into the political process, and courts have increasingly become more legislative in their functions. Yet each time judicially created rights overrule legislative acts, the principle of majority rule and self-government is weakened. Moreover, the liberal faith in the democratic process has atrophied as liberals have increasingly relied on the judiciary rather than the democratic legislatures for their political goals. Interest group liberals have become so focused on the courts that their democratic impulse has turned to the courts and has advocated greater citizen participation in the judicial decision-making process through more relaxed procedural requirements. Thus, rather than widening and improving the democratic political process, interest-group liberals have tried to democratize an inherently undemocratic institution—the courts.

This attempt, however, has contradicted the liberal tradition and has in fact more closely followed the conservative approach. During much of the nineteenth and early twentieth centuries, conservatives used the courts to enforce the rights of business and property owners that were at odds with the popular will and the common good. Conservatives relied on legalism to bypass the democratic process and attempted to govern society not by democratic majorities but by judicial decree. Their reliance on the courts for their political agenda indicated that they occupied the minority in society. From that experience Americans learned to be wary of those groups which primarily resort to the judiciary as their political forum in a democracy. Likewise, interest-group liberals risk the same reaction.

### A Distorted Federalism under Interest-Group Politics

Along with its focus on rights and the judiciary, interest-group liberalism distorts the nature of federalism in our democracy. Under interest-group liberalism, federalism has taken on a new meaning: instead of political power-sharing by different levels of government, power is shared among organized groups, and all government activity concentrates at the federal level. The causes of this distorted federalism lie in the nature of interest-group politics. From the New Deal and the civil rights movement, interest groups learned of the power of the federal government. This lesson, combined with the fact that groups could better concentrate their power at the federal level, wedded interest-group liberals to the exclusive use of federal power. Consequently, interest-group liberalism discouraged action at the state and local levels. Thus, any matter of government attention became a matter of *federal* government attention.

A concentration of government action at the federal level has tended to inhibit flexible, experimental action at the state and local levels. This in turn set liberalism against innovative change, since the primary changes during the 1980s were taking place within the states. The liberal goal, however, always had been responsive government action, not an intractable government institution. Both JFK and FDR were strong believers in innovative and experimental government action. Yet they did not attempt to concentrate all functions at the federal level.

The Madisonian vision of federalism understood that states are ordinarily better equipped than Congress to democratically evolve policies that best serve the people. The science of government was seen by Madison, as well as by Roosevelt and Kennedy, as the science of experimentation. Therefore, the problems confronting government can often be best addressed by drawing on the experiences of all the states. Not only are the states more flexible to experiment and have closer ties with people, but competition among the states also provides motivation for progressive social programs. As Justice

Thurgood Marshall recognized: "Local officials, by virtue of their proximity to, and their experience with, local affairs, are exceptionally well-qualified to make determinations of public good within their respective spheres of autonomy." In arguing against overturning a local set-aside program, Justice Marshall urged greater respect for and deference to the wisdom of local leaders in dealing with racial problems. Liberals would do well to once again pay such respect to the federalism of the American political system.

During the 1980s, Reagan glorified the efforts of state and local governments in addressing social problems with an activist style of experimentation. This is a liberal approach, the approach that brought about the New Deal. Yet liberals, acting within the interest-group orientation, hesitated in transferring political debate and action to the state level. This hesitancy results from two concerns or insecurities—one in keeping with the liberal tradition, and one not. First, liberals oppose such a movement if the effect is to cut out necessary funding of important social programs like education. The second reason for the opposition, however, lies with the fact that interest-group liberals, who focus on client interests rather than the public interest, seem to fear dialogue and grass-roots action on these issues. This fear is both surprising and shocking in light of the liberal tradition, which has always been closely associated with grass-roots democracy. This fear is also surprising given the liberal support of open debate and government experimentation.

### Interest-Group Liberalism and the Alienation
### of the Populist Spirit

The Reagan victories demonstrated, once again, the power of populism in American politics. Reagan's populism rebelled against big government. Because liberals were seen as in control of big government catering to privileged groups, they were identified with a stagnant status quo and in opposition to the populist spirit. The Reagan voter, who had once been the Roosevelt and Kennedy voter, saw the government being run by a "limousine liberal," an upper-class elite out of touch with the general public and imposing their cultural and social liberalism on the rest of America. With their children attending private schools and with no factory jobs to lose, such liberals were insulated from the effects of certain social changes like busing and affirmative action they were advocating for society. The liberal tradition, on the other hand, has stressed social inclusiveness and the direction of political change by those affected by and responsible for such change.

The unusual aspect of the Reagan populism in the 1980s was that the populism of the past had so often been associated with liberal reform. In fact, throughout American history, conservatives had usually occupied the position of the establishment and as the object of populist opposition. The populist spirit infusing the New Deal, for instance, called upon government to address needs—health care, home ownership, and educational opportunity—that applied to the majority of American society. This developed a sense of egalitarianism, political cohesion, and civic community.

As interest-group politics evolved in the 1960s and 1970s, however, the inclusionary nature of liberalism eroded.[6] The social solidarity impulse behind the New Deal gave way to a fragmented politics in which certain groups laid claim on social resources. In Robert Reich's terms, the New Deal liberal society of "we" was changed to one of "us" and "them." Politics became less a governing activity of the people and more a competition among groups. Special interests gained more power in the democratic process than the majority will.

Since the late nineteenth century, and until the 1960s, liberals have usually been the economic populists. The mistake, however, was to think that a permanent association with the New Deal coalition would forever put liberals on the right side of populist spirit. Now, as interest-group liberalism is seen as a protector of big government and special interests, it has become the object of a populist backlash extending beyond economic issues and grounded in an antagonism to the privileged and the specially protected. Under Reagan, a social and cultural populism sprang up among "average Americans" and was directed against liberals for their perceived pandering of feminist, gay, and civil rights organizations. Yet it was the perceived control by these organizations of liberal politicians, rather than the advocacy on behalf of the victims of discrimination, that prompted the populist attack. What liberals must recognize is that they cannot capture the populist spirit with a static approach of representing certain groups whose members may once have been populists. The populist grain in American politics is more fluid and broader; its energy comes from commitment to democratic equality and hostility to all forms of special privilege or protection.

Interest-group politics not only incited populist backlash, but it has also alienated the quiet but potent middle class. Apparently, the middle class has not constituted a sufficiently influential group within interest-group liberalism. However, the failure of liberalism in the 1980s to hold the middle class contrasts sharply with the historical pattern of the twentieth century. The liberalism of Roosevelt, Truman, and Kennedy identified closely with the middle class and focused on opening the middle class and its opportunities to all members of society—the disadvantaged, the discriminated, and the disenfranchised. Indeed, the connection of liberalism in the early 1960s to the middle class was far stronger than that of conservatism in the 1980s. For instance, a comparison of the Kennedy tax-cut with the Reagan tax-cut demonstrates the difference: instead of getting trickle-down benefits, the middle class in 1962 was more directly targeted as a beneficiary.

In the 1970s and particularly with the McGovern candidacy, however, liberals appeared to side with particular interests and groups at the expense of the middle class. For those Americans without a specific interest-group hold on politics, liberals seemed unconcerned. While the politics of FDR and JFK sought to bring society's fringe-groups into the heart of society—the middle class—the politics of the McGovern liberals eschewed any attempt at unifying and harmonizing society. It instead carved out permanent, separate social spheres for each group and gave them an armory of claims on the rest of society. Consequently, with the loss of the middle and the failure of competing groups to formulate much more than a list of demands, much less a coherent social vision, the dialogue and policies of liberalism came increasingly from the Left.

Throughout American history, populism has reflected the struggle of community against forces outside its control and threatening its existence. Populism has also been characterized by grass-roots political action and a suspicion of concentrated power. Therefore, just as populists in 1912 and 1932 reacted against private economic concentration, populists in 1988 reacted against a federal government bureaucracy which had supplanted and repressed local community institutions and alienated voters. Reagan-style populism saw American society as being governed from the top down out of Washington bureaucracies, rather than from the bottom up out of the local democratic community. A large part of the populist backlash against interest-group liberalism, then, was a movement asserting community and communal values.

### The Community Reaction against Interest-Group Liberalism

Interest-group liberalism, with its view of society as a fragmentation of various special interests, tends to contradict and antagonize the public's community values. In the 1980s, much criticism of liberalism focused on the failure of interest-group liberalism to express communal values. Reagan captured the American desire for community and exposed its feelings of alienation. This longing for community and criticism of liberalism found expression in books such as Alasdair MacIntyre's *After Virtue,* Roberto Unger's *Knowledge and Politics,* and Michael Sandel's *Liberalism and the Limits of Justice.* According to Unger, modern liberalism does not acknowledge communal values; and Sandal argues that citizens under an interest-group liberal state are doomed to a miserable isolation of strangers.

Conservatives throughout the 1980s have criticized liberalism for its denial of people as social beings with social identities and its belief in the primacy of rights.[7] Politics, according to the critics of liberalism, should aim political goals higher, toward something more inspiring and comforting than rights and entitlements. That "something higher" is community and a social consensus on the nature of a good society. Thus, to its communal critics, modern liberalism fails to provide what people yearn for most: fraternity, solidarity, harmony, and community. Interest-group liberalism has largely ignored the liberal commitment to self-government as well as to community. What liberals have forgotten is that self-government requires community, and that people could be "more entitled" but "less empowered" at the same time. Indeed, the real crisis in government today is not the protection of rights but the effective working of democracy. Voting rates and party participation, for instance, are dangerously low.

Just as democracy cannot exist without respect for individual rights and freedoms, those rights may not be guaranteed without a healthy democratic community. Fluctuating majorities and a flexible democracy provide protection for minorities, just as do judicially mandated rights. Yet to encourage political participation, there must be a communal vision that inspires the individual. Rights and entitlements do not offer such an inspiration nor such a unifying vision of self-government. A political philosophy, argues Sanford Levinson in *Constitutional Faith,* must recognize a particular conception of what America stands for. Indeed, a democratic society will not stay democratic if it does not teach the love of democracy to its citizens. Therefore, liberals must again recognize, as Levinson does, that contained within liberal thought is a deep commitment to the ideals of democratic citizenship and community that express the common identity and values of American society.

A new community activism is alive among those liberals who have been frustrated by the inadequacies and unresponsiveness of federal programs to provide social justice and to solve social problems. These community-minded liberals are troubled by the "all-consuming" emphasis of interest-group liberalism on individual rights. They argue that "communities have the same rights as individuals" and that people "must seize back control of their communities."[8] Such liberalism seeks to elevate community to a higher level of political consciousness and to protect communities from the intrusive power of both the federal government and large corporations.

Community-minded liberals are striving to reinvigorate the notion of the liberal community. With the social problems lying ahead in the 1990s, "there's a new recognition that the country's not going to be saved by experts and bureaucrats . . . but by some moral vision and some moral hope coming from the grassroots and the neighborhoods," argues Milton Kotler, director of the National Association of Neighborhoods.[9] A renewed belief in community democracy has also encouraged the proliferation of grass-roots organizations working for social betterment. Such grass-roots community activism has focused on liberal causes—environmental protection, better education, revitalization of urban housing—and has tried to instill communal responsibility for the social problems that trouble liberals.

What is emerging in the debates on liberalism and community is a changing view of the relationship between the individual and society. Community-minded liberals recognize that ordinary citizens participate in society through membership in different community institutions. A more balanced theory of liberalism, they claim, tries to understand how the individual is shaped by society while still retaining a sense of autonomy. Rejected is a model of liberalism which envisions people as isolated individuals who achieve their sense of identity all on their own. Participation in communal life helps give meaning to individual lives, yet the ties of community and family depend on individual choice and commitment. Liberalism must recognize that through such ties and bonds some of the individual's highest goals are fulfilled. Extreme individualism, on the other hand, creates an impersonal, isolated existence and prevents the transmission of community values and loyalties necessary for workable politics and for social cohesion.

Community-oriented liberals recognize the importance of social bonds to the individual and seek to redirect liberalism to a part of its tradition other than just the definition of individual rights. For instance, such liberal theorists as John Locke and John Stuart Mill valued social institutions that helped teach citizens to be virtuous, which in turn acted as a check on the seamier side of individualism. As first recognized by Locke and Mill, community organizations often constitute the prime transmitters of civic virtue. According to the community civic virtue ideal, communities should not hinge primarily on the principle that they have to respect each member's right to be different, but should be free to reach higher levels of civic virtue and common good.

When interest-group liberals have spoken of community, they have referred only to the national community. But America is too vast a nation to sustain more than a minimal commonality and too distant to permit more than occasional instances of participation. These liberals came to mistrust local communities after seeing in the New Deal and the Great Society that communities had failed to protect their members. But part of that failure was a lack of power. Indeed, there is nothing intrinsically conservative about family, neighborhood, or community. According to Michael Sandel, liberalism needs a "vision of community that embraces the right array of civic resources intermediate between the individual and the nation." Interest-group politics, conducted through organized interests concentrated in Washington, lost touch with these communities. The challenge to liberalism today is to seek new ways of defining and fostering community that transcend borders of race, ethnicity, and class. The words of Benjamin Franklin at the signing of the Declaration of Independence are, in this regard, as significant now as they were then: "We must indeed all hang together, or, most assuredly, we shall all hang separately."[10]

Although interest-group liberalism has in many ways ignored communal values, the community critique of liberalism has been somewhat misplaced. Indeed, the main threat to community values comes not from liberals but from the conditions of modern society. As society becomes more mobile and as television isolates individual households, the bonds of community loosen. Unquestionably, Americans today are more often alone than they were in the past. Neighborhoods and families are more distant and fragmented. But this reality arose more from the march of time than from any liberal policies.

## Interest-Group Liberalism
### and the Abandonment of Values

In connection with the criticism that it fails to recognize and support community, liberalism has received much criticism regarding its perceived lack of concern for values. It has been called a valueless political philosophy. Critics charge that modern liberalism has focused almost exclusively on process and procedure over substance, and on rights over values. Without values and a framework for ranking rights, liberal society loses its vision and its sense of good and bad, claim the critics. Even liberal Adolf Berle was troubled by the emerging nihilism in American culture in the 1970s and criticized fellow liberals for failing to "articulate any ideas of the civilization it wants or where it is going."[11] This criticism has continued in the 1980s as liberals have been accused of indifference to cultural degeneration and the moral struggles of ordinary people.

The values criticism of liberalism also occurs during a time in which the American public appears to have a renewed interest in fostering moral and ethical values. In a 9 April 1989 speech, Vartan Gregorian, president of Brown University, articulated a public need for a value-oriented, moral sense of politics. Without a public morality, Gregorian argued, democracy drifts without direction and without strength. He directly rebutted the liberal argument for removing morality from the political realm:

We cannot privatize public morality nor relegate it to the realm of private choice or so-called 'lifestyles.' Tension between morality and politics is real and we must confront it. . . . We cannot be social, political, and moral isolationists.

The absence of a sense of public morality, just as with an absence of justice, freedom, and choice, will "always weaken our social bonds and hence weaken our society and our democracy," according to Gregorian. A democratic society needs, along with freedom and choice, a moral center and not a moral enclosure.

We have no choice but to end the imprisonment of the self and concern ourselves with those outside our moral enclosures. We need a moral center, not a moral enclosure. We need to be capable of moral outrage and sensitive to the pain and sorrow of our fellow man and woman. It is important . . . to be willing to make public declarations of one's convictions and commitments and then translate them into actions and deeds.

Gregorian strives to inject moral passion into an increasingly listless liberalism. He advocates a moral sense, but not as defined by conservative beliefs. In contrast to the imposition of a "moral enclosure" on society through a denial of individual choice, the moral center should come from a public moral discourse and from the choices of individuals regarding moral values and social ideals. As in the liberal scheme, politics should implement our freely chosen values, not dictate them. To Gregorian, although we build meaning into our lives through our commitments, we become individual through our choices.

Vaclav Havel, the leader of Czechoslovakia's democratic movement, eloquently expresses the contemporary yearning for a politics based on values. In one of the most moving and compelling speeches delivered to Congress in recent years, Havel proclaimed that the world's salvation lies "in the human heart, in the human power to reflect, in human meekness and in human responsibility."[12] He reminded us that

> The only genuine backbone of all our actions—if they are to be moral—is responsibility. Responsibility to something higher than my family, my country, my firm, my success. Responsibility to the order of Being, where all our actions are indelibly recorded and where, and only where, they will be properly judged.

Havel's words offer inspiration to Americans who have become so cynical about politics that only half the electorate bothers to vote in presidential elections. And many of those who do vote lack conviction and vision of the connection between their political choices and their own daily lives.

Gregorian's and Havel's words speak to an America increasingly in search of values and of a more moral and ethical public order. For instance, a recent survey of college-educated, middle-income Americans found that they were more religiously active than the national average.[13] Seventy-five percent claimed that they attended religious services at least once a week; 73 percent said their reason for religious involvement was for moral guidance and strength. Furthermore, a Gallup Poll found that today's teenagers are more religiously active than their parents. Minority leaders have also begun to realize how the demise of sexual, familial, and marital values has caused more serious problems for the poor and uneducated than for the more wealthy and educated members of society.[14]

The surge of interest in moral and spiritual values also accompanies an increased awareness of ethics in public life. In the wake of the Wall Street scandals, the Iran-Contra affair, bribery scandals like the "Wedtech" scandal, and the all-too-frequent "conflict-of-interest" indictments in the Reagan administration, the public is becoming increasingly concerned with ethical behavior in all areas of public activity—in both business and government. During the decade of the eighties, ethics courses in colleges and graduate schools multiplied, as did books and seminars on ethical issues. Although public schools should not become the purveyors of religion, many educators have come to realize that children should learn integrity as well as economics, and civic morality as well as science. The history of political scandals alone has demonstrated that a healthy democratic society needs citizens grounded in a solid core of ethical values. Those values, however, are not a commodity or a body of information that can be quickly acquired. They are learned and formed throughout life and by education, choices, and commitments. Thus, despite all the courses and publication coverage, ethics cannot infuse public life without moral and ethical values entering our political dialogue. This absence in our political dialogue has reflected a weakness of modern interest-group liberalism.

Recent political experience suggests that America cannot govern itself without cultivating a public life based on some higher values and a common purpose larger than individual rights and interests. The candidacies of Jesse Jackson and Pat Robertson in 1988, though at opposite poles in their platforms, demonstrated the power of moral passion in American politics. The followings of the two candidates revealed that a significant number of Americans wish to establish a moral vision of a good society. However, over the last several decades liberals have become increasingly fearful of any moral values or choices. Their repulsion of traditional values has translated into a spurning of all moral values, except those moral statements from interest groups seeking acceptance and recognition of their own tailored agenda and interests.

Much of the modern liberal opposition to public values stems from the attitudes of the 1960s, when all traditional values were thrown off. The challenge now must be to engage in a selection process to determine which values society will incorporate and encourage and which it will not. To throw off all traditional values and structures simply because they are traditional is mindless and unjustified. Liberals, for instance, advocate a family policy recognizing and supporting nontraditional families. But liberals must not take a position of opposing or antagonizing traditional families just because they are traditional. More than one-third of all families with preschool children fit the "Ozzie and Harriet" model—homemaker mothers married to breadwinner fathers. The liberal tradition has strengthened and supported all families; it has not sought to discriminate against one type of family to the benefit of the other, as conservatives tend to do.

Interest-group liberals have not only failed to formulate, but have self-righteously objected to the recognition of, any kind of consensual political moral vision of a good society. They have seemingly taken joy in refusing to recognize the public yearning for values. Consequently, the fundamentalist Right has fed the public hunger for a politics grounded on higher values with its rigid, moralistic demands that create, in Gregorian's words, a "moral enclosure." Nonetheless, however troubling the intolerance of the Moral Majority, the liberal rejoinder is still inadequate and unresponsive. Washing their hands of any values discourse, liberals have simply claimed that mixing politics and moral values is illegitimate and a violation of church and state. They have tried to avoid recognition of any role for moral values by distinguishing between "private" versus "public" beliefs. However, this distinction is often irrelevant in a democratic society where individuals have political power and the freedom to inject their own beliefs and opinions into the political dialogue. Furthermore, the Constitution does not protect the public world from the onslaught of private beliefs; it protects the sanctity of private beliefs and freedoms from public regulations.

To the disappointment of Richard Neuhaus in *The Naked Public Sphere: Religion and Democracy in America,* interest-group liberals have been unable to articulate the moral basis of their political philosophy. Neuhaus argues that a "naked public sphere" empty of moral meaning is not sustainable and creates a political vacuum. He concludes that democracy's best answer to the Moral Majority is not to flee moral and religious discourse, but to engage it. Otherwise, he warns, the most intolerant voices will have a monopoly on the deepest sources of moral and political authority. Examples of such a "renewed democratic discourse" inspired by moral values might include the Catholic bishops' recent statements on nuclear weapons and the economy. These statements not only inject moral argument and values into public discourse, but they also translate those values into terms that are addressed to the wider community, and especially to those who do not share the same sectarian beliefs.

The liberal objection in the 1980s to mixing religion and politics has not been entirely true to the liberal tradition. Liberalism has in the past often invoked religious and moral themes. Examples include the New Deal reforms and the civil rights movements. Mario Cuomo has recently tried to reclaim religion for liberals by defining liberalism to include the concerns of the "social gospel," such as peace, compassion, and care for the needy. As liberals have believed throughout most of the twentieth century, a social conscience sustains a free society and provides the moral basis of a liberal social policy.[15] Indeed, the liberal notion of social justice requires a moral ingredient, because without a moral sense justice merely becomes the outcome of competing interests without any concept of right and wrong.

Religion in America has been historically liberal in its political messages.[16] Many of the virtues of liberal pluralism, such as respect for individual dignity and a belief in the equality of all persons, have strong roots in Judeo-Christian beliefs. Unlike Marxism, the Judeo-Christian theology believes that every individual matters and possesses incalculable worth.

The liberal church-state separation argument does not recognize the historical background of religion and politics in America. Indeed, the spirituality of politics was first affirmed by Plato at the very beginnings of Western political philosophy. Thomas Curry argues in *The First Freedoms: Church and State in America to the Passage of the First Amendment* that religion was a widely recognized cultural good and an important dimension of community in revolutionary America. This recognition of the role of religion in American life and values does not require, as conservatives seem to suggest or as modern liberals seem to fear, an ignoring of constitutional commands. As Leonard Levy argues in *The Establishment Clause: Religion and the First Amendment,* many modern conservatives who narrowly interpret the First Amendment to allow Congressional power to aid and support religious denominations in reality believe that "religion needs to be patronized and promoted by government."[17] However, religious institutions have long flourished in America without any such patronage, and even before our constitutional democratic government was established. Nonetheless, a constitutional opposition to government promotion or patronage of religious institutions differs entirely from the interest-group liberal's opposition to any presence of moral and religious values in political discourse.

The moral values and church-state debate always, to liberals, comes down to the issue of tolerance and diversity. But this can also be a means of avoiding the issue and ignoring the importance of values in democratic politics. Tolerance can be a trait of people who do not believe in anything: a tolerance by default. But another view of tolerance also exists—that beliefs and values are vital to a society and a democracy and that a respect of all beliefs will in turn promote a moral dialogue which will infuse a sense of values into the public realm. This latter view of tolerance has been the one that has characterized the American liberal tradition but which has been abandoned by interest-group liberals.

Toleration has long seen a staple of the American political tradition. In *On Liberty,* John Stuart Mill articulated the democratic need for tolerance and wrote that individual freedom could not be used to deprive others of their freedom to pursue their own good. Nonetheless, the liberal values of tolerance and freedom of choice have exposed liberalism to a charge of relativistic complacency. The refusal of modern liberals to incorporate the teaching of values into a liberal arts education, for instance, has drawn criticism from conservatives like Allan Bloom. According to Bloom, teaching the humanities means teaching about values. Although liberals may disagree with Bloom's specific claim that the Western classics contain timeless truths undergirding human life, they should agree that education should reveal the need to formulate moral and ethical visions and standards. Yet liberal America today tends to be a no-fault society in which strong philosophical views are discouraged, except for the view that no value system is superior to any other. Contemporary liberal opinion tends to mandate a laissez-faire approach toward moral values and a relativist attitude toward beliefs. It is this relativist attitude, void of any perceived moral meaning, which opens liberalism to attack.

Despite the relativistic criticism, liberalism in many ways is more capable of achieving a politics of values than is conservatism. Toleration and freedom of choice are liberal values. They allow individuals to cultivate and choose moral values and to develop values with other members of society. However, while tolerance is a necessary liberal virtue, it is not sufficient. To value only toleration and choice is to proceed halfway; to fully value freedom of choice is to value the result and outcome of that choice.

Although the achievement of tolerance is a necessary precondition of an enlightened moral vision for society, such a vision can only be acquired through a cultural process of confronting and choosing certain models of truths and values. Therefore, by valuing tolerance liberals stand poised to support a set of values freely chosen by society. Conservatives, on the other hand, often bypass the necessary choice and toleration stage and seek to impose a certain set of values on a somewhat uncommitted society.

The goal of liberal pluralism is not to prevent the formulation of any common moral vision; the goal is to allow each cultural and ethnic group to equally participate in the process of defining a moral vision for society. The goal is to achieve a moral vision through tolerance, not to avoid a moral vision. And the goal is to bring cultures together to build a common culture through shared values and visions, rather than to solidify the differences of the various groups.

The relativist predicament of liberalism lies in its affirmation of liberal principles—choice and toleration—without an embrace of any particular ends. It is difficult to "affirm certain liberties and rights as fundamental without embracing some vision of the good life, without enforcing some ends over others."[18] Liberalism cannot deny that certain moral values have influenced, and will continue to influence, public culture and political discourse. Consequently, liberals should not deny the political decisions which in some way reflect those values. This approach is much different from arbitrarily imposing certain values not freely chosen by society and then forging them into law. The latter scenario presents a dictation of ends without consideration of the means, while the former scenario is an acceptance and value of the ends which flow from legitimate means. It is a case of values through freedom versus values through imposition and forced obedience. The modern conservative position, which tends toward imposition, implies a mistrust in individuals to exercise a free will and to choose what is good.

Extreme relativism and a refusal to recognize the legitimacy of any moral values in the political realm have brought about a crisis of political authority within interest-group liberalism. This crisis has intensified because interest-group liberalism has also sought to do without another traditional source of political authority—the republican ideal of civic virtue. Besides religious or historical values, the concept of civic virtue provides another alternative to the "naked public sphere" and enables a society to create a public life larger than private pursuits and with a common purpose and identity. The civic virtue or republican ethic tradition is concerned less with religious moral values than with citizenship values and the pursuit of a common good beyond the sum of individual interests. The aim of interest-group liberalism, to the contrary, is perceived by its critics as simply pandering to individual desires and vulgar wants. With interest-group liberals, the notion of civic virtue has given way to self-centeredness. The value of America's civic virtue tradition, however, lies in its capacity for revitalizing our public life and restoring a sense of community, without relying on religious codes or the establishment of a "Christian America." In other words, perhaps we can clothe the naked public sphere with civic virtue rather than with religious values.

Many historians argue that civic republican ideals played an important role in the founding of the American democracy.[19] James Madison recognized the role of civic virtue and acknowledged that no form of government, without virtue among the people, could provide protection and security. Tocqueville likewise hoped that a sense of public morality would override short-term gratification and materialism and that individuals would learn that what is *right* is also *useful*. Tocqueville, as did Adam Smith, assumed that the pursuit of self-interest would operate within a moral context. Indeed, it has been the conservative elevation of economic self-interest as a supreme principle that has, certainly in the present era, drained the economy of its moral foundations.[20] In contrast, liberals throughout the twentieth century have feared the effects of a mass, industrialized society as a breeding ground for conformity, mediocrity, and passivity in its citizens, threatening republican citizenship and independence of judgment.

Despite this tradition of civic virtue, critics of liberalism argue that the liberal philosophy has no room for virtue. John Diggins is one such critic. In *The Lost Soul of American Politics: Virtue, Self-Interest, and the Foundations of Modern Liberalism,* Diggins associates liberalism with the unrestrained drive toward material wealth, the erosion of community and of political authority, and the tendency for wealth to replace work. Diggins equates liberalism with acquisitive materialism; and with the ascendancy of liberalism, he suggests that America lost its moral and virtuous vision. This characterization is misleading because its definition of liberalism is slanted and inaccurate. It ignores the fight of twentieth-century liberalism against the harms of unrestrained pursuit of material wealth. It ignores the focus of liberalism on production and on the working American. And it ignores the New Deal effort to provide a secure and safe community, the Fair Deal effort to bring a sense of justice and fair play into our society, and the New Frontier effort to motivate individuals to public service and to consider the common good over the private good.

The struggle of liberalism has been one of inspiring political concern for the common interest. This struggle has been reflected in the history and purpose of the liberal journal *The New Republic,* as first stated by the founders of the journal in 1914: "To transform American men and women into a citizenry dedicated to virtue, civic duty, and the public good."[21] Thus, the interest politics and materialism of interest-group liberalism contradict the original ideals, philosophy, and history of the American liberal tradition.

Unsurprisingly, Diggins's materialistic view of liberalism is a view common to conservatives in the 1980s. In *Revolt on the Right,* Senator Barry Goldwater argued that

> Liberals tend to stress the material man. Liberals tend to regard economic satisfaction as the dominant mission of society. Conservatism puts material things in their proper place, subsidiary to the spiritual side of man's nature. The primary concern of conservative political philosophy is the enhancement of man's spiritual nature. . . . No man or woman, if politically enslaved, can be economically free and efficient. People are responsible for their own spiritual and material development, and these should not be dictated by outside forces such as government. The conscience of a conservative opposes all who would debase the dignity of the individual.[22]

Contrary to this description of philosophies, however, American conservatism has throughout its history often been the advocate of materialism. Liberalism, on the other hand, has traditionally imposed a social conscience on the conservative belief in unrestrained pursuit of wealth. Yet Senator Goldwater suggests that the only concern of liberalism is for the material wealth and economic satisfaction of society. This statement would obviously not fit the decades of the twenties, the fifties, and the eighties during this century.

The abandonment by interest-group liberals of civic values and moral vision has therefore marked a sharp departure from the liberal tradition. The spark behind the lofty statements of freedom and democracy in the Declaration of Independence did not come from a negotiation of rights and entitlements. It came from the belief in liberal values. While the Declaration set America on its course to nationhood, the Constitution established its political and legal system. Through its constitutional democracy, America professes the promise of justice, equality, and opportunity to all its citizens. But the political system is not perfect—it has fallen short of its promise many times in the past, and will undoubtedly do so many times again. Political causes frequently fail, and law so often does not achieve justice. Therefore, if our hope for society rests strictly on the political process, on rights and entitlements, we will be often disappointed. We instead need a more timeless faith in democratic values—the kind of faith that inspired America's birth—if we are to retain our belief in the ideals and mission set forth in the Declaration of Independence.

## The Victim Mentality of Interest-Group Liberalism

Interest-group liberalism has fostered a "victim mentality" in American politics. Focusing as it does on rights and entitlements, interest-group liberalism positions itself with certain groups that are seen to have been "victimized" by society and in need of reparations. For instance, instead of inventing new ways to create jobs, interest-group liberals have sought to maintain existing jobs in out-of-date and declining industries.

Interest-group liberalism has allowed, or at least tolerated, certain groups to define themselves as "victims." Such a definition, however, keeps the group in a perpetual state of self-righteous anger and self-pity. Groups have found that, within interest-group liberalism, political power lies in proving that they are indeed victims. Yet the maintenance of this power requires that the victims continue celebrating their victimization, which in turn leads other groups— women, gays, ethnic and racial minorities, and even recently heterosexual white males—to compete for power by defining themselves as victims. This chain reaction of victimization creates divisiveness and undermines community and democratic responsibility.

The victim mentality has created a sort of "reactionary liberalism" expressing the envious whine of interest groups on the outskirts of the power they desire. Since interest-group liberalism looks to fragmented interests as its constituency, rather than the general public interest, it opposes the will of democratic majorities and instead favors whatever groups or interests have been "hurt" by society. This victim orientation shows up in the increasing attempts to use the courts to attain their political agenda and to bypass the democratic process.

In the area of poverty and welfare, interest-group liberals have characterized the poor as victims and hence have opposed any workfare programs that impose some responsibility on the recipient. They claim that such programs smack of "blaming the victim." Social policies which blame the victim, however, differ entirely from social policies based upon victimization. Moreover, the poor and disadvantaged are not just innocent victims, according to William Wilson in *The Truly Disadvantaged;* they make choices that help shape their lives, just as everyone else does. Jesse Jackson also rejects placing a victim stigma on the poor and preaches to poor urban blacks the need to assume a sense of obligation to one another, to live by responsible rules, and to avoid drug use and family breakdown.

In *Losing Ground,* Charles Murray articulates the conservative criticism of the victim-based social policies initiated in the 1960s and

1970s. He sums up the liberal position on poverty as believing that "the system is to blame." To Murray, liberals blame the social environment when poor people commit crimes; rather than blaming people who behave badly, liberals label them as victims. Murray's criticism has some merit: to construct a social policy on this "victim-basis" sends a self-defeating message to the individuals who are having the problems, especially to the youth living in poverty. In effect, individual effort is denied before it is even exerted. Indeed, the moral rhetoric employed by leaders like Jesse Jackson is often undermined by the modern liberal's admonition against "blaming the victim." William Wilson, for instance, argues that the liberal reluctance to blame African-Americans for anything that is happening in their communities has clouded the way of thinking about how they can improve those communities.

The victimization of interest-group liberalism signals a significant departure from the social contract theory of government. Without the social contract, individuals have no social obligations or responsibilities; and without responsibilities or duties, individuals necessarily become victims in a society over which they have no control. Government action then becomes patronizing, as illustrated by the shift in emphasis on jobs under FDR to an emphasis on welfare in the late 1960s. Contrary to the social contract, rights and entitlements have acquired a one-sided obligation—that of society to dispense. Any corresponding obligations or duties of the recipients are off-limits even for debate or discussion. This one-sided arrangement and the liberal acceptance of it further strains the once-stable relationship between liberalism and the social contract.

The victim mentality also accompanies a social guilt complex. On certain issues and for certain segments of the population, liberals feel a sense of guilt which prohibits them from advocating an open discussion of the issues. This, in turn, goes against the liberal belief in an open marketplace of ideas. For instance, liberals often refuse to discuss frankly the serious shortcomings of many programs aimed at disadvantaged African-Americans. This refusal results from a sense of social guilt, not necessarily from a constructive and realistic striving toward social justice. A neurotic sense of social guilt has replaced a constructive sense of social responsibility. It provides a paternalistic rationale for persons who are the object of that guilt to fail to take independent action and responsibility for their lives and their futures. This approach, however, contradicts the true needs of those for whom liberals feel guilt. During the civil rights movement, for instance, Dr. King not only opposed white injustice but preached for black self-improvement: less crime and drugs, better family life, more education, and a greater sense of community obligation. With many liberals today, however, the simple categorization of persons as minorities automatically kicks in the sense of guilt and prevents a rational assessment of controversial programs and human needs.

Crime is another area which brings out the liberal guilt. For most of our nation's history, people charged with crimes did not fare well. A fair trial and a presumption of innocence was more a myth than reality. In the 1960s, the Warren Court began recognizing and rectifying injustices in our criminal system. Yet the knowledge of these injustices also produced an underlying sense of guilt in modern liberals. This guilt has consequently clouded liberals' attention to the rights of the victims of crimes. Despite the fact that one in sixteen urban Americans has been a victim of property or violent crime, liberals today continue to see the criminal as the primary victim. With this type of outlook, little meaningful progress on law enforcement and crime prevention can occur.

Vietnam had a particularly profound effect on the victim orientation of American liberalism. In Vietnam, the liberal foreign policy of the postwar period had, in the liberal view, "degenerated into a ruinous adventure, leading to a widespread loss of confidence in the legitimacy of America's purpose in global politics and . . . a wave of neoisolationist sentiment that pointed toward withdrawal from the rest of the world."[23] From the experience of Vietnam, liberals came to believe that American foreign policy was inherently corrupt and oppressive. Whenever America took sides on an international issue, the opposite side was viewed by liberals as the oppressed innocent victim. This view has been called the "devil theory" of American foreign policy: America is bad and wherever there is suffering and injustice, America is to blame. Under this view of America, no positive action is possible, since by definition any American action will only produce victims. Furthermore, with the victim mentality, liberals have focused more on picking adversaries than on picking allies. Therefore, the heart of American liberal foreign policy in the 1970s and 1980s became not constructive progress but reactionary resentment, not the longing for justice but the desire for revenge. Action was paralyzed by the constant suspicion that it was wrong and victimizing.

The victim mindset in domestic politics has likewise acted as a brake on progress and innovation at home. Liberals like Franklin Roosevelt and John Kennedy believed in attaining the common good through positive, innovative action. To move all of society forward, they stressed the social goals of investment, production, and progress. The emphasis of interest-group liberalism has been far more tilted toward consumption in the present than toward investment for the future, since present consumption "buys off" the social and economic victims.

Compared with their predecessors twenty-five years ago, liberals today lean toward victim compensation rather than opportunity creation. The difference in focus is clear: welfare versus jobs; protector versus enabler; and consumption versus production. This victim-based mentality also retards the development of a progress-oriented vision and divides society, as it serves to isolate groups rather than assimilate or harmonize them into the rest of society. In interest-group politics, the group looks skeptically on society. The group strives to cement its rights within society as a secure claim immune from political negotiation. Not only does the group not share in a common interest or purpose with society, it attempts to avoid any risks or adversities borne by society. It seeks to lower its risks by insulating itself from society.

This risk-aversion combines with the victim mentality to further stifle action. Action is viewed from a victim's point of view, and the relevant inquiry is about the risks, not about the benefits because a victim point of view always presumes failure and injury. In the 1970s, with the environmental and consumer movements and the proliferation of interest groups, a loss of faith in American technology occurred among liberals and solidified America's risk aversion. Today, government often seems obsessed with eliminating risk and with elevating safety so high that innovation becomes impossible. Lawyers, rather than engineers, have come to characterize the American economy. Indeed, with 5 percent of the world's population, America has almost 70 percent of the world's lawyers; and from 1973 to 1983, the number of lawyers increased 85 percent.[24] Currently, litigation is increasing five to seven times faster than our population. Yet it is the engineer who makes the economic pie grow larger; the lawyer only decides how to carve it up. However, the emphasis on lawyer versus engineer and the increasing risk-aversion of our society could inevitably threaten both economic and scientific progress.

The interest-group liberal's aversion to risk and association with the "victim" represent a sharp departure from the focus of twentieth-century liberalism. They create a philosophy reluctant to change, pessimistic toward action, and obsessed with the present. This type of liberalism is a far cry from the bold calls to action of risk-taking liberals like Franklin Roosevelt, Harry Truman, and John Kennedy.

# Conclusion:
# The Importance of Ideology

## The Liberal Ideology and the American Identity

The liberal tradition has guided American history for almost three centuries. It is this tradition that fully defines the liberal philosophy for the 1990s and the next century. According to this tradition, liberalism contains several basic tenets, the first of which is a respect for the dignity and freedom of the individual. The second basic liberal belief lies in the democratic system and in the role of self-government as the only legitimate form of government and as the highest civil authority in society. To liberals, no social institution should eclipse in power the democratic institutions in which all citizens have a voice. And finally, liberalism contains an optimistic faith in the power and capability of a democratic government to solve social problems and to engineer progressive change. In America, liberalism has always been the philosophy of optimism and of the future, emitting a faith in the power of rationally directed change to bring about a better society.

In *The Crosswinds of Freedom,* James MacGregor Burns brings to a conclusion his account of "the American experiment," his term for the American attempt to expand both individual liberty and equality of opportunity for everyone. To Burns, this attempt to expand liberty and opportunity represents the supreme promise of the Declaration. Burns's description of the American experiment also serves as a concise description of the liberal tradition. Almost forty years ago, Earl Warren, then the Republican vice-presidential nominee, gave a similar description of liberalism. He wrote in 1948 that civil rights, representative government, and equality of opportunity constituted the liberal tradition and that most Americans believed in that tradition.

In 1988, these glowing descriptions of American liberalism gave way to campaign slogans charging that liberalism was un-American and outside the mainstream of American life. At the same time, however, conservatives admit that "American conservatism has never been . . . particularly American."[1] Moreover, it is ironic that while conservatives in America were downgrading liberalism as a political philosophy, proponents for greater freedom and democracy in Soviet Russia, Europe, and China were hailing liberal thought and liberal thinkers. In those regions, liberalism has a heroic image; however, in America, conservatives speak of liberalism as being a festering wound on society.

Historically, many of the emotion-charged attacks on political liberalism have resulted from social forces independent of the liberal political philosophy. For instance, ever since the conservative reaction against Darwin's theory of evolution, attacks on liberalism during the twentieth century have sometimes been, in reality, reactions against modernity. Conservatives in the early 1900s, as did conservatives in the 1980s, became alarmed at the changes in life-styles of the youth and blamed such "modern" changes on the permissiveness of liberals. Indeed, throughout the last two centuries, strong leaders and movements in American history have opposed the effects of modernism. William Faulkner was one such American. Faulkner, according to Frederick Karl in *William Faulkner: American Writer,* saw modernism as a form of anarchism which swept away the past, destroyed history, and defied custom and community.

Other writers have similarly articulated suspicions about modernism and have connected liberalism with the negative consequences of modernism, such as the breakdown of values and communities, while associating the positive effects, such as scientific progress and enlightened beliefs, with conservatism. In *The Conquest of Politics: Liberal Philosophy in Democratic Times,* Benjamin Barber examines the vices of modernism—alienation, nihilism, and meaninglessness—and notes the "inconsolable coldness" of modernity. John Murrin has also noted the association between modern and liberal.[2] In a pejorative sense, "modern" has been used to describe the discarding of classical and fundamental American principles—principles which form the heart of the liberal philosophy. Therefore, conservative attacks on liberalism must be examined in terms of whether those attacks relate to the liberal political philosophy or whether they relate strictly to the effects of modernization brought on by a changing world.

The vicious conservative crusades against liberalism throughout the 1980s also obscure the vital interdependence of conservative and liberal creeds. Both conservatism and liberalism play a vital role in American politics. Liberalism provides the energy for change and a vision of the future, while conservatism nurtures the past and protects valuable tradition. As Schlesinger argues in *Cycles of American History,* the public needs and desires periods of rest in between periods of change and activism. Indeed, conservatives often protect much of what liberals achieve. Likewise, liberals need to define the part of the past worth saving and refining. America could not have succeeded as it has in its great "democratic experiment" without the influences of both conservative and liberal philosophies. Recognizing this interdependence, liberals have never actively campaigned to smear conservatism with "un-American" labels like "fascism," even though conservatives have so often engaged in such attacks by equating liberalism with radicalism or communism. To degrade one of the political philosophies is to degrade the American political tradition of which the other philosophy is a vital part. Perhaps, however, the tension between liberalism and conservatism is increasing because, as many of the longstanding ethnic and religious divisions dissipate, the liberal versus conservative distinction is becoming the primary one for most Americans in defining their views of morality and politics.[3]

Despite its long and accomplished tradition in American political history, liberalism has drifted from that tradition in recent decades and has consequently lost some of its focus and direction. Interest-group liberalism has over the last two decades contradicted the basic tenets of the liberal tradition. The emphasis on "rights against the state" has protected some individuals but has failed to empower them in a democratic society. Self-government has weakened from a weakening of community and of a sense of common purpose. Judicial activism has replaced political activism. Lawyers, rather than community and political activists, have been the agents of political change. And by concentrating political activity in the federal government, where interest groups can most effectively lobby, interest-group liberalism has eroded local activism and community building. For instance, in *The Living City* Robert Brandes Gratz argues that large federal urban programs tend to crush small neighborhood initiatives, which have usually been more successful than the federal programs.

The result of interest-group liberalism has been to focus on what separates, rather than on what unites, American society. It has precluded the recognition and celebration of any common culture or tradition. Indeed, as Arthur Schlesinger notes, the bonds of social cohesion are sufficiently fragile that we should not strain them by excessive worship at artificial shrines of ethnicity, bilingualism, global cultural base-touching and the like. Let us take pride in our own distinctive inheritance as other countries take pride in their distinctive inheritances; and let us understand that no culture can hope to ingest other cultures all at once, certainly not before it ingests its own.

Despite their populist attacks on elitism and privilege, Americans have long cherished the vision that the country will unite on a common consensus of higher principles to insure civic virtue. This desire for consensus, a desire by Americans to participate in the national experience, has been ignored by interest-group liberals. Yet as the historian Richard Hofstadter once recognized, "It has been our fate as a nation not to have ideologies but to be one." This sense of national unity and common purpose must once again return to the liberal philosophy.

The success of twentieth-century liberalism has revolved around its vision of the future and its embrace of political experimentation to meet social problems. Yet in the decade of the eighties, conservatives tapped the public's mood for change and the "populist" spirit. Conservatives convinced the public that liberals are elitist, powerful, and contemptuous—the way bankers used to be portrayed. This image of liberal elitism encouraged the perception that conservatives, and not liberals, are the true believers in popular government. Reinforcing this image was the loss of faith in grass-roots democratic action and in the wisdom of public opinion on the part of interest-group liberals.

## Debate within the Liberal Ranks:
## Neoliberalism and the Liberal Tradition

Interest-group liberals have also resisted change and debate within the liberal ranks. In the past, liberalism has thrived on its openness to change and its embrace of debate even about the liberal philosophy itself. The rich tradition of American liberalism has resulted from its ability to incorporate the prescriptions it gave to society as a whole— the encouragement of robust debate and a belief in the constructive role of a "marketplace of ideas." In the 1980s, however, liberals discouraged a wide-open, internal debate about the meaning of American liberalism and refused to accept dissenters and reformers as liberals. A liberal with questions or reservations about contemporary liberalism was branded as a "new conservative," even though most New Deal and New Frontier supporters would today probably describe themselves as liberals—with reservations. This defensive and reactionary stance has stagnated liberalism and has consequently produced a liberalism difficult to define, as exemplified by Dukakis's adamant resistance to assume the liberal label.

The modern reformers and dissenters within the liberal ranks have been termed "neoliberals," as though they are not quite true or pure liberals, or as if they do not want to assume the same label as that used by interest-group liberals. However, the rejection of neoliberals from the liberal camp reflects the exclusionary and narrowing effect of interest-group liberalism, as well as furthering the elitist image of liberals. Yet liberalism would be strengthened by welcoming all believers and by broadening consensus on the basic beliefs of liberalism. The question is whether the "interest-group liberals" or the "neoliberals" in their political philosophies conform more closely with the American liberal tradition.

In 1984, Randall Rothenberg published *The Neoliberals,* in which he defined the basic policy themes of the neoliberals. According to Rothenberg, they believe in investment and economic growth to create a larger economic pie as opposed to redistribution of a shrinking pie, they favor a mixture of governmental and private incentives rather than government programs alone, and they believe in cooperative problem-solving ("the national interest") rather than us-against-them politics ("special interests"). Neoliberals, in opposing both big bureaucratic government and corporations, also favor decentralization of government and entrepreneurial small business.[4]

Rothenberg noted that neoliberalism, rather than constituting a dramatic break with traditional liberalism, directly followed from New Deal liberalism in that both philosophies responded to new structural problems of the economy and to the need to overcome stagnation of the economy. Like the older liberalism, neoliberalism still wanted the same goals: equal opportunity and economic justice. Just as the New Deal liberals turned to the power and resources of the federal government to handle the Great Depression, which was beyond the power of the states to handle, neoliberals look to the states in the 1990s to provide the flexible, experimental action needed to combat complex, nonuniform social problems which cannot be adequately addressed through bureaucracies in Washington. The neoliberal critique of interest-group liberalism as surrendering control over public policy to organized private groups, defining the public interest as the sum of group claims, and strangling the economy with ever-increasing group entitlements also coincides with the liberalism of FDR.[5] Neoliberalism expressly affirms Roosevelt's philosophy that the public interest is greater than the sum of group claims.

The neoliberal advocacy of the entrepreneur and of the growth potential of the market also fits in with traditional liberalism. A socialist or command economy has never been a vision of American liberalism. To the contrary, liberals were the initial sponsors and advocates of a free enterprise, freely competitive economy. But that Adam Smith type of economy no longer exists. Industrial concentration has long since filled the market with inequities and rigidities. The history of American business, contrary to the vision of Adam Smith, has been the history of attempts to escape competition. Thus, liberals have not tended to view the modern economy as the "infinitely sensitive, frictionless, impartial, self-equilibrating mechanism imagined by conservatives."[6] Like the New Deal liberals, the neoliberals value the market economy for its productive potential, but do not rely on it alone to solve all social problems.

Neoliberals tend to be antiestablishment, unorthodox, reform-minded, and yet pragmatic.[7] They favor government action to solve problems, but they want efficiency and financial accountability in those programs. The neoliberal outlook, while recognizing an active role for government, rejects an approach assuming that government solutions are *always* the appropriate solution. Interest-group liberals, according to Senator Bill Bradley, have slipped into the rut of answering every problem with a government department. Echoing the social contract theory of the American liberal tradition, Bradley states that there exists a web of social obligations that citizens owe each other. Sometimes the obligations can be best met through a government program and sometimes through a private or charitable association effort. Either way, activism and innovation are the crucial keys to solving the social problems.[8] This brand of liberalism in many ways reflects the basic outlook of twentieth-century liberalism.

Neoliberals also look to all levels of government, as demonstrated by David Osborne in *Laboratories of Democracy,* in which he describes the activist and innovative strategies of neoliberal governors. As governor of Arizona, Bruce Babbitt, for instance, envisioned federal government as a partner with the states and private sector in restructuring the economy and in delivering services. In striving to make government more responsive and flexible, he advocated decentralized means to achieve national goals, as in his proposal for food stamp–like child-care vouchers. Babbitt attacked Washington for getting involved in too many things, such as education, that should be handled by state and local governments.[9] He also called for a clearer federalism. In the past, according to Babbitt, federal-state relations were like a layer cake; now they are like a marble cake, with all the functions intermixed. Under interest-group politics, Babbitt lamented, nothing seemed too trivial to involve the federal government.

In contrast to the divisive nature of interest-group liberalism, neoliberals reject an adversarial approach to politics and the separation of society by interest group, which has in turn produced a politics of group selfishness. To restore a sense of unity and common purpose, neoliberals rely heavily on two policy goals: economic growth and education. Like the Progressives during the early years of this century, neoliberals shun social division and seek to define values that all Americans can endorse—values like reform, progress, and good government. Neoliberals also recognize the importance of civic values in a democratic society. For instance, Jerry Brown described the California Conservation Corps, a program putting urban youth to work in conservation projects, as an attempt "to counter the loss of values and inspire people with discipline." Through bringing together people from a whole variety of backgrounds, the CCC "reflected the idea of inclusion, of environmental values, of community, and of serving some larger purpose."[10]

Advocacy of a return to the social contract also characterizes neoliberalism. Government programs should not dole out benefits as a matter of right and should help create social opportunities rather than social dependence. According to many neoliberals, government benefits should bring reciprocal duties and responsibilities from the recipients. Furthermore, government benefits ought only to go to the truly needy and should not be used to buy off the middle class with entitlements.

The neoliberal outlook offers a valuable and constructive input to the liberal philosophy. The challenge to liberalism lies in encouraging the debate on neoliberal ideas and incorporating the useful ideas. Neoliberalism is consistent in many ways with traditional liberalism, and it offers new ideas on how to solve problems with which liberals have always been concerned. This source of debate and dissent within the liberal ranks provides necessary fuel for future growth. For its growth and vitality to continue, liberalism cannot become conservative within itself by refusing to incorporate new ideas and encourage dissenting debate.

While neoliberalism brings a certain pragmatic outlook to liberal policies, the task ahead for liberalism is still to articulate and strengthen itself as an ideology. This task carries great importance, since much of the unpopularity of liberalism in the 1980s was due to negative images or definitions of the liberal ideology. However, public opinion polls have shown that there has been no shift to the Right in public opinion regarding government programs during the Reagan era.

Although the interest-group liberalism of the last twenty years has confused or shaken the liberal ideology, liberals must not altogether abandon ideology. No political philosophy can thrive without an ideology, a vision for the future, and a moral purpose. As Bernard Bailyn has argued, the concept of ideology has exerted a powerful influence in America's origins and political development. An ideology is more than just propaganda, it brings together into a coherent creed all the opinions and attitudes that are otherwise too diverse and scattered and vague to be acted on. Indeed, pragmatism is necessary as a tool to achieve a vision, but it cannot be an ideology in itself. Citizens demand more than problem solving from their political leaders. As history has shown, Americans look to their political leaders for vision and hope—the bureaucrats provide the pragmatism.

## Liberalism and the Democratic Tradition

In articulating its ideological core, liberalism must reaffirm its commitment to and passion for democratic government. This passion was muted by the interest group politics of the last two decades. Yet democracy has reflected America's highest political traditions and aspirations; and because of the liberal espousal of democratic values, even conservatives recognize that "it has too often been the liberals who have known the magical words needed to unlock our highest traditions." Conservatism, on the other hand, "has not been very good either at understanding or practicing democratic statesmanship."[11] What liberals must now remember, however, is that democracy is as fundamental a belief of liberalism as is individual freedom. Rights and freedom are interwoven with, not set apart from, democratic society.

Liberals who have for so long concentrated on rights and entitlements to the exclusion of democratic processes and majority rule should examine closely what has recently occurred in many Communist countries. In a single day in May of 1989, more than one million people demonstrated in Beijing in support of democracy. On the same day, half a million people demonstrated in Shanghai and 300,000 rallied in the city of Xiam. Unfortunately, a sobering reality for Americans existed in these Chinese democratic movements. As reported by observers of the demonstrations, President Gorbachev's visit to China and his call for greater political change were "widely viewed as having more of an impact on the democratic movement than President Bush's visit earlier in the year." Indeed, "It was Mr. Gorbachev's photos and not Mr. Bush's portraits that enlivened the demonstrators' posters."[12]

The American response to the democratic movements in China and Eastern Europe has been surprisingly weak for the strongest and oldest democratic nation on earth. While the Reagan conservatives were eager and anxious to militarily intercede in Nicaragua on behalf of somewhat dubious forces, the Bush response to the massacre of the Chinese democratic protestors was that "we don't want to be too critical of the Chinese Government."[13] In comparison with the billions of dollars in military aid given to the Contras by the Reagan administration in the name of democracy, the initial commitment by the Bush administration to provide only 1 percent of the total aid requested by Poland's democratically formed government was paltry and disappointing. Though President Bush is willing to pursue a "new world order" through a military defeat of Iraq, he is not willing to ensure that this new order is one of international democracy under the leadership of the United States. What is needed is the type of commitment to democratic values shown by liberals like Wilson, Roosevelt, Truman, and Kennedy. Indeed, the democratic movements in China and Eastern Europe in 1989 demonstrate the human passion for democratic ideals and values which has infused the American liberal tradition. It is this passion to which American liberalism must return.

Modern liberalism has learned what separates and differentiates Americans; it must now relearn what unites and binds American society. The interest-group liberal preoccupation with the rights and entitlements of its constituent groups has caused an imbalance in the liberal view away from democracy and toward individual rights. Indeed, the political problem with liberal democracy has always existed in the conflict between majority rule and individual freedom. Two views relate to this conflict and have, until recently with interest-group liberalism, found a balance within the liberal tradition.

The Madisonian view of liberal democracy sees popular rule as a restraint, through the ballot box, on government officials. This view defines democratic freedom as a "negative liberty"—the absence of interference by government in one's life. The positive liberty or populist theory of democracy, on the other hand, believes that through popular participation democratic governments embody the will of the people and therefore cannot oppress.[14] Populists do not fear tyranny by the majority as do advocates of the Madisonian view. If a government or its officials infringe on liberty, the voters will simply elect new officials. Thus, populists equate democracy with positive liberty—the freedom to rule and govern.

The difference between the Madisonian and populist views is that the latter trusts the opinions of the majority because the will of the people is the liberty of the people. The Madisonian view, however, attaches no special value or moral character to decisions of the majority. For the Madisonian, since democracy generates liberty simply by restraining officials, there is no need to treat democratic decisions as the embodiment of liberty itself. The populists, on the other hand, believe that democratic action, like voting, generates liberty by participation and that therefore democratic decisions are themselves the exercise of liberty.

During the last several decades, liberals have leaned far toward a Madisonian view of democracy. Such a view focuses on the independence of and differences among individuals. It reflects a realization of what separates us. Democracy also, however, reflects what unites and joins us. This latter view has, in balance with the Madisonian view, played a vital role in the American liberal tradition.

To resurrect its democratic spirit and sense of common purpose, liberalism must assert a vision of community. A community, even as defined by conservative George Will, "consists of people held together by a broad, deep consensus about justice under a common sovereignty." Such a community is vital not as a means to impose moral conformity but as a means of social cohesion necessary for a democratic society. To connect government with community, liberals should "make it clear that all of the specific tasks of government are undertaken in the cause of patriotism; thus every success of the government will have the effect of increasing Americans' faith in their country and each other."[15] Liberalism must embody the idea that a popularly elected government can be the instrument of the common purpose of a free people and can embrace great causes.

The liberal vision of society, as it has been in the past, should be inclusionary; the aim of both liberalism and community should be to broaden, not to narrow. An example lies in the American immigrant experience. The American "melting pot" has worked because most immigrants eagerly adopted the American communal values, not because the immigrant was separated from the rest of society and provided with certain distinct rights and entitlements.

Above all else, liberals must reenter the ideological fray and stand by a liberalism consistent with its traditional foundations. The answer is not to make a reactionary shift to the right just because of the unpopularity of interest-group liberalism. Instead, liberalism must be reinvigorated with basic traditional liberal values and with the new challenges of the present age. It is no answer to simply and naively wish for a return to the days of past heroes like FDR and JFK. Likewise, liberals must disassociate their beliefs from those of other creeds sometimes associated with liberalism and which distort certain traditional liberal values. The libertarianism of the American Civil Liberties Union, for instance, does not often reflect the liberal view of the public good and the social contract.

Liberalism for the last two decades has been a "philosophy in exodus." The crisis of liberalism in the 1980s, however, arose from more than just the effects of interest-group liberalism. A confusion occurred in the 1970s over the purposes of the liberal tradition: for instance, did it aim to achieve equality of opportunity, or equality of result; did it favor a liberal capitalist democracy, or a socialist democracy? This confusion stemmed from the emergence in the 1960s of the "New Class." The New Class—"highly mobile professionally and geographically, anticommercial by career choice and strong conviction, attracted instinctively to the novel and unconventional, and prone to depict itself as the protector of the oppressed"—took liberalism far to the Left during the several years preceding Kennedy's death and McGovern's campaign.[16]

The strong anticommercial bias of the New Class contrasted sharply with the liberal tradition. From Jefferson to Truman, liberalism had proclaimed the virtues of an open, competitive capitalist system and represented the aspirations of the small entrepreneur against the power of entrenched wealth and monopoly. By the 1970s, however, liberalism came to express the view of the intelligentsia, those less likely to romanticize small business and more apt to criticize the entire capitalist ethos. The "once firm distinction between liberalism and socialism had all but evaporated."[17] According to Hamby, this inroad of socialist thought and hostility toward business led to a repudiation of the older liberal goal of equality of opportunity and to an adoption of the newer goal of equality of results. Furthermore, with their antibusiness bias and their lack of concern with economic growth, New Class liberals refused to face the problem of funding social programs in a stagnant economy, which in turn created even more clients for social welfare programs. From the Fair Deal to the New Frontier, liberals had generally acknowledged that major advances in social welfare required strong economic growth. This commitment to growth, however, evaporated in the liberalism of the 1970s.

Thus, to view liberalism only from the vantage point of the last decade or two would be to miss the primary thrust and vision of the American liberal philosophy. Despite the historical oddity of interest-group liberalism, and despite the emotionally laden, distorted attacks on liberalism in the 1980s, the American liberal tradition is neither dead nor outmoded. It continues to form a substantial part of the American identity. Furthermore, as America moves through the 1990s, it will need the guidance of liberal thought perhaps as much as it ever has in the past.

Throughout its history, America has symbolized youth, dreams, and opportunity. It has been the nation of action and progress. The long decade of the 1980s, however, departed from that image. Though not necessarily a sick or decadent decade, it was a static decade. While the rest of the world seemed charged with passion and renewal, America seemed capable of only paranoia about the present and nostalgia toward the past. Its obsession with the present focused on status concerns—how did America compare with Japan? Its nostalgia revealed itself in the intensive effort to relive the past. More and more radio stations played the "oldies," and most of the rock groups of the sixties and seventies played reunion concerts to sold-out crowds.

The eighties' obsession with the past was not confined to popular culture. In many ways, the political mood of the decade centered on a nostalgia for the 1950s. The traditional and narrow values of the 1950s were hailed as America's true identity. The national deference to business governance of society—"What is good for GM is good for the country"—was revived, but this time it focused more singularly on the amassing of huge wealth not by contributing to a corporation's success but by putting its stock into play. And the national political apathy, even greater than that of the 1950s, contributed to a stagnant, "do-nothing" political system. Without a vision for the future and a national energy to pursue that vision, the decade of the eighties reverted to the pursuit of hedonistic lifestyles and a superficial glorification of the past. Accompanying this nostalgia came the frightening prospect that America had outgrown its youth and settled into a sedentary middle age.

In looking back on the 1980s, there is concern that the decade will never command any special nostalgia or passion among future generations. The haunting question is whether the American idealism and drive for progressive change will return to energize the nation, as it has so often in the past. It will—if the liberal vision returns. America's youthful vigor and optimism will be revived—if the liberal vision returns. And the liberal vision will return when liberals, particularly the Democratic party, renew their ideological identity and historical convictions. They must convince a nation adrift in political apathy that government and politics matter to each individual and that a government guided by liberal principles will improve the health of both individual and society. Americans hold these ideals and convictions deep in their souls; but these ideals will not resurface simply by waiting for the past to return. Liberalism must activate them.

# Notes

## Introduction:
### The Task Ahead—Rediscovering the Liberal Tradition

1. Ann Devroy, "There's no homecoming for Bush," 12.
2. Walter Shapiro, "Are the Democrats Cursed?" 58.

## Chapter 1
### The Decline of Liberalism in the Eighties

1. *Minneapolis Star Tribune*, 13 Oct. 1988; *New York Times*, 16 Oct. 1988.
2. *Minneapolis Star Tribune*, 13 Oct. 1988; *New York Times*, 16 Oct. 1988.
3. *Minneapolis Star Tribune*, 13 Oct. 1988.
4. "Democratic Party: Left Behind in the Dust," *Christian Science Monitor*, 10 Feb. 1989; "Lectern to Lectern," *Newsweek*, 21 Nov. 1988, 124.
5. "A Reaffirmation of Principle," signed by leading liberals, *The New Republic*, 17 Oct. 1988, 13; L. Larsen, "When the Label Liberal Didn't Scare Politicians," *Minneapolis Star Tribune*, 27 Oct. 1988.
6. See Kevin Phillips, "The Democrats and Republicans: Dead from the Neck Up?" 6–7.
7. Everett C. Ladd, Jr., and Seymour M. Lipset, "Public Opinion and Public Policy," in *Conflict and Consensus in Modern American History*, ed. Allen F. Davis and Harold D. Woodman, 534.
8. Ideological terms and labels are discussed in David Green, *Shaping Political Consciousness: The Language of Politics in America from McKinley to Reagan.*
9. Arthur M. Schlesinger, Jr., *The Politics of Hope*, 91–92.
10. Ladd and Lipset, "Public Opinion," in *Conflict and Consensus*, 508.
11. *New York Times*, 21 Jan. 1989.
12. Tim Smart, "Regulation Rises Again," 58–59.
13. *New York Times*, 11 Dec. 1988; ibid., 12 Mar. 1989; Tim Smart, "A Blacklash against Business," 30–31.
14. *New York Times*, 22 Jan. 1989; ibid., 30 Oct. 1988; "91% favor 7-day wait for handgun purchases," *Minneapolis Star Tribune*, 30 Oct. 1988; "Americans say reducing budget deficit is top priority," ibid., 6 Nov. 1988: Majorities of more than two to one favor government aid to the elderly and poor, to improve education and health

care, and to protect the environment. Americans also think the tax system favors the wealthy at the expense of the average person. *Washington Post*, 14 Feb. 1986; ibid., 15 May 1985.

15. Ladd and Lipset, "Public Opinion," in *Conflict and Consensus*, 543, 548.

16. Ibid., 543, 544, 546.

17. Thomas Ferguson and Joel Rogers, "The Myth of America's Turn to the Right," 43, 44; Ladd and Lipset, "Public Opinion," in *Conflict and Consensus*, 539; *New York Times*, 6 Nov. 1988.

18. Ferguson and Rogers, "The Myth," 44. Also see George Wills's column in *Newsweek*, 31 Nov. 1988.

## Chapter 2
## A History of Attacks on Liberalism: Patterns of Hysteria and Reaction

1. See Robert Remini, "Election of 1832," 509.

2. Henry Pringle, *Theodore Roosevelt: A Biography*, 556; Sidney Ratner, *American Taxation: Its History as a Social Force in Democracy*, 260.

3. Paul F. Boller, Jr., *Presidential Campaigns*, 197.

4. Francis Russell, *The Shadow of Blooming Grove: Warren G. Harding in His Times*, 347.

5. One preacher declared, "If you vote for Al Smith you're voting against Christ and you'll be damned." Edmund A. Moore, *A Catholic Runs for President: The Campaign of 1928*, 188.

6. Boller, *Presidential Campaigns*, 235; Handlin, *Al Smith*, 159.

7. Boller, *Presidential Campaigns*, 242, 248; Arthur M. Schlesinger, Jr., *The American as Reformer*, 84.

8. Alonzo Hamby, *Liberalism and Its Challengers: FDR to Reagan*, 122.

9. Schlesinger, *The Politics of Hope*, 69; Louis Hartz, *The Liberal Tradition in American*, 221.

10. Schlesinger, *The American as Reformer*, 74.

11. Peter N. Carroll and David W. Noble, *The Free and the Unfree: A New History of the U.S.*, 114, 187, 188; Schlesinger, *The American as Reformer*, 75.

12. W. P. and F. J. Garrison, *William Lloyd Garrison* 1:336, 3:32–33. Sources include E. N. Elliott, ed., *Cotton Is King and Pro-Slavery Arguments*, and W. S. Jenkins, *Pro-Slavery Thought*. Schlesinger, *The American as Reformer*, 78.

13. David Bennett, *The Party of Fear: From Nativist Movements to the New Right in American History*, 13.

14. Arthur Schlesinger, Jr., *The Vital Center*, 194, 196.

15. Ibid., 208, 210, 192.

16. Bennett, *The Party of Fear*, 388.

17. See Richard Curry, ed., *Freedom at Risk: Secrecy, Censorship, and Repression in the 1980s*.

18. "Looking for Mr. Right," *Newsweek*, 21 Nov. 1988, 35.

## Chapter 3
## The Liberal Political Philosophy

1. William Riker, *Liberalism against Populism: A Confrontation between the Theory of Democracy and the Theory of Social Choice*, 3.

2. Schlesinger, *The Politics of Hope*, 71.

3. Ibid., 67; Schlesinger, *The American as Reformer*, 68.

4. Schlesinger, *The Vital Center*, 172, 174.

5. Robert Reich, "Toward a New Public Philosophy," 68–79.

6. E. J. McCarthy, *A Liberal Answer to the Conservative Challenge*, 8.

## Chapter 4
## The Liberal Tradition in America

1. This debate is discussed in Daniel T. Rodgers, *Contested Truths: Keywords in American Policy since Independence*.

2. Carroll and Noble, *The Free and the Unfree*, 394.

3. Ibid., 393.

4. Schlesinger, *The Politics of Hope*, 65.

5. A general discussion of classical liberalism appears in D. J. Manning, *Liberalism*.

6. Ibid., 127; Hartz, *The Liberal Tradition*, 132.

7. Hartz argues this point in *The Liberal Tradition in America*.

8. For a discussion of the liberal focus on "citizenship rights," consult Ralf Dahrendorf, *The Modern Social Conflict: An Essay on the Politics of Liberty*.

9. The liberal beliefs of Tocqueville are discussed in Roger Boesch, *The Strange Liberalism of Alexis de Tocqueville*.

10. John J. Waters, *The Otis Family in Provincial and Revolutionary Massachusetts*, 22; M. H. Smith, *The Writs of Assistance Case*, 554.

11. A. J. Langguth, *Patriots: The Men Who Started the American Revolution*, 24.

12. Ibid., 32.

13. James Otis, *Rights of the Colonies Asserted and Proved*, 73; Pauline Maier, *From Resistance to Revolution*, 82.

14. Langguth, *Patriots*, 99, 95, 115.

15. Robert Kelly, *The Cultural Pattern in American Politics: The First Century*, 33.

16. Ibid., 42.

17. The political nature of the movement for independence is examined in Edward Countryman, *The American Revolution*.

18. These views may be seen in Merrill D. Peterson, *Thomas Jefferson and the New Nation: A Biography*, and in Adrienne Koch, *The Philosophy of Thomas Jefferson*.

19. Peterson, *Thomas Jefferson*, 667.

20. Jefferson's views are outlined in Forrest McDonald, *The Presidency of Thomas Jefferson*. Kelly, *The Cultural Pattern*, 117.

21. Linda K. Kerber, *Federalists in Dissent: Imagery and Ideology in Jeffersonian America*, 130.

22. Kelly, *The Cultural Pattern*, 122. See also Kerber, *Federalists in Dissent*, 91.

23. Kelly, *The Cultural Pattern*, 127.

24. Robert Walker, *Reform in America: The Continuing Frontier*, 20; Kelly, *The Cultural Pattern*, 163.

25. Mary Beth Norton et al., *A People and A Nation: A History of the United States*, 185; Eric Foner, *Free Soil, Free Labor, Free Men: The Ideology of the Republican Party before the Civil War*, 19.

26. John Diggins, *The Lost Soul of American Politics: Virtue, Self-Interest, and the Foundations of Liberalism*, 147.

27. Kelly, *The Cultural Pattern*, 198.

28. Don E. Fehrenbacher, *Lincoln in Text and Context: Collected Essays*, 142.

29. Foner, *Free Soil*, 38, 23, 21; Kelly, *The Cultural Pattern*, 200, 204, 206; *Springfield Republican*, 19 December 1857.

30. Kelly, *The Cultural Pattern*, 244, 247. See George M. Fredrickson, *The Inner Civil War: Northern Intellectuals and the Crisis of the Union*, 55-81.

31. Fredrickson, *The Inner Civil War*, 231; Kelly, *The Cultural Pattern*, 282, 250. See also Richard Allan Gerber, "The Liberal Republicans of 1872 in Historiographical Perspective," 40-73, and Matthew T. Downey, "Horace Greeley and the Politicians: The Liberal Republican Convention in 1872," 727-50.

32. Qtd. in Schlesinger, *The American as Reformer*, 85; D. D. McKean, *Party and Pressure Politics*, 659.

33. Robert H. Wiebe, *The Search for Order: 1877-1920*, 52; see also Lawrence Goodwin, *Democratic Promise: The Populist Movement in America*.

34. Wiebe, *The Search for Order*, 102.

35. See Niels Aage Thorsen, *The Political Thought of Woodrow Wilson, 1875-1910*.

36. Diggins, *The Lost Soul of American Politics*, 145.

37. Much of the following discussion of the Great Depression and the New Deal is taken from William E. Leuchtenburg, *Franklin D. Roosevelt and the New Deal*.

38. The effects of the Depression are discussed in Robert S. McElvaine, *The Great Depression: America 1929-1941*; Leuchtenburg, *The New Deal*, 3.

39. Norton et al., *A People and a Nation*, 714.

40. Leuchtenburg, *The New Deal*, 17.

41. Ibid., 33.

42. These views on the connection between the American economic and political systems are examined in Martin J. Sklar, *The Corporate Reconstruction of American Capitalism: The Market, the Law, and Politics*.

43. Jordan A. Schwarz, *Liberal: Adolf Berle and the Vision of an American Era*, 374.

44. Leuchtenburg, *The New Deal*, 69, 77.

45. Ibid., 90.

46. Ibid., 121, 37.

47. Ibid., 126.

48. Ibid., 131; Carroll and Noble, *The Free and the Unfree*, 350-51.

49. Leuchtenburg, *The New Deal*, 154.

50. Ibid., 164.

51. Ibid., 176.

52. Ibid., 193; Kelly, *The Cultural Pattern*, 286.

53. Robert H. Ferrell, *Harry S. Truman and the Modern American Presidency*, 98-99.

54. Ibid., 104.

55. Hamby, *Liberalism and Its Challengers*, 59.

56. Ibid., 88, 107, 111.

57. Ibid., 203; Schlesinger, *The Vital Center*, 469.

58. Kelly, *The Cultural Pattern*, 288.

59. Hamby, *Liberalism and Its Challengers*, 214.

60. Louis S. Gerteis, *Morality and Utility in American Antislavery Reform*, 148.

61. For a discussion of Adams's efforts at railroad reform, see Thomas K. McCraw, *Prophets of Regulation: Charles Francis Adams, Louis D. Brandeis, James M. Landis, Alfred E. Kahn*. Stefan Lorant, *The Glorious Burden: The American Presidency*.

62. Wiebe, *The Search for Order*, 192.

63. Ibid., 201. For criticism of Roosevelt in the 1912 election, see Boller, *Presidential Campaigns*, 192, 197. Pringle, *Theodore Roosevelt*, 560; Charles W. Thompson, *Presidents I've Known*, 220-22.

64. Carroll and Noble, *The Free and the Unfree*, 356, 357.
65. Hamby, *Liberalism and Its Challengers*, 121; Norton et al., *A People and a Nation*, 855.
66. Norton et al., *A People and a Nation*, 131.
67. *Minneapolis Star Tribune*, 16 June 1989.


## Chapter 5
## Liberalism and Affirmative Government

1. I have drawn much of this discussion from chapter 9 of Arthur M. Schlesinger, Jr., *The Cycles of American History*. E. A. J. Johnson, *The Foundations of American Economic Freedom: Government and Enterprise in the Age of Washington*, 153, 200, 260, 312; Joyce Appleby, *Capitalism and a New Social Order: The Republican Vision of the 1790s*, 88.
2. For a discussion of government economic activity, consult Louis Hartz, *Economic Policy and Democratic Thought: Pennsylvania, 1776–1860*.
3. Henry Adams, "The New York Gold Conspiracy," 189.
4. Norton et al., *A People and a Nation*, 482.
5. Hartz, *The Liberal Tradition*, 228; Schlesinger, *The Politics of Hope*, 68.
6. Schlesinger, *The Vital Center*, 177.
7. Peter Berger argues that an intrinsic link between capitalism and political democracy exists in *The Capitalist Revolution: Fifty Propositions about Prosperity, Equality and Liberty*.
8. Herbert Hoover, *State Papers and Other Public Writings* 2:8–9; Franklin D. Roosevelt, *Public Papers and Addresses*, 458.
9. Roosevelt, *Public Papers*, xxix–xxx.
10. Schlesinger, *The Politics of Hope*, 68.
11. Lester C. Thurow discusses the existence of oligopolies and the absence of any behavior of pricing theory for oligopolies in *Dangerous Currents: The State of Economics*.
12. William H. Rehnquist, *The Supreme Court: How It Was, How It Is*, 32, 133, 177.
13. "The Quiet Crusader," *Business Week*, 18 Sept. 1989.
14. See Lester C. Thurow, *The Zero-Sum Solution*.
15. George Lodge, "It's Time for an American Perestroika," 36.
16. Schlesinger, *The Vital Center*, 182. The partnership argument is made by Stuart Bruchey in *Enterprise: The Dynamic Economy of a Free People*. Roosevelt, *Public Papers and Addresses* 2:164.
17. *New York Times*, 27 Aug. 1989.
18. Michael Parenti, *Democracy for the Few*, 48.
19. Schlesinger, *Cycles*, 248.
20. Ronald Grover, "Fighting Back: The Resurgence of Social Activism," 34–35.
21. Ladd and Lipset, "Public Opinion," in *Conflict and Consensus*, 523.
22. "The Can't Do Government," *Time*, 23 Oct. 1989, 15–16.
23. For a discussion of economic performance in the 1980s, consult Peter Peterson, "The Morning After," 43.
24. Ibid., 61.
25. McCraw, *Prophets of Regulation*, 154.
26. Robert Kuttner, *The Life of the Party: Democratic Prospects in 1988 and Beyond*, 4.

27. See Peter N. Carroll, "The New Populists, the New Right, and the Search for the Lost America," in *Conflict and Consensus in Modern American History*, ed. Allen F. Davis and Harold D. Woodman.

28. See Harlan Lane, *When the Mind Hears: A History of the Deaf*, and Peter L. Tyor and Leland V. Bell, *Caring for the Retarded in America: A History*.

29. Kuttner, *Life of the Party*, 5.

30. *Minneapolis Star Tribune*, 25 June 1989.

31. Schlesinger, *The Vital Center*, 183.

32. This statement, sponsored by the Economic Policy Institute, appeared in *The New Republic*, 7 Aug. 1989.

33. Jonathan Rauch, "Kids as Capital," 57.


## Chapter 6
## Lessons from History: A Comparison of Liberalism and Conservatism

1. Kelly, *The Cultural Pattern*, 285.

2. Schlesinger, *The Vital Center*, 24.

3. William F. Buckley and Charles R. Kesler, eds., *Keeping the Tablets: Modern American Conservative Thought*, 14.

4. Robert Reich, "Corporation and Nation," 79.

5. Roosevelt, *Public Papers and Addresses*, xxix–xxx.

6. Nicholas Lemann, "The Culture of Poverty," 38. During Reagan's administration, programs for the poor suffered even more severe cutbacks than programs aimed at the middle class.

7. Woodrow Wilson, "Bryce's American Commonwealth," 153–69.

8. Reich, "Toward a New Public Philosophy," 75.

9. See Leslie Dunbar, *The Common Interest: How Our Social-Welfare Policies Don't Work, and What We Can Do about Them*. The poverty rate of people under thirty has nearly doubled since 1973 to 22 percent. Also, the real average income of families headed by people under thirty has plunged 14 percent since 1973, according to Children's Defense Fund. For a further discussion on income inequality and poverty in America, see Robert Reich, "As the World Turns," 23–28.

10. Jonathan Rauch, "Is the Deficit Really So Bad?" 42.

11. *Skinner v. Railway Labor Executives' Association*, No. 487 U.S. 602 (1989).


## Chapter 7
## The Recognition and Role of Values in the Liberal Tradition

1. See John Judis, *William F. Buckley, Jr., Patron Saint of the Conservatives*.

2. Schlesinger, *Cycles*, 41.

3. Richard H. Pells, *The Liberal Mind in a Conservative Age: American Intellectuals in the 1940s and 1950s*, 403.

4. Allen F. Davis and Harold D. Woodman, eds., *Conflict and Consensus in Modern American History*, 455; Godfrey Hodgson, "Triumph and Failure of a Cultural Revolution," 486.

5. *Time*, 25 May 1987, 26.

6. Diggins, *The Lost Soul of American Politics*, 340.

7. Ibid., 335.

8. A. Bartlett Giamatti, former president of Yale University, also makes this point in *A Free and Ordered Space: The Real World of the University*.

9. The drift of the Communist bloc countries has been well documented. See "Poland Flirts with Pluralism," *New York Times*, 4 June 1989. At the same time, conservatives like Richard A. Epstein, at the commencement exercises of the University of Chicago Law School on 10 June 1989, praised pluralism and warned against forcing too much consensus. John Silber, *Straight Shooting: What's Wrong with America and How to Fix It*.

10. *Minneapolis Star Tribune*, 8 June 1989.

11. Lee Bollinger, in *The Tolerant Society*, discusses the social benefits of tolerance.

12. For a discussion of Madison's views, see Drew McCoy, *The Last of the Fathers: James Madison and the Republican Legacy*.

13. For an anthology of the classic statements of American liberal Protestantism, see William Hutchinson, *American Protestant Thought in the Liberal Era*. Patricia U. Bonomi, *Under the Cope of Heaven: Religion, Society, and Politics in Colonial America*, 160.

14. Schlesinger, *Cycles*, 17.

15. The political influence of religion is discussed in Robert Wuthnow, *The Restructuring of American Religion: Society and Faith since World War II*.

16. Sanford Levinson, *Constitutional Faith*, 10. For further discussion on civil religion, see Russell E. Richey and Donald G. Jones, eds., *American Civil Religion*.

17. *New York Times*, 19 March 1989.

### Chapter 8
### Liberalism and Community

1. Hamby, *Liberalism and Its Challengers*, 163, 165.

2. Michael Sandel, "A Public Philosophy for American Liberalism," 23.

3. *Time*, 29 May 1989, 40.

4. Michael Walzer, "The Communitarian Critique of Liberalism," 6.

5. Stephen Holmes "The Philosophers' War on the L-word," 26.

6. Robert Reich, *Tales of a New America*, 168; John Rawls, *A Theory of Justice*.

7. "If You See Families Staging a Comeback, It's Probably a Mirage," *Wall Street Journal*, 25 Sept. 1986.

8. In *Rediscovering America's Values*, Frances Moore Lappe emphasizes individual development through interaction with others and individual opportunity as dependent on social environmental factors.

9. William Schneider, "The Democrats in '88," 37–39.

10. Michael Sandel, "Morality and the Liberal Ideal," 17.

### Chapter 9
### A Liberal Approach to Four Contemporary Issues

1. "The New Abortion Wars," *The New Republic*, 8 Aug. 1989.

2. "Nobody's Children," *Time*, 9 Oct. 1989.

3. See Karl Zinsmeister, "The Poverty Problem of the Eighties," 8–12.

4. "Poverty in America," *Public Opinion*, June/July 1985.

5. Described by Albert O. Hirschman in "Reactionary Rhetoric," 63.

6. See Sheldon H. Danziger and Daniel Weinberg, eds., *Fighting Poverty: What Works and What Doesn't*. Studies have shown that from 1965 to 1980, when Medicaid and other health programs were instituted, infant mortality fell by 50 percent. Similarly, life expectancy rates for individuals over sixty-five rose as a result of Medicare. Furthermore, the compensatory education program for disadvantaged children improved the test scores of low-income schoolchildren; the Head Start Program correlates with increased employment and reduced welfare, crime, and teenage pregnancy. See also Lawrence M. Mead, *Beyond Entitlement: The Social Obligation of Citizenship*.

7. See the Family Support Act of 1988 incorporating "workfare" provisions, Public Law No. 100–485, 102 Statutes 2343 (1988). *New York Times Magazine*, 7 May 1989, 38.

## Chapter 10
## The Crisis of Liberalism and the Challenges for the Future

1. Hamby, *Liberalism and Its Challengers*, 344.
2. Theodore J. Lowi, *The End of Liberalism: Ideology, Policy, and the Crisis of Public Authority*, 58.
3. Ibid., 72.
4. Stephen L. Newman, *Liberalism at Wit's End*, 161.
5. Schlesinger, *The Vital Center*, 159.
6. Kuttner, *The Life of the Party*, 11.
7. Holmes, "The Philosophers' War," 25–26.
8. Ibid., 25.
9. Carroll, "The New Populists," in *Conflict and Consensus*, 518.
10. Sandel, "A Public Philosophy for American Liberalism," 23.
11. Schwarz, *Adolf Berle*, 371.
12. 20 Feb. 1990 speech to Congress.
13. In *Constitutional Faith* (60), Levinson ponders the relationship between the Constitution and morality. *Better Homes and Gardens*, Jan. 1988.
14. The effects of a lack of values on black poverty are discussed in William J. Wilson, *The Truly Disadvantaged: The Inner City, the Underclass, and Public Policy*.
15. Schlesinger, *Cycles*, 245.
16. This argument is made by Glenn Tinder in "Can We Be Good Without God: On the Political Meaning of Christianity."
17. Leonard W. Levy, *The Establishment Clause*, 118.
18. Sandel, "Morality and the Liberal Ideal," 16.
19. This argument receives detailed attention in Gordon Wood, *The Creation of the American Republic*.
20. Fred Hirsch, *Social Limits to Growth*, 11–12, 143.
21. "The New Republic and Its Times," *The New Republic*, 10 Dec. 1984, 73.
22. Barry M. Goldwater, *Goldwater*, 120–21.
23. Hamby, *Liberalism and Its Challengers*, 6.
24. Henry Fairlie, "Fear of Living," 14–19; "The Limits of Risk," *New York Times*, 19 Mar. 1989.

## Conclusion:
## The Importance of Ideology

1. Buckley and Kesler, *Keeping the Tablets*, 10.

2. John Murrin, "Self-interest Conquers Patriotism: Republicans, Liberals, and Indians Reshape the Nation," in *The American Revolution: Its Character and Limits,* ed. John P. Greene, 225.

3. As recognized by Robert Wuthnow in *The Restructuring of American Religion.*

4. For instance, Robert Reich, in *The Next American Frontier* and in *Tales of a New America,* articulates a liberalism combining entrepreneurship and social comity.

5. Schlesinger, *Cycles,* 251.

6. Ibid.

7. William Schneider, "JFK's Children: The Class of '74," 39.

8. Schneider, "The Democrats in '88," 52.

9. Hendrik Hertzberg, "Stand-up Guy," 22–23; Fred Barnes, "Sunbelt Democrat," 9–15.

10. The basic neoliberal themes are also set forth in Charles Peters, "Neo-Liberal's Manifesto." Schneider, "JFK's Children," 55.

11. Buckley and Kesler, *Keeping the Tablets,* 11, 14.

12. *New York Times,* 21 May 1989.

13. Ibid.

14. Riker, *Liberalism against Populism,* 9.

15. Nicholas Lemann, "Winning an Election," 30–32.

16. Hamby, *Liberalism and Its Challengers,* 345, 346.

17. Ibid., 346, 347.

# Bibliography

## Books

Adams, Henry. "The New York Gold Company." In *The Great Secession Winter of 1860–61 and Other Essays,* edited by G. E. Hochfield. New York: N.p., 1958.

Appleby, Joyce. *Capitalism and a New Social Order: The Republican Vision of the 1970s.* New York: New York Univ. Press, 1984.

Bennett, David. *The Party of Fear: From Nativist Movements to the New Right in American History.* Chapel Hill: Univ. of North Carolina Press, 1988.

Berger, Peter. *The Capitalist Revolution: Fifty Propositions about Prosperity, Equality and Liberty.* New York: Basic Books, 1986.

Boesche, Roger. *The Strange Liberalism of Alexis de Tocqueville.* Ithaca: Cornell Univ. Press, 1987.

Boller, Paul F., Jr. *Presidential Campaigns.* New York: Oxford Univ. Press, 1985.

Bollinger, Lee. *The Tolerant Society.* New York: Oxford Univ. Press, 1988.

Bonomi, Patricia U. *Under the Cope of Heaven: Religion, Society and Politics in Colonial America.* New York: Oxford Univ. Press, 1986.

Bruchey, Stuart. *Enterprise: The Dynamic Economy of a Free People.* Cambridge: Harvard Univ. Press, 1990.

Buckley, William F., and Charles R. Kesler, eds. *Keeping the Tablets: Modern American Conservative Thought.* New York: Harper and Row, 1988.

Carroll, Peter N., and David W. Noble. *The Free and the Unfree: A New History of the U.S.* New York: Penguin, 1988.

Countryman, Edward. *The American Revolution.* New York: Hill and Wang, 1985.

Curry, Richard, ed. *Freedom at Risk: Secrecy, Censorship, and Repression in the 1980s.* Philadelphia: Temple Univ. Press, 1989.

Dahrendorf, Ralf. *The Modern Social Conflict: An Essay on the Politics of Liberty.* New York: Weidenfeld and Nicolson, 1988.

Danziger, Sheldon H., and Daniel Weinberg, eds. *Fighting Poverty: What Works and What Doesn't.* Cambridge: Harvard Univ. Press, 1986.

Davis, Allen F., and Harold D. Woodman, eds. *Conflict and Consensus in Modern American History.* Lexington, Mass.: D. C. Heath, 1984.

Diggins, John. *The Lost Soul of American Politics: Virtue, Self-Interest, and the Foundations of Liberalism.* Chicago: Univ. of Chicago Press, 1984.

Dunbar, Leslie. *The Common Interest: How Our Social-Welfare Policies Don't Work, and What We Can Do about Them*. New York: Pantheon, 1988.

Elliot, E. N., ed. *Cotton Is King and Pro-Slavery Arguments*. New York: Negro Univ. Press, 1860.

Fehrenbacher, Don E. *Lincoln in Text and Context: Collected Essays*. Stanford: Stanford Univ. Press, 1987.

Ferrell, Robert H. *Harry S. Truman and the Modern American Presidency*. Boston: Little, Brown, 1983.

Foner, Eric. *Free Soil, Free Labor, Free Men: The Ideology of the Republican Party before the Civil War*. New York: Oxford Univ. Press, 1970.

Fredrickson, George M. *The Inner Civil War: Northern Intellectuals and the Crisis of the Union*. New York: Harper and Row, 1965.

Garrison, W. P. and F. J. *William Lloyd Garrison*. New York: Arno Press, 1969.

Gerteis, Louis S. *Morality and Utility in American Antislavery Reform*. Chapel Hill: Univ. of North Carolina Press, 1987.

Giamatti, A. Bartlett. *A Free and Ordered Space: The Real World of the University*. New York: W. W. Norton, 1989.

Goldwater, Barry M. *Goldwater*. New York: Doubleday, 1988.

Goodwyn, Lawrence. *Democratic Promise: The Populist Movement in America*. New York: Oxford Univ. Press, 1976.

Green, David. *Shaping Political Consciousness: The Language of Politics in America from McKinley to Reagan*. Ithaca: Cornell Univ. Press, 1987.

Hamby, Alonzo. *Liberalism and Its Challengers: FDR to Reagan*. New York: Oxford Univ. Press, 1985.

Handlin, Oscar. *Al Smith and His America*. Boston: Northeastern Univ. Press, 1958.

Hartz, Louis. *Economic Policy and Democratic Thought: Pennsylvania, 1776–1860*. Cambridge: Harvard Univ. Press, 1948.

——— . *The Liberal Tradition in America*. New York: Harcourt, Brace, 1955.

Hirsch, Fred. *Social Limits to Growth*. Cambridge: Harvard Univ. Press, 1976.

Hofstadter, Richard. *The Paranoid Style in American Politics and Other Essays*. New York: Alfred A. Knopf, 1965.

Hoover, Herbert. *State Papers and Other Public Writings*. Edited by W. S. Myers. New York: Doubleday, Doran, 1934.

Hutchison, William. *American Protestant Thought in the Liberal Era*. New York: Harper and Row, 1986.

Jenkins, W. S. *Pro-Slavery Thought*. Chapel Hill: Univ. of North Carolina Press, 1935.

Johnson, E. A. J. *The Foundations of American Economic Freedom: Government and Enterprise in the Age of Washington*. Minneapolis: Univ. of Minnesota Press, 1973.

Judis, John. *William F. Buckley, Jr., Patron Saint of the Conservatives*. New York: Simon and Schuster, 1988.

Kelly, Robert. *The Cultural Pattern in American Politics: The First Century*. New York: Alfred A. Knopf, 1979.

Kerber, Linda K. *Federalists in Dissent: Imagery and Ideology in Jeffersonian America*. Ithaca: Cornell Univ. Press, 1970.

Koch, Adrienne. *The Philosophy of Thomas Jefferson*. New York: Columbia Univ. Press, 1943.

Kuttner, Robert. *The Life of the Party: Democratic Prospects in 1988 and Beyond*. New York: Penguin, 1987.

Lane, Harlan. *When the Mind Hears: A History of the Deaf.* New York: Random House, 1984.

Langguth, A. J. *Patriots: The Men Who Started the American Revolution.* New York: Simon and Schuster, 1988.

Lappe, Frances Moore. *Rediscovering America's Values.* New York: Ballantine, 1989.

Leuchtenburg, William E. *Franklin D. Roosevelt and the New Deal.* New York: Harper and Row, 1963.

Levin, N. Gordon, Jr. *Woodrow Wilson and World Politics: America's Response to War and Revolution.* New York: Oxford Univ. Press, 1968.

Levinson, Sanford. *Constitutional Faith.* Princeton: Princeton Univ. Press, 1988.

Levy, Leonard W. *The Establishment Clause.* New York: Macmillan, 1986.

Lorant, Stefan. *The Glorious Burden: The American Presidency.* New York: Harper and Row, 1968.

Lowi, Theodore J. *The End of Liberalism: Ideology, Policy, and the Crisis of Public Authority.* New York: W. W. Norton, 1969.

McCarthy, E. J. *A Liberal Answer to the Conservative Challenge.* New York: Praeger, 1965.

McCoy, Drew. *The Last of the Fathers: James Madison and the Republican Legacy.* New York: Cambridge Univ. Press, 1989.

McCraw, Thomas K. *Prophets of Regulation: Charles Francis Adams, Louis D. Brandeis, James M. Landis, Alfred E. Kahn.* Cambridge: Belknap Press, 1984.

McDonald, Forrest. *The Presidency of Thomas Jefferson.* Lawrence: Univ. Press of Kansas, 1976.

McElvaine, Robert S. *The Great Depression: America 1929–1941.* New York: Times Books, 1985.

McKean, D. D. *Party and Pressure Politics.* Boston: Houghton Mifflin, 1949.

McLoughlin, William G. "The Role of Religion in the Revolution." In *Essays on the American Revolution,* edited by Stephen Kurtz and James Hudson. Chapel Hill: Univ. of North Carolina Press, 1973.

Maier, Pauline. *From Resistance to Revolution: Colonial Radicals and the Development of American Opposition to Britain.* New York: Alfred A. Knopf, 1972.

Manning, D. J. *Liberalism.* New York: St. Martin's Press, 1976.

Mead, Lawrence M. *Beyond Entitlement: The Social Obligation of Citizenship.* New York: Free Press, 1986.

Moore, Edmund A. *A Catholic Runs for President: The Campaign of 1928.* New York: Ronald Press, 1956.

Murrin, John. "Self-interest Conquers Patriotism: Republicans, Liberals, and Indians Reshape the Nation." In *The American Revolution: Its Character and Limits,* edited by Jack P. Greene. New York: New York Univ. Press, 1987.

Newman, Stephen L. *Liberalism at Wit's End.* Ithaca: Cornell Univ. Press, 1984.

Norton, Mary Beth, David M. Katzman, Paul D. Escott, Howard P. Chudacoff, Thomas G. Paterson, and William M. Tuttle, Jr., eds. *A People and a Nation: A History of the United States.* Boston: Houghton Mifflin, 1982.

Otis, James. *Rights of the Colonies Asserted and Proved.* Boston, 1864.

Parenti, Michael. *Democracy for the Few.* New York: St. Martin's Press, 1988.

Pells, Richard H. *The Liberal Mind in a Conservative Age: American Intellectuals in the 1940s and 1950s.* New York: Harper and Row, 1985.

Peterson, Merrill D. *Thomas Jefferson and the New Nation: A Biography.* New York: Oxford Univ. Press, 1970.

Pringle, Henry. *Theodore Roosevelt: A Biography.* New York: Harcourt, Brace, 1931.

Ratner, Sidney. *American Taxation: Its History as a Social Force in Democracy.* New York: W. W. Norton, 1942.

Rawls, John. *A Theory of Justice.* Cambridge: Harvard Univ. Press, 1971.

Rehnquist, William. *The Supreme Court: How It Was, How It Is.* New York: Morrow, 1987.

Reich, Robert. *The Next American Frontier.* New York: Penguin, 1984.

———. *Tales of a New America.* New York: Vintage, 1987.

Remini, Robert. "Election of 1832." In *A History of Presidential Elections,* vol. 1, edited by Arthur M. Schlesinger, Jr. New York: Chelsea House, 1971.

Richey, Russell E., and Donald G. Jones., eds. *American Civil Religion.* New York: Harper and Row, 1974.

Riker, William. *Liberalism against Populism: A Confrontation between the Theory of Democracy and the Theory of Social Choice.* San Francisco: W. H. Freeman, 1982.

Rodgers, Daniel T. *Contested Truths: Keywords in American Policy since Independence.* New York: Basic Books, 1987.

Roosevelt, Franklin D. *The Public Papers and Addresses of Franklin D. Roosevelt.* New York: Random House, 1938–50.

Russell, Francis. *The Shadow of Blooming Grove: Warren G. Harding in His Times.* New York: McGraw-Hill, 1968.

Samuelson, Paul. *Economics from the Heart: A Samuelson Sampler.* New York: T. Horton, 1973.

Schlesinger, Arthur M., Jr. *The American as Reformer.* Cambridge: Harvard Univ. Press, 1950.

———. *The Cycles of American History.* Boston: Houghton Mifflin, 1986.

———. *The Politics of Hope.* Boston: Houghton Mifflin, 1963.

———. *The Vital Center.* Cambridge: Riverside Press, 1962.

Schwarz, Jordan A. *Liberal: Adolf Berle and the Vision of an American Era.* New York: Free Press, 1987.

Silber, John. *Straight Shooting: What's Wrong with America and How to Fix It.* New York: Harper and Row, 1989.

Sklar, Martin J. *The Corporate Reconstruction of American Capitalism: The Market, the Law, and Politics.* New York: Cambridge Univ. Press, 1989.

Smith, M. H. *The Writs of Assistance Case.* Berkeley: Univ. of California Press, 1978.

Stewart, James Brewer. *Holy Warriors: The Abolitionists and American Slavery.* New York: Hill and Wang, 1976.

———. *Wendell Phillips: Liberty's Hero.* Baton Rouge: Louisiana State Univ. Press, 1986.

Thompson, Charles W. *Presidents I've Known.* Indianapolis: Bobbs-Merrill, 1929.

Thorsen, Niels Aage. *The Political Thought of Woodrow Wilson, 1875–1910.* Princeton: Princeton Univ. Press, 1988.

Thurow, Lester C. *Dangerous Currents: The State of Economics.* New York: Random House, 1983.

———. *The Zero-Sum Solution.* New York: Simon and Schuster, 1985.

Tyor, Peter L., and Leland V. Bell. *Caring for the Retarded in America: A History.* Westport, Conn.: Greenwood Press, 1984.

Walker, Robert. *Reform in America: The Continuing Frontier.* Lexington: Univ. Press of Kentucky, 1985.

Waters, John J., Jr. *The Otis Family in Provincial and Revolutionary Massachusetts.* Chapel Hill: Univ. of North Carolina Press, 1968.

Wiebe, Robert H. *The Search for Order: 1877–1920.* New York: Hill and Wang, 1967.

Wilson, William J. *The Truly Disadvantaged: The Inner City, the Underclass, and Public Policy.* Chicago: Univ. of Chicago Press, 1988.
Wood, Gordon. *The Creation of the American Republic.* New York: W. W. Norton, 1969.
Wuthnow, Robert. *The Restructuring of American Religion: Society and Faith since World War II.* Princeton: Princeton Univ. Press, 1988.


## Magazine and Journal Articles

Barnes, Fred. "Sunbelt Democrat." *The New Republic,* 27 May 1985, 9–15.
Devroy, Ann. "There's no homecoming for Bush." *Washington Post National Weekly Edition,* 12 July 1991, 12.
Downey, Matthew T. "Horace Greeley and the Politicians: The Liberal Republican Convention in 1872." *Journal of American History* 53 (March 1967): 727–50.
Fairlie, Henry. "Fear of Living." *The New Republic,* 23 January 1989, 14–19.
Ferguson, Thomas, and Joel Rogers. "The Myth of America's Turn to the Right." *The Atlantic Monthly,* May 1986, 43–53.
Gerber, Richard Allan. "The Liberal Republicans of 1872 in Historiographical Perspective." *Journal of American History* 62 (June 1975): 40–73.
Grover, Ronald. "Fighting Back: The Resurgence of Social Activism." *Business Week,* 22 May 1989, 34–35.
Hertzberg, Hendrik. "Stand-up Guy." *The New Republic,* 4 January 1988, 20–23.
Hirshman, Albert O. "Reactionary Rhetoric." *The Atlantic Monthly,* May 1989, 63–70.
Holmes, Stephen. "The Philosophers' War on the L-Word." *The New Republic,* 28 November 1988, 24–28.
Lemann, Nicholas. "The Culture of Poverty." *The Atlantic Monthly,* September 1984, 26–41.
———. "Winning an Election." *The Washington Monthly,* March 1989, 30–32.
Lodge, George. "It's Time for an American Perestroika." *The Atlantic Monthly,* April 1989, 35–36.
Peters, Charles. "Neo-Liberal's Manifesto." *Washington Monthly,* March 1982, 6–9.
Peterson, Peter. "The Morning After." *The Atlantic Monthly,* October 1987, 43–69.
Phillips, Kevin. "The Democrats and Republicans: Dead from the Neck Up?" *Washington Post National Weekly Edition,* 9–15 October 1989, 6–7.
Rauch, Jonathan. "Is the Deficit Really So Bad?" *The Atlantic Monthly,* February 1989, 36–42.
———. "Kids as Capital." *The Atlantic Monthly,* August 1989, 56–61.
Reich, Robert. "As the World Turns." *The New Republic,* 1 May 1989, 23–28.
———. "Corporation and Nation." *The Atlantic Monthly,* May 1988, 76–81.
———. "Toward a New Public Philosophy." *The Atlantic Monthly,* May 1985, 68–79.
Sandel, Michael. "Morality and the Liberal Ideal." *The New Republic,* 7 May 1984, 15–18.
———. "A Public Philosophy for American Liberalism." *The New Republic,* 22 February 1989, 23.
Schneider, William. "The Democrats in '88." *The Atlantic Monthly,* April 1987, 37–59.
———. "An Insider's View of the Election." *The Atlantic Monthly,* July 1988, 40.
———. "JFK's Children: The Class of '74." *The Atlantic Monthly,* March 1989, 35–58.

Shapiro, Walter. "Are the Democrats Cursed?" *Time*, 21 November 1988, 58.
Smart, Tim. "A Backlash against Business." *Business Week*, 6 February 1989, 30–31.
———. "Regulation Rises Again." *Business Week*, 26 June 1989, 58.
Tinder, Glen. "Can We Be Good without God: On the Political Meaning of Christianity." *The Atlantic Monthly*, December 1989, 69–85.
Walzer, Michael. "The Communitarian Critique of Liberalism." *Political Theory* 18 (February 1990): 4–19.
Wilson, Woodrow. "Bryce's American Commonwealth: A Review." *Political Science Quarterly* 4 (March 1889): 153–69.
Zinsmeister, Karl. "The Poverty Problem of the Eighties." *Public Opinion*, June/July 1985, 8–12.

# Index